Family and Consumer Sciences

Family and Consumer Sciences

PREVENTATIVE AND RESTORATIVE EDUCATION

MELINDA SWAFFORD AND ELIZABETH RAMSEY

cognella®

SAN DIEGO

Bassim Hamadeh, CEO and Publisher
Amy Smith, Senior Project Editor
Arielle Lewis, Editorial Assistant
Celeste Paed, Associate Production Editor
Emely Villavicencio, Senior Graphic Designer
Natalie Piccotti, Director of Marketing
Kassie Graves, Vice President of Editorial
Jamie Giganti, Director of Academic Publishing

Printed in the United States of America.

3970 Sorrento Valley Blvd., Ste. 500, San Diego, CA 92121

To my father, David Delk, who throughout his life modeled a strong work ethic, commitment to goals, and decency toward others. I thank you for your love and support. I miss you and our conversations.

Melinda Swafford

To my father, Gene Brown, who taught me to love education and to excel. I miss your sunny disposition, our talks, your laugh, and your wisdom. Dad, you've been gone 2 years, but you are still the voice in my head telling me I can do anything.

Elizabeth Ramsey

BRIEF CONTENTS

DETAILED CONTENTS

CHAPTER 3   Adverse Childhood Experiences and Trauma-Informed Classroom Approach   49

Elizabeth Ramsey, PhD; Rufaro A. Chitiyo, PhD; and Melinda Swafford, PhD

CHAPTER 4   Learning Theories and Educational Psychology   73

Elizabeth Ramsey, PhD, and Melinda Swafford, PhD

CHAPTER 5   Curriculum, Standards, and Philosophy of Education   91

Melinda Swafford, PhD; Elizabeth Ramsey, PhD; and Kayleigh Beasley, MA

CHAPTER 6   Planning Lessons   105

Melinda Swafford, PhD; Elizabeth Ramsey, PhD; and Kayleigh Beasley, MS

CHAPTER 9   Planning and Implementing Labs and Other Action-Oriented Strategies   171

Hannah Upole, PhD; Elizabeth Ramsey, PhD, CFLE; Melinda Swafford, PhD; Samantha Hutson, PhD; and Caitlin Williams, MS

PREFACE

The American Association of Family and Consumer Sciences (AAFCS, 2020) states that family and consumer sciences (FCS) is a people-centered, problem-solving profession that provides education to help individuals and families address the challenges faced in society. This text supports the mission of the FCS profession of preparing quality educators to help individuals and families improve their quality of life (AAFCS, 2020). *Family and Consumer Sciences: Preventative and Restorative Education* reflects current requirements of national teacher education accreditation requirements, national licensure exams, state and university teacher preparation requirements, and legislative requirements of career technical education. Furthermore, this text will provide you with content on the philosophy and mission of the profession. Throughout this text, you will be instructed on how to plan engaging lessons using a variety of methodologies to address the ever-changing societal issues facing individuals and families.

There are several reasons for writing this textbook. First, there was a need to have a current text in preparing preservice students in FCS education, a viable and needed career. Our goal was to ensure that preservice FCS educators are prepared to meet legislative requirements, as well as meet the diverse needs of individuals and families in society. Therefore, the content includes research, preventative approaches, current legislative requirements, as well as evidence-based methods and strategies for the applied science of FCS education. Throughout the text, personal experiences from FCS educators are included. Finally, this textbook allows us to give attention to pressing questions of society that we often see posed by social media and press outlets: What happened to home economics, and what is family and consumer sciences?

Home economics has evolved and changed into a discipline called family and consumer sciences. Although the name changed years ago, the mission remained the same: FCS education works to improve the lives of individuals, families, and communities. In other words, FCS education is preventative and restorative. Concerning preventive education, FCS educators help individuals and families identify practices of interactions that strengthen family relationships and identify how to use resources to meet needs during everyday life and during times of stress. Through education, individuals may prevent everyday stressors from becoming overwhelming and traumatic. Likewise, teaching and equipping high school students' with knowledge of child development, in turn, prevents child abuse because one day, those students will be parents, and when a parent has developmentally appropriate expectations for their children, they are less likely to abuse them. In regard to restorative, through education, families gain strength-building practices, modeled by professionals, that promote wellness, healing of relationships, resources acquisition, and restoration of family functioning.

It was our intention to add content that was limited or previously not included in past FCS education textbooks. These concepts included a strong focus on diversity, advocacy, adverse childhood experiences (ACEs), and trauma. FCS professionals currently address the major societal issues of today, including the landmark research on ACEs. Considering the prevalence of ACEs and the related physical and mental health outcomes and behavior risks associated with ACEs, along with the prevalence of trauma, the FCS profession serves as both preventative and restorative because FCS professionals work in every area of the original 10 ACEs, including the various types of abuse: physical abuse, emotional abuse, and sexual abuse; types of neglect: physical and emotional; and types of household dysfunction: mental illness, incarcerated relative, mother treated violently, substance abuse, and divorce (Tennessee Department of Education, 2018).

Furthermore, professionals in the area of counseling, social work, and the medical field are beginning to understand the importance of FCS education for individuals and families, as it is becoming ever more clear that the content not only prevents major societal issues but also provides restoration for individuals and families. From a national standpoint, there is a shortage of FCS professionals to fill available positions (Werhan & Whitbeck, 2017). Knowing the importance of FCS demonstrates the need for university and college programs in FCS education to fill the shortage. A current, up-to-date textbook in FCS pedagogy will help improve and hopefully increase programs. Thank you for joining us on this mission!

REFERENCES

American Association of Family and Consumer Sciences. (2020). *What is FCS?* http://www.aafcs.org/aboutus/what-is-fcs

Tennessee Department of Education. (2018). *Six-hour building strong brains for secondary schools: Facilitator guide.*

Werhan, C. A., & Whitbeck, D. A. (2017). Family and consumer sciences teacher shortage inaccuracies: Collaborating to set the record straight. *Journal of Family and Consumer Sciences Education, 34*(special edition 2), 24–28. http://www.nate-facs.org/pages/v34 se2 Werham.pdf

ACKNOWLEDGMENTS

Completing this project required commitment, support, and talent. This was possible with the support of family, colleagues, and FCS teachers (who were former students). Dr. Swafford would like to thank her family—husband, Blake; children, Brad and Megan; daughter-in-law, Amy; granddaughter, Sadie; and her mother, Bernice—for their love and support. She would also like to thank her mentors Dr. Sue Bailey, Dr. Cathey Hix, Dr. Linda Richey, the late Dr. Dean Richey, and Filomena Palmer for encouragement and opportunities. Each one has greatly impacted her as a professional educator working with children and families. Thank you to Dr. Elizabeth Ramsey, cowriter and friend, for your hard work on this project.

Dr. Ramsey would like to thank her husband, Paul, and her children Rita, Pete, Ruth Ann, and Sarah Bette who offer their constant love and support. She would also like to thank her father who is no longer here on Earth but whose constant love and support continue to be the voice in her head telling her she can accomplish great things. Dr. Ramsey would also like to thank her dear mentor, friend, and cowriter, Dr. Melinda Swafford, for inviting her to this project and for her years of support and encouragement.

The authors would like to thank all the individuals who assisted in the development of this text. Among them are their invited contributors who were colleagues and FCS teachers. Their willingness to collaborate as a team and share their expertise and experiences in FCS contributed to the success of this project.

- Melinda Anderson, PhD, RD, LDN, director of the School of Human Ecology, and professor, Nutrition and Dietetics at Tennessee Technological University
- Kaleigh Beasley, TTU, MA and FCS educator in Tennessee
- Rufaro Chitiyo, PhD, associate professor of Human Ecology at TTU in Child Development and Family Relations concentration
- Samantha Hudson, PhD, RD, LDN, graduate program director of the MS in Community Health and Nutrition, assistant professor, Nutrition and Dietetics at TTU
- Caitlin Roach Williams, MS, technology integration coach and FCS educator
- Hannah Upole, PhD, assistant professor of Human Ecology at TTU in Merchandising and Design and Consumer Economics

Throughout the textbook, many of the spotlights, textboxes, and example handouts were contributed by former students. We would like to thank them for sharing their resources.

- Stephanie Birdwell Ross, BS, FCS educator
- Chelsea Groover, residency student TTU, Human Ecology
- Kristen Giordano, M.Ed., owner, The Market, and FCS educator

We would also like to thank Jessica Broh who created the artwork for the cover during her senior year at TN Tech.

We would like to thank our reviewers Beau Weston, PhD, of Centre College, and Cherly Robinson, PhD, of the University of Tennessee at Chattanooga. Their insight and careful review of our chapters and feedback resulted in clarification of content. Finally, we would like to thank the team at Cognella Publishing: Kassie Graves, vice president editorial, Amy Smith, senior project editor, and Celeste Paed, associate production editor, who provided support throughout the entire process.

ARTIST STATEMENT

Jessica Broh

In my artwork, used on the over of this textbook, I depicted a diseased tree with butterflies. The rotting in the tree symbolizes a "Nest," which symbolizes the household. Butterflies depicted as stained glass are inside the rotten part of the tree. I used glass because a family is fragile. It only takes one traumatic event or adverse childhood experience (ACE) to change the entire family dynamic. The colors in the stained glass symbolize the everlasting impact of the trauma, which is generational trauma. Each marking represents a specific traumatic or adverse event, which is why the larger (parental) butterflies created a butterfly with the same markings. On the other hand, the butterflies on the outside of the tree appear to be vibrant butterflies. That is because these butterflies live in a healthy family dynamic and have the proper resources to thrive. A child in a broken family dynamic can become one of these thriving butterflies; however, it takes restorative intervention on the entire household to make this a possibility.

When working with individuals and families, it is imperative to look at the family unit as a whole. Bronfenbrenner's ecological theory is the foundation of family and consumer science (FCS) content areas. It emphasizes looking at a family in a broader sense so we can understand how the entire family system operates. Those in FCS professions look at how several types of communities (extended family, friends, media, religious organizations) influence a family. While these communities often positively influence families, they can also be a source of stress. If not managed properly, everyday stressors can lead to bigger problems, such as ACEs, which can become a source of trauma. The good news is FCS education can help prevent ACEs and other societal issues because the content that is taught in FCS education is both preventative and restorative.

FCS education is incredibly important for the prevention of many of the societal issues that we face today. With proper FCS education, individuals and families are given resources that aid in building a healthy family dynamic. An important step in this education is understanding how to use effective interpersonal interactions, as taught in FCS programs. Furthermore, it is crucial for everyone to understand the consequences (both intended and unintended) of their interactions with children. FCS educators teach individuals and families to understand and manage stress effectively, recognize healthy coping strategies, mitigate ACEs, aid in healthy human development, and so much more.

FCS is composed of several concentration areas that work to better the lives of individuals and communities. Professionals working in every FCS content area apply knowledge in their day-to-day interactions with individuals and families. These professionals teach healthy, meaningful interactions by modeling skills that support wellness and capacity building. As someone whose concentration is housing and design, I use the knowledge taught to make better design choices. The skills that I am developing are a direct result of a better understanding of people—both on an individual and societal basis. I use botanical elements and personalized layouts to create a fully functional and comfortable space. Furthermore, I have learned to understand light and color theory in a way that creates a feeling of content in those who encounter the space. This is very similar to the way merchandising students must understand the consumer to generate revenue. Beyond revenue, however, they must also understand the average consumer to determine the complexities of day-to-day life. If successful, they can create products that make the consumer's life easier or otherwise offer them something they will enjoy.

Additionally, those following the nutrition and dietetics concentration must apply effective interpersonal communication skills to better understand the client. Besides creating meal plans, it is important to understand the client's background. The client might have limited financial resources, and the dietician must account for this. Therefore, a cost-effective yet nutritious meal plan must be generated. This client might not have much time to cook, so an alternate meal plan must be created without sacrificing quality and effectiveness. This is also crucial for those with extreme dietary restrictions because they must learn to manage the condition while still properly nourishing the body. Therefore, when prior FCS education is used, the dietician is able to provide a better personalized, more effective treatment plan.

Ultimately, the goal of FCS is to improve individual and family life amid changing social, political, economic, and physical influences. Implementation of FCS content areas in universities aids in developing a deeper understanding of individuals and communities, thus instilling knowledge that is useful throughout one's career. Therefore, when implemented, FCS education can help prevent negative societal issues and helps bring restoration to individuals and families, making our communities stronger.

PART I

Foundation of FCS Education

Overview of Chapters 1–6

In higher education programs, the profession of family and consumer sciences (FCS) is currently referred to by other names, such as human ecology, human studies, family sciences, and human sciences. Internationally, the content is known as home economics. Regardless of the title, FCS professionals have one major similarity: FCS they apply science to solve problems, thus improving the way individuals relate to their environment.

FCS professionals practice in a variety of diverse settings, applying math, science, communication, and social skills to the content that impacts the everyday lives of individuals. Within FCS are the content categories of finance/consumerism, food/nutrition/food safety, health/wellness, individual/family development/family relations/well-being, home interiors/design, sustainable resources and fabrics/fashion, and merchandising, each having national standards (AAFCS, 2020). "The diversity in our field is essential because the challenges of everyday life are not one dimensional" (Uphole et al., 2021, p. 31).

The focus of this text is to prepare preservice students for a career in FCS education in either community extension programs or in public schools. Topics and content included will enhance students' ability to be successful with the PRAXIS exams and prepare them for success with nationwide teacher performance assessments, edTPA. This text is designed to be used for an introduction to teaching FCS education as well as a course in materials and methods of teaching FCS. This text will also serve as a reference for students during their' practicum and residency/student teaching experiences.

The first part of this text, Chapters 1–6, consists of content on background, principles, theoretical frameworks, learning theories, addressing the diversity of learners, and other issues impacting the FCS education profession. The authors' intent is to provide a solid foundation for becoming an effective FCS education professional. Chapter 1, "The Foundation of the Family and Consumer Education," includes an overview of the mission, history of FCS, and specific legislation that has impacted the profession of FCS education.

Chapter 2, "Respecting and Embracing Diversity," provides FCS professionals with appropriate strategies to work with a wide variety of learners. Key elements of accepting differences in others, fostering a learning environment that promotes acceptance of others, addressing English language learners, and implementing individualized education program requirements are addressed. Embracing and respecting diversity is not only a moral obligation to our educational system but also an obligation that every individual living in our country deserves. Furthermore, legislative requirements, federal mandates of Perkins reauthorization, IDEA, ADA, and the 14th Amendment to the Constitution support inclusive education.

Chapter 3, "Adverse Childhood Experiences and Trauma-Informed Classroom Approach," covers the impact of trauma on brain development and individual behavior. In this chapter, preservice educators and current educators will learn how to implement a trauma-informed classroom, along with understanding how to build resilience and avoid trauma triggers for individuals who have experienced ACEs and trauma.

Chapter 4, "Learning Theories and Educational Psychology," covers the content on how knowledge is acquired, processed, and maintained in the learning process. Understanding learning theories is essential for the preservice educator when planning appropriate lessons that incorporate various instructional methodologies to enhance learning. In this chapter, several learning theories are summarized and categorized with commonalities.

Chapter 5, "Curriculum, Standards, and Philosophy of Education," provides the reader with a focus on curriculum development and the collaborative effort with FCS professionals that were used to develop appropriate standards for teaching FCS content. The learner will be exposed to the 16 career clusters that encompass career technical education. Chapter 5 includes content about how course standards are used to develop courses, how learning segments are created, and how standards support lesson plans. In addition, this chapter introduces the learner to how knowledge of educational philosophy and developing one's personal philosophy of education.

Chapter 6, "Planning Lessons," provides the learner with an overview of the importance of planning. This chapter places emphasis on the stages of learning as well as using a backward process in planning. A standard lesson plan template that meets a national teacher performance assessment is used, and each component is described. Furthermore, an example is provided in each section for guidance in the planning process. Also, a completed lesson plan is included in Appendix C for the learner to use as a guide. The authors recognize the time commitment for the learner to become proficient in planning. It is recommended that this chapter be reviewed and coordinated with Chapters 7–11 for continuity in the planning process.

REFERENCE

American Association of Family and Consumer Sciences. (2020). *What is FCS?* https://www.aafcs.org/about/about-us/what-is-fcs

Upole, H., Ramsey, E., & Swafford, M. (2021). Advocating is essential: Recommendations based on a case study of the state of family and consumer sciences secondary education in Tennessee. *Contemporary Family Magazine (Winter 2021)*, 30–31.

An Overview of Family and Consumer Education

Melinda Swafford, PhD, and Elizabeth Ramsey, PhD

FIGURE 1.1 The Betty Lamp, Symbol of the American Association of Family and Consumer Sciences, Means to Enlighten

Chapter 1 Objectives

Upon completion of the chapter, the learner should be able to

- summarize the history of family and consumer sciences (FCS), including the founder of the profession;
- identify the components of the FCS body of knowledge (BOK);
- analyze how the FCS BOK impacts quality of life for individuals and families;
- analyze the impact of major legislation on FCS education;
- define and give examples of occupational and traditional FCS courses; and
- compare and contrast careers in the FCS education profession.

Introduction

This chapter includes a brief overview of the FCS education profession, which includes the mission, foundation/history, careers, and impact of the profession on quality of life for individuals and families. Major legislative acts that resulted in changes in the profession will be summarized, with particular attention to the current status. FCS is the science of living and working well in our complex world. This problem-solving profession incorporates various strategies to address the challenges faced by individuals in society (AAFCS, n.d.-c).

What Is FCS Education?

The name "FCS education" has evolved from domestic sciences, home economics, vocational home economics education, and consumer and homemaking education, to family and consumer sciences education. Throughout the evolution of the profession's name, the mission has remained the same: to improve individual and family life amid changing social, political, economic, and physical influences. FCS, a people-centered profession, acknowledges the various environmental influences that impact quality of life for individuals and families (AAFCS, n.d.-e).

What is **quality of life**? As defined by the American Association of Family and Consumer Sciences (AAFCS, n.d.-c), it is the ability to meet needs in life such as home, family, work, school, and community while using available resources and opportunities. Therefore, quality of life is connected with social, economic, physical, and psychological well-being. Quality of life varies among individuals and families. When collaborating with individuals and families, FCS professionals apply science when helping individuals work to solve problems and achieve goals in life. FCS professionals do not use a single response to solve all problems. Research-based knowledge and resources are shared, and skill development is taught to help individuals relate to their environment. These skills are vital to the success of individuals, families, and communities.

The ecological theory is the foundation of the FCS profession. In ecological theory, the environmental settings are viewed as a series of layers that range from the immediate setting, like home and family, to the more remote setting of culture and time (Bronfenbrenner, 1979). Knowledge of ecological theory augments the professional's understanding of the uniqueness of each family, as problems and decision-making skills are impacted by all contextual layers in the family's environment (Swafford et al., 2020).

See Figure 1.2 for Bronfenbrenner's ecological theory model. The model depicts how the layers build upon one another and are integrated with reciprocal interactions, which means a change or conflict in one layer impacts other layers. Furthermore, each layer has a set of norms, rules, and routines that impact the individual and their interactions with others (Sontang, 1996). These environmental settings greatly influence the individual's access to resources and decision making. As explained by the ecological theory, each individual functions within a microsystem that likewise is connected to a mesosystem embedded in the exosystem while being influenced by the encompassing exosystem and chronosystem (Bronfenbrenner, 1979; Swafford et al., 2015). The microsystem includes behavior, family roles, and activities in an individual's immediate surroundings, like the home. For example, some students in your class may be responsible for taking care of younger

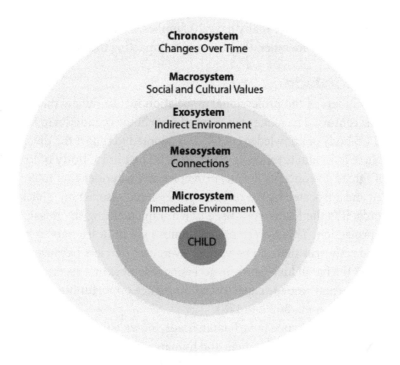

FIGURE 1.2 Ecological Theory Model (The Psychological Notes Headquarters)

siblings before and after school (often viewed in society as a parental role). This responsibility may impact the social, academic, and extracurricular activities of your student. Therefore, it is imperative for FCS educators to know their students. The mesosystem refers to interrelationships that form among the microsystems in the person's daily environment (home, peers, siblings, schools, etc.). The stronger the relationship, the more influence it will have on the individual or family. For example, a close relationship between the child care program and the home may result in the teacher having a greater impact on suggestions to have a print-rich home. The exosystem refers to external factors influencing the individual. These factors are not directly a part of an individual's daily life. This would include school board policies, school calendars, insurance policies, and so on. The macrosystem is the larger cultural context that influences the individual, such as ideologies (ways of thinking) or values and cultural norms of society. The chronosystem includes a change in the individual or the environment that occurs over time. The change can be from an external event like a catastrophe, such as the pandemic, or can be internal, such as puberty and cognitive development. This change, however, greatly influences individual development.

When applying the ecological theory to practice, do not view families or individuals in isolation. We must consider that our interactions, knowledge, and support or lack of the aforementioned have an impact on the entire family seeking to achieve quality of life. By doing so, professionals recognize the uniqueness of each individual and family. Therefore, it is crucial to remember that when we have 20 students in our class, we really have 20 families. When a registered dietitian explains a therapeutic diet to one family member, they are really impacting the entire family's diet.

FCS Body of Knowledge

In the late 1990s, members of the professional association met to review the current status of the profession in the 21st century. The name was changed from home economics to family and consumer sciences, and the FCS body of knowledge (BOK) was adopted to reflect the diversity of society and the emerging needs of individuals (Nickols et al., 2009). The phrase **body of knowledge** refers to a "complete set of agreed-to concepts, terms, principles and activities that make up a professional domain, as defined and advocated by the relevant professional association" (Nickols et al., 2009, p. 107). In other words, it is the framework used when implementing the mission by applying the knowledge of the profession. This framework facilitates FCS professionals to identify individual/family strengths and resources that can be used to overcome barriers because of policies and procedures that may limit the individual/family in accessing resources and services. Addressing barriers is vital, as these barriers may impede capacity building since opportunities for active participation may be affected (Swafford et al., 2020, p. 128).

The core concepts of BOK include basic human needs, individual well-being, family strengths, and community vitality. Life-course development and human ecosystems are the theoretical foundation of the BOK. The five cross-cutting themes in the FCS BOK include capacity building, global interdependence, resource development and sustainability, appropriate use of technology, and wellness

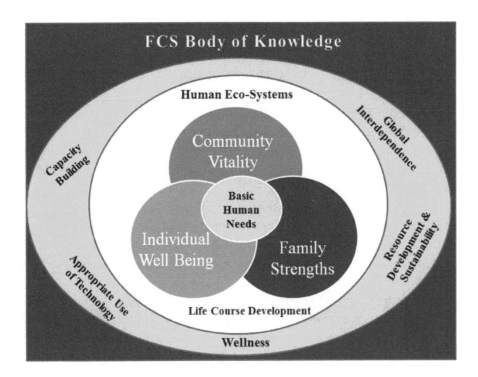

FIGURE 1.3 FCS BOK (Nickols et al., 2009)

(Nickols et al., 2009). All these concepts and themes are essential to our mission and vital as we implement the knowledge base of the FCS profession (Poirier et al., 2017). See Figure 1.3 for a visual of how these concepts are connected. See the Spotlight section to gain an understanding of how an FCS professional puts theory into practice for improving quality of life for individuals and families.

The following spotlight illustrates how an FCS educator incorporates the principles of BOK with the knowledge of ecological theory into everyday practice. These two entities are supportive and may appear to overlap in areas. However, each entity has a purpose in providing quality services to individuals and families as they improve their quality of life. The theory is used as the knowledge base, and the BOK is the principle of implementing the practice. It may be helpful to do a quick review of the BOK and ecological theory before completing the activities in the spotlight.

SPOTLIGHT: IMPLEMENTING ECOLOGICAL MODEL AND THE FCS BOK

Example: You are an FCS educator in an occupational early childhood education classroom. You have 20 high school students who work with young children and families in the school-based nursery school program. Objective: Teaching your high school students to enhance language acquisition and prereading skills for young children in the program and collaborate with families to enhance language acquisition and prereading within the home.

Applying the Knowledge Base of the Ecological Theory

Recalling the concept of the ecological theory, a change in one level impacts the other levels of the environment. In the microsystem when a home has a print-rich environment, the home has generous amounts of children's literature. Parents who read to their children, as well as provide opportunities for children to interact with written words throughout everyday life, make lasting gains on their children's cognitive development. In doing this, the family also models the enjoyment of reading. Language acquisition and learning to read are also influenced by the entities outside the family (microsystem), such as school board decisions; political and legislative decisions, such as educational testing; teacher preparation programs (exosystem); and the value society and culture put on reading (macrosystem).

When applying the principles of the BOK, the teachable moment for language acquisition and prereading is during the earlier stages of young children's lives; this represents using life-course development theory. Language acquisition and prereading are viewed as a cognitive basic need that contributes to positive individual/family well-being and community vitality, therefore impacting how basic needs are met, which is a core value of the BOK. During professional interactions to help others, professionals observe those living in a print-rich home with family members who model reading and use technology as a strength of the family. These family attributes may contribute to resources development/sustainability and capacity building, as individuals may gain and apply knowledge. If the home is not a print-rich environment, FCS educators and preservice students should model "serve and return" interactions for the family and share information from various studies about the correlation between mothers' vocabularies and children's vocabularies, as chil-

(Continued)

dren from low socioeconomic levels speak fewer words because fewer words are spoken to them by their mothers (Brent & Siskind, 2001; Hart & Risley,1995; Huttenlocher et al., 1998; Schmitt et al., 2011). Applying the human ecosystem theory, language acquisition and prereading are influenced by the entities outside the family (macroenvironment), such as school board decisions; political and legislative decisions, such as educational testing; teacher preparation programs; and the value society and culture puts on reading. All of these entities are enhanced and impacted by a print-rich environment within the family and home (microenvironment).

ACTIVITY 1.1: APPLICATION OF THE BOK

Discussion:

1. How can parents provide opportunities for their children to develop a strong vocabulary?

2. Consider the adage, which comes first, the chicken or the egg? Do you think this applies to families when considering vocabulary? If so, what can professionals do to help families?

3. In the macroenvironment, consider the value that the culture puts on reading. Explain how our culture values or disvalues reading.

4. In the chronosystem, consider the age of the child when one begins teaching concepts of reading. Also, consider any catastrophic or unusual events that may impact reading (e.g., the COVID-19 pandemic, school systems going to remote learning, and the closing of local libraries). Give other examples of catastrophic or unusual events that impact reading, giving real-life solutions for families and educators.

Tasks:

1. Create developmentally appropriate activities for parents to interact with their children at home that will enhance vocabulary.

2. In the mesosystem, consider the relationship between the home and school. How might a strong relationship between home and school create a more positive reading outcome for a child?

3. Within the exosystem, a decision was made by the school board to fund a program to enhance reading and vocabulary. Consider the program and decide what components are needed to enhance reading and vocabulary. For example, does the program use sight words or phonics? Also consider any political and legislative matters that impact reading, such as testing and licensure requirements for becoming a teacher.

4. Considering the cross-cutting themes, identify technology that may be used to enhance language and prereading skills.

5. Reading is highly valued globally. Resources such as libraries and curricula are used to teach prereading. Reading well promotes capacity building and wellness. For resources and sustainability, consider how the family uses community resources like the library. Reach out to your local library and discover what resources it offers to young children and families.

6. Programs like the Dolly Parton Imagination Library provide free books to children. Do an internet search and see if free books are available for your area through the Imagination Library. If not, check to see if there are other free book resources. If so, what are they? Does the occupational child care program provide any platforms that support reading to your child for 20 minutes each day or family reading events?

Foundation of FCS

Studying the foundation or history of the profession brings awareness of how the profession has evolved. This awareness also allows one to see the impact of society and culture on the profession, as well as clear up any misconceptions such as the **Matilda effect**, which is the underrecognition of the contribution of women in science (Kershner, 2017). For example, early leaders in the profession were progressive women. Catharine Beecher, activist/advocate for equal education opportunities for women, also wrote the first FCS textbook.

Ellen Swallows Richards, an early feminist (Wylie, 1975) and pioneer for the environment and women in science, established the profession of home economics and its professional organization, the American Home Economics Association (AAFCS, n.d.-a). "Richards believed women would spark a change that would resonate beyond the kitchen table and transform society" (McNeills, 2018, para. 3). Her thoughts and ideas far surpassed the knowledge of her time, as environmental science was not accepted until nearly a century and a half after her death. Richards was also the first person to create the term *oecology*, which is now known as **ecology**, the branch of the study of the biology of organisms interacting with each other and their surroundings. In her forward way of thinking, she recognized that people's interactions with the environment could potentially lead to a future environmental crisis (Kato & Elias, 2015).

SPOTLIGHT: THE LIFE AND LEGACY OF ELLEN SWALLOW RICHARDS

Ellen Swallow Richards (see Figure 1.4) was the first woman to attend and graduate from the Massachusetts Institute of Technology (MIT), beginning her enrollment in 1873 (Britannica, 2020). With the passing of the Morrill Act, higher education at land grant colleges and universities became available to women (Kato & Elias, 2015). Considering this was a time when females were not educated or were only educated in finishing school, an academic program designed especially for girls, Ellen Swallow Richards blazed a trail for women by becoming an excellent scholar in chemistry at MIT, proving her competence in a world that was only reserved for men (Kato & Elias, 2015).

(Continued)

Richards (1842–1911) lived in a time when men were heads of households and women played a subordinate role. Women did not have the right to vote until 10 years after her death, yet Richards longed for more than the farm life that she knew as a young girl. Her parents were former educators and tutored her from home. When they realized that her intellectual abilities far surpassed their capacity to continue tutoring, they sold the family farm in Massachusetts and moved to the town of Westford, which had an academy that Richards attended (Kato & Elias, 2015).

The road to MIT was not easy, as she had dreams of attending Vassar College; however, she instead cared for her ailing mother, cleaned houses, taught school, and tutored over the course of about 2 years (Kato & Elias, 2015). However, this dream of attending Vassar eventually became a reality. In 1870, Richards graduated from Vassar, where she had been admitted as a "special student" because she was female and was permitted to study church history, the Bible, Latin, Greek, astronomy, and calculus (Kato & Elias, 2015). After graduating, she was continuously turned down on her attempts to gain employment as a chemist. However, one chemist recognized her abilities and recommended that she seek more education from MIT, which reluctantly agreed to permit Richards to study at the elite college. MIT regarded her admission as an "experiment" and closely observed her for indications that she was being "wrecked as a woman" (Hunt, 1942). Richards succeeded and graduated with a degree in chemistry from MIT, later writing her master's thesis and fulfilling all of the requirements for a PhD in chemistry from MIT, but unfortunately, she was never awarded a PhD. It is suspected that MIT did not want to be the first to award a PhD to a woman (Kato & Elias, 2015).

Richards used her knowledge and education to apply science to everyday living. She began the New England Kitchen in 1890 under the guidance of Robert H. Richards, who was head of the engineering department at MIT and offered training to families to prepare low-cost, nutritious food (Britannica, 2020). The New England Kitchen provided school lunches as requested by the Boston school committee. Richards also spoke for the inclusion of domestic science and chemistry courses in schools in her state.

FIGURE 1.4 Ellen Swallows Richards Circa 1870

Lake Placid

In 1899, Richards's work expanded beyond Massachusetts and New England. She formed a meeting of all the newfound workers in the new field of domestic sciences in Lake Placid, New York, with the objective of improving home sanitation and living conditions (McNeill, 2018). It was at this historic gathering that the field of home economics was born (Britannica, 2020). Over the following years, the Lake Placid groups of home economists created standards, bibliographies, and course outlines and lobbied Congress for funds to study the nutrition of our country (McNeills, 2018).

Richards, a pioneer in applying science to daily living, conducted research that led to the first Purity Laws for food labeling in our country; this was before the 1906 Food and Drug Act when foods purchased contained harmful chemicals and nonfood items. Furthermore, many legislative and consumer actions that protect the environment from manufacturers/industry pollutants begin with Richards's work (McNeill, 2018). Because of her scientific work, Richards has earned a place in the Smithsonian as one of the most influential women in America, and the Women's Hall of Fame credits her as the founder of ecology as a specialty of study (Kato & Elias, 2015).

AAFCS

In 1900, during one of the Lake Placid conferences, Richards and the members at the conference formally organized a professional organization for home economics, named American Home Economics Association (AAFCS, n.d.-a). The name was later changed to American Association of Family and Consumer Sciences in 1994 (AAFCS, n.d.-a). In the early 1920s, the Betty Lamp was adopted as a symbol of the profession (see Figure 1.1). The name is from the German words "besser" or "bete," meaning "to make better" (AAFCS, n.d.-b). The Betty Lamp represents a symbol of learning for the profession of FCS to enlighten others to education.

Today, several content areas are represented within the AAFCS professional organization, including child care and parenting, nutrition, finances, family systems, personal relationships, career preparation and exploration, management of family resources, merchandising and design, apparel industry, interior design, and environmentally friendly construction (AAFCS, n.d.-a). The AAFCS shares knowledge, research, and experience to help members stay current with best practices and provides leadership and professional development opportunities and collaboration (AAFCS, n.d.-a).

The Impact of Legislation on the Profession

Since the beginning, FCS education has focused on skills needed for successful living in our complex society. Legislation has impacted the profession of FCS and continues to be ever influential in the implementation. Legislation has even impacted the name change of vocational education to **career technical education (CTE)**, which provides specific career training for occupations requiring an academic foundation and practical experience (Association for Career and Technical Education [ACTE], 2019). These broad careers include professions in agriculture, FCS, electricians, mechanics, and medical professionals, such as respiratory therapists, nursing, and medical records. This training can be in middle school, high school, and postsecondary CTE institutions

The **Morrill Land Grant Act of 1862** established grants to purchase land for public colleges and universities in each state. This legislation stressed that education should be practical and accessible for people of all socioeconomic levels. The purpose of educating men in agriculture and mechanics and women in home economics is to meet the country's economic needs. Prior to this legislation, colleges and universities were unattainable for the working class and individuals living at lower socioeconomic levels (Staley, 2013). Ultimately, this legislation established the profession of FCS as an academic field of study. In connection with the Morrill Land Grant Act of 1862, other legislative acts have greatly impacted the profession while addressing the needs of our country. The **Smith-Lever Act of 1914** established community extension through outreach programs with land grant universities. The purpose was to provide education to rural areas about advancements and technology available in agriculture and home economics.

During the Industrial Revolution, our country was experiencing rapid economic growth; however, a shortage of skilled labor was noted. The **Smith-Hughes Act of 1917** provided federal funding to establish vocational education classes and cooperative extension programs to address this problem. In addition to industrial education courses, home economics and agriculture education courses were specifically identified in this legislation, resulting in the establishment of these courses in public high schools (ACTE, 2019). Funding was also provided to train teachers in higher education institutions to teach these courses and prepare extension educators. This legislation also supported the development of student leadership organizations, such as FFA and the former Future Homemakers of America (FHA; currently Family, Career and Community Leaders of America [FCCLA]) to promote leadership and problem-solving skills in youth. See Chapter 12 for more information on FCCLA.

The **Vocational Education Act of 1963** provided funding to expand and improve vocational education in high schools through training, program development, and work-study opportunities. In fact, this was the largest investment to date in high school programs (Stone, 2014). This legislation led to the establishment of occupational programs in FCS, such as food service and child care (currently known as culinary/hospitality and early childhood education, respectively). The education for employment act (Mason, 1968) occupational programs were developed to prepare students for entry-level positions in a specific occupation. Reauthorization of the legislation resulted in serving individuals with disabilities and individuals at risk, those that live at lower socioeconomic levels (ACTE, 2019).

SPOTLIGHT: CONTRIBUTIONS OF MARJORIE BROWN

Majorie Brown (1914–1996) was a practicing home economist FCS professional for over 65 years. She cowrote with Beatrice Paolucci five documents that provided a mission statement for the profession, as well as reconceptualized the philosophy of the profession. Her work promotes a change in the focus from daily problems to **perennial problems** faced by individuals/families in society (McGregor, 2014). Perennial problems are influenced by environmental factors (contextual) and often are long term, such as developing respectful family interactions, parenting/caregiving children in a nurturing manner, or solving issues of food insecurity in the family. Brown urged FCS professionals to take a critical look to broaden the values of the profession and to be more inclusive of society and its unique needs. Brown's work is currently found in professional standards, curriculum changes, and the inclusion of course standards in public education (Laster & Johnson, 2001).

The FSC BOK includes Brown's concepts of human ecosystem theory, family strengths, capacity building, and individual well-being. When applying Brown's work, FCS professionals, instead of just providing solutions or solving the problem themselves, incorporate family strengths and capacity building as a means to promote individual/family well-being. **Capacity building** occurs when acknowledging family strengths and incorporating the strengths into the individuals/families' active engagement in the solution of the problem. This leads to increased self-esteem in the individual and a willingness to solve future problems. Research by Dunst (2014) states that professionals create capacity building when they provide opportunities for individuals/families to develop new skills to address problems and needs while enhancing existing strengths, therefore building self-efficacy. By fully implementing her work, FCS professionals can alleviate the myths and misconceptions that many have about the profession.

The **Vocational Act of 1984** (referred to as **Carl D. Perkins/Perkins I**) legislation supported vocational programs with funding by ensuring that underserved populations would have equal access to educational courses, occupational programs of study, and work-based learning. The economically and educationally underserved population included individuals with disabilities, those living in poverty, and English language learners (ELLs). Perkins I also required coordination between vocational education with special education services and vocational rehabilitation services to ensure the vocational education supports the student's individualized education program (IEP). IEPs, goals, academic integration into vocational education courses, and elimination of gender bias in courses were key components of this legislation (see Figure 1.5).

In 1990, the reauthorization of the Carl D. Perkins Act became known as **Perkins II**. Through increased funding, courses were organized into a sequence that would better prepare individuals for paid employment that did not require postsecondary education or unpaid employment. This legislation also required that courses have standards, and the students would be measured on how they attained the content of the standards.

In 1998, the reauthorization of Perkins to **Perkins III** updated the definition of vocational education and began preparing students for postsecondary education. Additional funding through Tech-Prep was provided (ACTE, 2019). Funding was also provided for technology in the classroom, vocational counselors/administrators, and professional development for teachers.

In 2006, **Perkins IV**, the **Carl D. Perkins Career and Technical Education and Improvement Act**, changed the name of vocational education to career and technical education. Funding was provided to incorporate academic integration into CTE courses (ACTE, 2019). The focus was to prepare students for college and career readiness by linking with postsecondary institutions with articulation agreements to provide dual credit or dual enrollment opportunities for students. This legislation established programs of study within the courses that supported one of the 16 career clusters, as well as a strong focus on industry certification or a postsecondary associate or baccalaureate degree (ACTE, 2019). To receive funding, states must have one program of study. The programs of study resulted in course content changes to reflect more of a career focus.

In 2018 **Perkins V, Strengthening Career and Technical Education for the 21st Century**, was passed. Emphasis was still placed on the programs of study within the 16 career clusters. This legislation provided states with a common definition of a CTE concentrator, expanded the definition of special populations, and provided more flexibility with stakeholders to use data from a local needs assessment to make decisions for program revisions and development. Funding was also provided to middle school programs for career development courses (ACTE, 2019). See Table 1.1 for a summary of CTE legislation.

TABLE 1.1 Summary of Legislation

Legislation	Date	Action
Morrill Land Grant Act of 1862	1862	Funded land purchases for universities and colleges; made education available for all social classes
Smith-Lever Act of 1914	1914	Establishment of extension through land grant universities providing education to rural areas
Smith Hughes Act of 1917	1917	Addressed the shortage of skilled workers by funding vocational education and cooperative extension, including high schools
Vocational Education Act of 1963	1963	Funding to further high school and vocational education; later reauthorizations included individuals with exceptionalities and at high risk
Vocational Act of 1984 (referred to as Carl D. Perkins/Perkins I)	1984	Ensured equal access to educational courses, occupational programs, and work-based learning
Reauthorization of Carl D. Perkin act (Perkins II)	1990	Increased funding, courses organized in sequence to better prepare students, required standards, and measured student acquired knowledge of standards
Perkins III	1998	Updated the definition of vocational education, prepared students for postsecondary education, provided funding for Tech-Prep, and provided funding for classroom technology, vocational counselors/administrators, and teachers
The Carl D. Perkins Career and Technical Education and Improvement Act (Perkins IV)	2006	Changed name to career and technical education, provided funding for academic integration into CTE courses, established programs of study within 16 career clusters and industry certification, postsecondary associate, or baccalaureate degree
Strengthening Career and Technical Education for the 21st Century (Perkins V)	2018	Common definition of a CTE, provided flexibility for local needs assessments for program revision and development, funding of middle school programs, and expansion of the definition of special populations

Information taken from Association for Career and Technical Education (2019).

Funding for CTE classrooms is provided according to how CTE programs address the legislative requirements. CTE educators are required to complete a program **quality indicator report** every year to document the following: teacher quality, FCCLA activities, academic integration with other educators, how the program offers dual credit/dual enrollment opportunities, and how the classroom activities are connected to careers. See Table 1.2 for current quality indicators for CTE programs. Also, each year, or at the end of the semester term (depending on the school system), CTE educators are required to report on how students attained competency on course standards, how many students are completers, and how many are concentrators. CTE educators also document how many students are ELLs, how many have IEPs, and the number of students who live at lower socioeconomic status. These reports are sent to the local CTE director and then on to the state level, where they are reported to the national level. When placed in a practicum or student teaching/residency placement, make sure to ask your mentor about these reports. Funding from Perkins may be used for

> activities such as improving programs, providing professional development, supporting the integration of academics and technical education, articulating secondary and postsecondary programs, implementing programs of study, purchasing equipment, providing students with career guidance, and ensuring access to CTE for youth with disabilities and other special populations. (College and Career Readiness and Success Center, 2013, p. 3)

TABLE 1.2   Current Quality Indicators of Programs for Perkins Funding

Teacher Quality	Programs have certified appropriately endorsed teachers.
Dual Credit/Dual Enrollment	Programs have state-approved articulation agreements.
Program Completers	Provide a number of students with two or more courses in a program of study sequence.
State Standards	Program uses state-approved curriculum standards.
Career Clusters	Program is aligned with state career clusters.
Sequence of Courses	Program must offer three or more courses in a program of study.
High Demand Career Education	Program is supported by current labor market data.
Career Education	Programs teach all aspects of an industry.
Active Advisory Panel	Members provide direction for growth or program.
Academic Integration	CTE and integration with Science, Technology, Engineering, Arts and Mathematics (STEAM) and other programs
Student Leadership Organization	Identify FCCLA activities.

Information taken from College and Career Readiness and Success (2013)

SPOTLIGHT: CARL D. PERKINS

Carl D. Perkins (see Figure 1.5) was born in October of 1912 in Hindman, Kentucky, where he attended school, including a junior college in Knox County (Dent, 2015). He later taught school in Knox County before he attended and graduated from Jefferson School of Law in Louisville, Kentucky (Dent, 2015). He served in World War II in combat and later married Verna Johnson (Dent, 2015). Carl D. Perkins became a member of the U.S. House of Representatives in 1948 during the Truman administration. For years, he served as the Democratic member on the House Education and Labor Committee (Dent, 2015). Additionally, he served as the chairperson of the General Subcommittee on Education and is best known for his landmark work (The Vocational Education Act of 1963) of bringing federal money to fund vocational programs (now under CTE) to help schools, including vocational schools (Dent, 2015), among many other humanitarian efforts. Perkins was a supporter of welfare programs under the New Deal. He was a champion of increasing Social Security benefits, Medicare, the war on poverty, school lunches, and public works (Dent, 2015). In 1972, Berea College awarded Perkins with an honorary degree: doctor of laws (Dent, 2015). Legislation impacting CTE since 1984 has been referred to as the Perkins Act in honor of Carl D. Perkins and his contribution to supporting CTE programs with an emphasis on providing marginalized individuals opportunities for education and job training.

FIGURE 1.5 Carl D. Perkins

Careers in FCS Education

FCS education is a problem-solving profession that incorporates various strategies to address the many challenges faced in society (AAFCS, n.d.-f). FCS education is an interdisciplinary field that provides opportunities for students to see real-world application of other subjects. FCS educators integrate knowledge from research-based resources of social science, physical and biological sciences, math, art, and humanities to help students identify, understand, and solve problems in life. The content is covered through public education in middle and high school programs of study and through community-based educators in cooperative community extensions, with each branch of FCS education requiring a baccalaureate or master's in FCS sciences education. See Table 1.3 for potential careers in FCS education.

Formal Education

Educators in public schools (formal traditional education) are required to be licensed in the educators' respective states. This license is from grades 6–12. In public schools, educators teach state course standards from the programs of study in the appropriate career cluster. Common courses include lifespan development, nutrition, family studies, independent living, fashion design, and

TABLE 1.3   Potential Careers in FCS Education

FCS high school teacher or FCS occupational teacher	Family crisis centers	Community agencies
FCS middle school teacher	Interior and fashion designers	Fund development agencies
Prevention and wellness education	Merchandising: equipment development and design	Improved product and services development
Managers of hotels, restaurants, spas	Merchandising: apparel design	Appliance, fabric, and furniture design
Foods: product development and public policy	Early childhood professionals	Extension agent
Foods: marketing, research, consumer affairs, planning	Human resource and youth programs	Dependent care

Information taken from AAFCS (n.d.-d).

interior design, which are grades 9–12, and a middle school curriculum including teen living or social health for grades 6–8.

On the other hand, educators can choose to become certified family life educators (CFLE) through the National Council on Family Relations (NCFR). Although this endorsement is not a state license to teach in middle and high schools, it is a certification that endorses candidates in 10 content areas of family life education, furthering their credentials to work in the human services field. The 10 content areas are (1) families and individuals in societal contexts, (2) internal dynamics of families, (3) human growth and development across the life span, (4) human sexuality across the life span, (5) family resource management, (6) parenting education and guidance, (7) family law and public policy, (8) professional ethics and practice, and (10) family life education methodology (NCFR, 2020). Many university programs have this certificate embedded in their coursework, and students gain the CFLE endorsement after graduating from one such endorsed program. For a complete list of universities that offer the CFLE, see NCFR CFLE approved programs at the NCFR website (https://www.ncfr.org/cfle-certification/cfle-approved-programs).

Occupational Education

Occupational licensure is for grades 9–12 and involves teaching skills that are directly related to a specific career. The most common occupational licenses in FCS are in food production and management, early childhood education, and fashion and fabrics. To obtain an occupational license, one must first hold licensure in FCS education and then add the appropriate coursework required to hold an occupational license. Currently, there is a nationwide shortage of licensed teachers in FCS education (Werhan & Whitbeck, 2017). The National Center for Educational Statistics (2009) reported that 90% of high school students take at least one CTE course. This shortage is causing a delay in the retirement of FCS educators and the closure of some FCS programs.

Master's and doctorate degrees are available in FCS education. Master's degrees are required for community college educators and adjunct university educators. Doctorate degrees are required for researchers and university researchers and professors.

Informal Education

Community-based educators working in **community cooperative extension services** provide FCS research-based knowledge and are funded by the U.S. Department of Agriculture and land grant universities. This information is shared in a nonformal setting to individuals and communities in adult programs across the nation. FCS topics include family relationships, nutrition, food safety, sanitation, money management, adult development, aging, food preservation, and gardening. Youth programs such as 4-H were also created with this legislation. For ages 9–19, 4-H research-based education emphasizes leadership skills/civic and service-learning by incorporating the values of "head, hand, heart, and health" into engaging activities with FCS content, such as family relations, leadership development, nutrition, money management, and career development (4-H, n.d.)

Other Careers Involving FCS Education Content

FCS professionals who work in social service agencies, such as the Department of Human Services, Department of Children Services, and health departments and agencies, help families who face trauma or individual/families at risk to meet basic needs by finding resources and making decisions to address needs. In industry, with companies that produce goods and services, FCS professionals are researchers and consultants helping to grow the field and provide necessary data on how programs and initiatives affect the lives of individuals, families, and communities.

SUMMARY

Regardless of the setting, the goal of every FCS education professional is to help individuals, families, and communities to make informed decisions to improve the quality of their lives. Through formal education, FCS allows students an opportunity to see how other subjects they study have real-world applications. Throughout the history of FCS, education legislation has impacted the profession to meet the needs of individuals, families, and society. Ellen Swallows Richards played a major role in the progressive era in U.S. history by using her skills for scientific research to improve and educate others on water quality, food preparation, sanitation, and quality of life. Richards's work created a new field that has evolved over time and continues to improve the lives of individuals, families, and communities. Nationally, there is a shortage of FCS educators in public schools, extension programs, and higher education (Werhan & Whitbeck, 2017). FCS educators are greatly needed to fill positions and to help individuals achieve optimal quality of life.

KEY TERMS

Quality of life

Smith/Hughes Act of 1917

Body of knowledge

Vocational Education Act of 1963

Morrill Land Grant Act of 1862

Community Cooperative Extension Services

Smith-Lever Act of 1914

Matilda effect

Quality indicator report

Career technical education (CTE)

Carl D. Perkins Act and subsequent
  reauthorizations, Perkins I–V

Ecology

Capacity building

Perennial problems

QUESTIONS AND ACTIVITIES

1. View the following webinar for information on how to use the BOK in the classroom. Open Access Webinars—FCS Body of Knowledge in the Classroom—FCS Education: https://www.fcsed.net/fcsed/support/support-webinars/open-access-fcsbok.
2. Briefly summarize the components of the FCS BOK.
3. Discuss five changes in FCS education that have resulted from legislation.
4. Conduct a web search of your state Department of Education and identify courses in FCS that are either occupational or traditional.
5. After reading the spotlight on Marjorie Brown, identify family strengths in each of the suggestions given. How can FCS promote capacity building?

REFERENCES

4-H. (n.d.). *About 4-H.* https://4-h.org/about/history/

American Association of Family and Consumer Sciences. (n.d.-a). *About AAFCS.* https://www.aafcs.org/advertise/about-aafcs

American Association of Family and Consumer Sciences. (n.d.-b). *Our symbol.* https://www.aafcs.org/about/about-us/aafcs-logos

American Association of Family and Consumer Sciences. (n.d.-c). *What is FCS?* https://www.aafcs.org/about/about-us/what-is-fcs

American Association of Family and Consumer Sciences. (n.d.-d). *Family and consumer sciences education: Issue in brief.* National Coalition of Family and Consumer Sciences Education. http://www.aafcs.org/Students/CareerFCS.asp

American Association of Family and Consumer Sciences. (n.d.-e). *Family and consumer sciences: The people-centered sciences.* https://www.aafcs.org/about/about-us/what-is-fcs

American Association of Family and Consumer Sciences. (n.d.-f). *National standards for family and consumer sciences.* http://www.leadfcsed.org/national-standards.html

Association for Career and Technical Education. (2019). *A brief history of CTE.* www.acteonline.org/wp-content/uploads/2019/06/BriefHistoryofCTE-Timeline-June2019.pdf

Brent, M. R., & Siskind, J. M. (2001). The role of exposure to isolated words in early vocabulary development. *Cognition, 81,* 33–34.

Bronfenbrenner, U. (1979). *The ecology of human development.* Harvard University Press.

College and Career Readiness and Success Center. (2013). *How career and technical education can help students be college and career ready: A primer.* American Institutes for Research. Retrieved February 28, 2022, from https://www.aypf.org/wp-content/uploads/2013/04/CCRS-CTE-Primer-2013.pdf

Dent, H. (2015). *Perkins, Carl D.: Home* (K. Grindstaff, Ed.). Berea College, Hutchins Library. https://libraryguides.berea.edu/carldperkins

Dunst, C. J. (2014). *Family capacity-building practices I: Foundations and conceptual model* [Oral Presentation]. Australian Early Childhood Program.

Hart, B., & Risley, T. R. (1995). *Meaningful differences in the everyday experience of young American children.* Paul H. Brookes Publishing Company.

Hunt, C. (1942). *The life of Ellen H. Richards.* American Home Economics Association.

Huttenlocher, J., Levine, S., & Vevea, J. (1998). Environmental input and cognitive growth: A study using time period comparisons. *Child Development, 69,* 1012–1029.

Kato, S. L., & Elias, J. G. (2015) *The foundations of family and consumer sciences* (2nd ed.). The Goodheart-Wilcox Company, Inc.

Kershner, K. (2017). *Why we should not forget Ellen Richards, founder of home ec movement.* How Stuff Works. https://howstuffworks.com/historicalfigures

Laster, J. F., & Johnson, J. (2001). Major trends in family and consumer sciences. In *Curriculum Handbook: Family and Consumer Sciences.* Association for Supervision and Curriculum Development. https://education.stateuniversity.com/pages/1976/Family-Consumer-Sciences-Education.html

Mason, L. (1968). School-work programs: The vocational education act in action. *The Clearing House, 42*(5), 294–296. http://www.jstor.org/stable/30180668

National Center for Educational Statistics. (2009). *Tables: Secondary/high school.* https://nces.ed.gov/surveys/ctes/tables/h123.asp

McGregor, S. T. (2014). Marjorie Brown's philosophical logic: Contemporary relevance. *Kappa Omicron Nu, 19*(1). https://www.kon.org/archives/forum/19-1/mcgregor3.html

McNeills, L. (2018, December 18). The first female student at MIT started an all women chemistry lab and fought for food safety. *Smithsonian Magazine.* https://www.smithsonianmag.com/science-nature/first-female-student-mit-started-women-chemistry-lab-food-safety-180971056/

National Council on Family Relations. (2020). *Family life education content areas: content and practice guidelines (2020).* https://www.ncfr.org/sites/default/files/2021-03/FLE%20Content%20and%20Practice%20Guidelines%202020.pdf

Nickols, S. Y., Ralston, P. A., Anderson, C. L., Browne, L., Schroeder, G. A., Thomas, S. L., & Wild, P. (2009). The family and consumer sciences body of knowledge and the cultural kaleidoscope: Research opportunities and challenges. *Family and Consumer Sciences Research Journal, 37*(3), 266–283.

Poirier, S., Remsen, M. A., & Sagen, R. (2017). Teaching and learning in family and consumer sciences education: Thriving in challenging times. *International Journal of Home Economics, 10*(2), 17–29.

Schmitt, S., Simpson, A. M., & Friend, M. (2011). A longitudinal assessment of the home literacy environment and early language. *Infant and Child Development, 20*(6), 409–431.

Sontang, J. C. (1996). Toward a comprehensive theoretical framework for disability research: Bronfenbrenner revisited. *Journal of Special Education, 30,* 319–344.

Staley, D. J. (2013). Democratizing American higher education: The legacy of Morrill land grant act. *Origins, 6*(4). https://origins.osu.edu/article/democratizing-american-higher-education-legacy-morrill-land-grant-act

Stone, J. R. (2014). More than one way: The case for high quality CTE. *American Educator.* https://www.aft.org/sites/default/files/stone.pdf

Swafford, M., Palmer, F., & Sisk, C. (2020). Research to practice enhances ecological theory and family capacity-building in home economics program practices. *International Journal of Home Economics, 13*(1), 127–136.

Swafford, M., Wingate, K., Zagumny, L., & Richey, D. D. (2015). Families living in poverty: Perceptions of family-centeredness. *Journal of Early Intervention, 37*(2), 138–154.

The Psychology Notes Headquarters. (2020, January 30). *Bronfenbrenner's ecological theory model.* http://thepsychologynotesheadquarters.com

Werhan, C. A., & Whitbeck, D. A. (2017). Family and consumer sciences teacher shortage inaccuracies: Collaborating to set the record straight. *Journal of Family and Consumer Sciences Education, 3* (special edition 2), 24–28. http://www.natefacs.org.Pages/v34se2 Werhan.pdf

Wylie, F. E. (1975). *M.I.T. in perspective: A history of the Massachusetts Institute of Technology.* Little, Brown.

Figure Credits

Embracing and Respecting Diversity

Rufaro Chitiyo, PhD; Melinda Swafford, PhD; and Elizabeth Ramsey, PhD, CFLE

FIGURE 2.1 Concepts of Diversity

Chapter 2 Objectives

After reading this chapter, you will be able to

- describe diversity and its importance,
- summarize the nondiscriminatory resolution of the American Association of Family and Consumer Sciences (AAFCS),
- identify the microcultures of diversity,
- identify the six principles of the Individual with Disabilities Education Act,

- summarize the principles of response to intervention,
- define and identify the purpose of the least restrictive environment and free appropriate public education,
- describe how educators promote a culturally competent classroom, and
- analyze how respecting diversity benefits preparing students for life.

Introduction

The mission of family and consumer sciences (FCS) education is to help individuals, families, and communities make decisions that improve quality of life. FCS education has focused on skills needed for successful living in our complex society. Consequently, FCS professionals need to be prepared to work with individuals and families of diverse backgrounds. Arnett (2012) reported that most FCS educators feel average in addressing diversity in the classroom, as education on diversity is often conducted in fragmented ways in teacher education programs.

The authors agree with Newsom et al. (2021) that learning must happen in culturally responsive environments for it to be both personal and meaningful. In our practice as FCS professionals in public schools, community extension, and higher education, we hold the philosophy that all individuals contribute to society and should be valued. It would be ideal if people accepted diversity as "normal." Diversity should not only be embraced but also respected. However, for individuals who derive comfort from commonality and sameness, the idea of diversity is often the root of anxiety (van Onselen, 2012).

This chapter will focus on promoting the acceptance of all students enrolled in FCS educational settings. The chapter will begin by defining diversity, covering the microcultures of diversity, and discussing terms associated with diversity. The chapter will continue with content on legislation that has provided educational opportunities. Finally, the chapter will include some suggestions to help the FCS educator create a culturally competent learning environment. Fostering a learning environment that is culturally competent promotes acceptance of others while avoiding stereotypical concepts and myths. According to Rehm and Allison (2006), all learners are diverse, even those from the same cultural background.

Diversity

Rice (2020) beautifully explained diversity as a rich blend of differences that includes "all the dimensions that make each person one of a kind, including ethnicity, race, age, style, gender, personality, beliefs, experiences, sexual orientation and more" (para. 1). We propose that when there is diversity, it means variety in the social and cultural characteristics at play within societies. Previous research has proven that diversity has a plethora of personal and educational benefits both in the short and long term (Farnsworth et al., 2004; Gurin et al., 2002; Hu & Kuh, 2003; Misra & McMahon, 2006).

The last few years have ushered in a widespread focus on both cultural competency and diversity in the United States (Newsom et al., 2021). In 2018, the U.S. Census Bureau projected that the United States will become a "White minority" nation in 2045. In 2019, the U.S. Census Bureau published data showing that diversity in the United States is growing at a faster rate than previously projected, implying that there will be more diverse families in this country than the typical White family. It is safe to speculate that because families have diversified in the past that diversity will continue with time. Worth noting is the fact that the U.S. Census Bureau (2019) specifically highlighted that diversity is higher among youths.

Reflecting on Sherbin and Rashid's (2017) work, we must mention that diversity is often used synonymously with inclusion, and that is problematic because while the two are somewhat related, they are distinctively different from each other. According to Segal (2019), when people hear the word "diversity," what often comes to mind is race or culture, and of course, these are among the key components of the diversity of ethnicity. "But diversity is much broader … and cuts across all facets of our lives" (Segal, 2019, para. 1). Diversity, therefore, is variety and does not equal deficient since it includes a number of factors and each factor can influence the relationships between teacher, student, family, and community. Inclusion, on the other hand, means empowering individuals so they not only feel a sense of belonging but can also openly contribute and engage as part of a group (Guyton, 2019). In Myers's (n.d) words, "Diversity is being invited to the party. Inclusion is being asked to dance" (para. 1).

Diversity is crucial because, as mentioned earlier, the United States is increasingly composed of non-White groups, and as such, there is a need to understand and respect each other. That understanding helps eliminate negative stereotypes and personal biases that we may have about different groups of people (Purdue University, 2021). In addition, diversity is essential because it introduces people to new experiences, as well as new ideas and perspectives as they learn and interact with each other (Segal, 2019). Based on O'Boyle's (2020) work, diversity is important because it increases acceptance and decreases discrimination, allows us to expand (and sometimes change) our perspectives, helps us become better global citizens, and enriches our life experiences.

Respecting and embracing diversity is necessary if we are to have a moral, unified society. The knowledge that we learn from our interactions with others may prevent stereotypes, myths, and discrimination by encouraging acceptance.

AAFCS Nondiscrimination Resolution

To embrace diversity and to implement ethical practice in our work with individuals, families, and communities, our professional organization (AAFCS) passed a nondiscrimination resolution at the 2006 annual meeting:

> Whereas AAFCS supports diversity and has consistently advocated to end discrimination, and whereas AAFCS is a professional society rooted in scientific principles and knowledge generated by research. Therefore be it resolved that the American Association of Family and Consumer Sciences does not tolerate discrimination with respect to an individual's or group's race, ethnicity, gender, religion, sexual orientation, marital status, age or disability, and therefore be it resolved that the American Association of Family and Consumer Sciences endorses the concept that all persons, regardless of individual's or group's race, ethnicity, gender, religion, sexual orientation, marital status, age or disability are entitled to equal protection and privilege under the law. (as cited in Crouch & Alexander, 2009).

This resolution was an important move to signify that AAFCS's professional organization embraces and respects the diversity of all individuals and families. With this resolution, state and local FCS programs have a model. FCS educators are the catalyst for providing FCS content, instructional activities, knowledge, and skills that will empower all learners regardless of diversity, gender, age, and exceptionality to become proficient in society.

Microcultures

Essential to a quality and culturally responsive FCS program, educators must have an understanding of the various **microcultures** that exist in the macroculture of the United States. Microculture refers to "identifiable groups of people who share the set of values, beliefs, and behaviors of the macroculture, possess a common history, and use a common verbal and nonverbal symbol system" (Neuliep, 2020, p. 84). Macroculture is the dominant culture of a society (Hall, 2005). Microculture may include race, age, gender **disability**, geographic location, and other identifying factors. As such, most Americans are members of a microculture, such as those depicted in Figure 2.2. While these groups may have things in common with the larger culture, they are united by specific traits, history, experiences, and values. Effective FCS educators should include personal and cultural connections within various microcultures to enhance student learning, as concepts will have relevance to the learners. This chapter will include content on how FCS educators respect various microcultures in FCS educational programs.

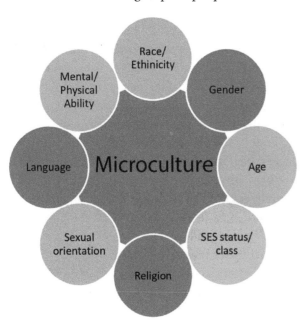

FIGURE 2.2 Microculture

Gender

FCS educators who are aware of gender bias in the classroom ensure that everyone is equally welcomed and represented positively in the family FCS classroom. The programs of study within the FCS provide content and an appropriate educational setting for students to explore independent and supportive gender roles in current society.

FCS has often been equated with women only. This belief may have contributed to the profession not being viewed by some as a relevant profession. As FCS professionals, we have witnessed the professional name not included in the legislation, cuts in funding, and courses that were originally FCS being taught by other educators. This belief and these practices need to change. Society benefits when all members become proficient in the multiple roles within the family and learn to balance work-life responsibilities (Swafford & Dainty, 2009). Our role as FCS professionals is to demonstrate how imperative the profession is to the well-being of society and its members.

Social Class/Socioeconomic Status

The socioeconomic status (SES) of a student includes not only income but also the educational level of the family members, as well as the status associated with the family's occupation. According to the Children's Defense Fund (2020), 1 in 6 American children lives in poverty. However, the poverty rate for children who are a minority and those with disabilities is higher (Parish et al., 2010).

Learners living in lower SES/social class levels face additional factors, such as poor health, less nutritious diets, fewer educational resources at home, resulting in a home that does not have a stimulating environment and often come from families with little formal education that impacts school readiness and learning opportunities (Hochschild, 2003). Often parents of children in lower SES have decreased self-esteem and increased stress, which results in increased parental depression, increased marital conflict, decreased nurturing of children, and harsh/ineffective child guidance. This type of home environment often results in learners with decreased self-esteem, challenging behaviors, poor cognitive development, and decreased language skills (Williams et al., 2016).

Social class is grouping individuals by wealth, influence, and status. The social class of a community often defines the student population of the school. Furthermore, social class influences the student's approach to learning, what is taught, and student expectations. Social class impacts how students are grouped. Schools often use ability tracking, which is not supported by research and correlated with SES (Hochschild, 2003), for placement in classes.

Ability tracking occurs by categorizing students by test scores, prior placements, and teachers' judgments (Hochschild, 2003) and should be avoided in quality FCS programs. Ability grouping impacts how teachers educate students and may lead to a self-fulfilling prophecy, which occurs when individuals or teachers have expectations that actually come to pass (Schaedig, 2020). For example, if a teacher does not expect quality work from a student and makes the student feel like they are not capable of quality work, the expectation, in essence, becomes a self-fulfilling prophecy, and the student will not strive to perform quality work. In the case of ability grouping, teachers might have a low expectation of their lowest ability group, and the students live up to that low expectation. Therefore, it is best not to use ability grouping in FCS classrooms and to maintain realistically high expectations for all students. Research documents that students in lower ability grouping receive instruction that is rote and mechanical, whereas students from upper class/SES level often receive instruction that encourages critical thinking and student-directed learning opportunities, such as projects (Marion, 2011). Classroom management also differs, as students in lower ability grouping often experience more teacher-directed lessons, and students from upper class/SES level often have input and discussion of classroom expectations (Marion, 2011). Also, a correlation exists between SES, race, and special education placement (Harry, 2008). These practices result in **systematic discrimination.**

Family Structure

As previously stated, minority and exceptionality are microcultures that intersect with lower SES/social class. Family structure is also a factor. Single-parent families are at high risk of living in lower social class/SES and often face food insecurity, fewer housing options, and utility shutoffs (Swafford et al., 2015). Diverse family structures are often not represented well by social policies and media (Fujiura & Yamaki, 2000; Harry et al., 2005). FCS educators must make sure to include diverse family structures in case studies, examples, and other teaching strategies instead of focusing only on the nuclear family in class. Failure to include a variety of family structures may result in a stigmatizing experience for the students and result in a "we-they" mentality (Harry et al., 2005).

Age

FCS educators may work with a variety of ages during their entire careers. It is important for you to understand the learner's intellectual, social, emotional, and physical development. As a community extension agent, one may work with fourth grade through high school students with 4-H. FCS educators notice we can expect certain intellectual, social, emotional, and physical skills to emerge during the time of middle childhood and adolescents. Furthermore, licensed FCS educators in public schools span the age range from sixth grade through senior year in high school. Each learner brings to the classroom a unique set of needs, abilities, and interests. FCS content can help ease the transition from middle childhood and adolescence to adulthood.

In community extension programs, FCS educators who work with adults as learners will note unique characteristics that may differ from working with adolescents. These characteristics include limited time, intrinsic motivation to learn, and requiring relevant content to meet learners' interests. Most adults do well with problem-centered learning or independent learning projects. Adults learn best in a student-centered, participatory, and collaborative environment, as many have established opinions, values, and beliefs about their experience with families, relationships, work, community, politics, and so forth. These views should not be dismissed but be respected. Learning more about these characteristics through human development courses will build an effective educator.

English Language Learners

English language learners (ELLs), by definition, are learners who have already acquired at least one language and are currently acquiring English (Lightbown & Spada, 2011). Typically, younger children are much more comfortable trying out their newly acquired language without fear of making a mistake when compared to adolescents and adults, who often find learning a new language stressful. This is an important concept to remember for FCS educators, as the adolescent students might feel intimidated using their newly acquired language skills and may not readily feel comfortable speaking in the classroom.

The behaviorism and innatist theoretical perspectives inform language acquisition, while cognitive theoretical perspectives inform how the mind perceives, organizes, retains, and retrieves information (Lightbown & Spada, 2011). The behaviorism approach was popular and widely used in the middle part of the 20th century and emphasized memorization and mimicry. Using this approach, children were taught to memorize basic scripts and dialogues (Lightbown & Spada, 2011). Nearing the 1970s, researchers found that behaviorism was inadequate for explaining second language acquisition, and the innatist approach began to become popular.

Chomsky, the forerunner of the innatist approach, rejected behaviorism and maintained that there are universal grammar principles that govern innate knowledge, which allows all children to acquire the language spoken in their environment during critical periods of development (Lightbown & Spada, 2011), which are early infancy to puberty (Papalia et al., 2012).

Later, Stephen Krashen, influenced by Chomsky, and dissatisfied with the behaviorism approach, developed the monitor model, which included five hypotheses (Lightbown & Spada, 2011). Included in the monitor model approach were acquisition-learning hypothesis, monitor hypothesis, natural order hypothesis, input hypothesis, and affective filter hypothesis (Lightbown & Spada, 2011, pp. 36–37). These five hypotheses demonstrated that (1) language learners acquire what they are exposed to; (2) language learners make adjustments and changes over time and are eventually able to produce language with relevant rules; (3) language acquisition follows a predictable sequence (e.g., grammar rules may be easy to state but not easy to add to spontaneous talk and therefore take time); (4) if a learner has already acquired a certain level, they need exposure to the next level; and (5) how a learner feels about a language matters, as their motives, feelings, and attitudes can prevent them from acquiring a language (Lightbown & Spada, 2011).

Considering cognitive perspectives, the information-processing model would propose that with language acquisition, declarative knowledge is learned first and later turns into procedural knowledge. Oftentimes, language development presents as a sudden burst of knowledge, where students seem to have "aha moments" but can also have moments of backsliding in their newly acquired skills.

SPOTLIGHT: ELL IN THE SCHOOL SYSTEM

In 1970, under civil rights laws, schools were obligated to provide equal access for ELLs to education (National Clearinghouse for English Language Acquisition, n.d.). Although specific services and modifications are not specified by state or federal law, the legislation provides a broad outline for schools to follow. The memo written by the Federal Office for Civil Rights states,

> Where the inability to speak and understand the English language excludes national origin minority group children from effective participation in the educational program offered by a school district, the district must take affirmative steps to rectify the language deficiency in order to open its instructional program to these students. (National Clearinghouse for English Language Acquisition, n.d., para. 4)

Although this memo does not explain the steps, it does explain how the law can be violated: (1) The law is violated if students are excluded from participating due to their inability to speak English; (2) the law is violated if minority students are inappropriately assigned to special education classes because of their inabilities in English; (3) the law is violated if programs to teach English are not provided immediately or if the programs lead nowhere; and (4) the law is violated if parents do not receive communication in the language they understand (National Clearinghouse for English Language Acquisition, n.d.).

Later, Congress passed the Equal Educational Opportunity Act, which required that no state should deny an individual equal opportunity. The following guidelines, borrowed from the National Clearinghouse for English Language Acquisition, exist for school districts regarding service of ELLs:

1. Identify potential ELLs.
2. Assess individual's need for ELL services.

(Continued)

3. Develop ELL program informed by experts in the field.
4. Necessary staff, curriculum materials, and facilities should be in place and properly used.
5. Develop evaluation standards, exit criteria, and methods to measure success.
6. Assess program success and modify as needed.

As an FCS teacher, you will have students in your classroom who are ELLs. You will need to make accommodations for them and support their learning. You may also need to collaborate with the English as a second language (ESL) teacher to help the students in your classroom. It is important to develop a good working relationship with the ESL teacher. Many times, the ESL teacher can support your teaching units if you will simply communicate your plans and student activities. Table 2.1 gives a helpful list of strategies for working with ELL students.

TABLE 2.1   Strategies for Working With ELL Students

Use modeling.	Demonstrate and explain actions.
Use think alouds.	Describe actions as you model.
Show examples.	Use visual student examples.
Use wait-time.	Be sure to wait ample time for responses or before calling on someone.
Speak slowly and clearly.	Don't rush; speak slow and clear.
Use visuals.	Show student examples, gestures, pictures.
Give verbal and written instructions.	Give written instructions along with verbal instructions. Include examples and pictures if needed.
Check for understanding.	Periodically check for understanding using thumbs up/down/sideways, Post-it® notes, red/green/yellow light method.
Incorporate group work.	Place children in small groups whenever possible so that they will have an opportunity to practice speaking to their peers in a less intimidating setting than the whole class.
Respect the silent period.	Do not force students to talk.
Honor their first language.	Allow students to use vocabulary from their first language or ask a question in their first language to a peer. If they are not capable of writing a response in English, allow them to write it in their first language instead of not participating.
Use sentence frames.	Give students sentence frames to aid discussions, for example, "I agree with _____, and would like to add _____".
Pre-teach.	Whenever possible, send material and links ahead of time to ESL students. This helps them feel empowered and ready to learn.
Learn and respect the culture.	Take time to learn about the culture of your ESL students but avoid making generalizations about their culture.

Informed by Ferlazzo (2012) and Gonzalez (2014)

Microcultures History

Regarding race and ethnicity in the United States, we are focusing on American Indians, African Americans, Hispanic/Latino Americans, Asian Americans, and Arab Americans as microcultures represented in school systems across the nation. The Office of Management and Business (1997) defined the first four microcultures as follows:

- *American Indian:* A person having origins in any of the original peoples of North and South America (including Central America) and who maintains tribal affiliation or community attachment.

Looking back at history, there have been multiple inappropriate attempts to educate American Indian children. For example, these children were forced to attend boarding schools run by religious organizations whose mission was to "assimilate Native children to the dominant American culture's language, values, and behaviors through a process of deculturalization" (Lynch, 2016, para. 3). To accomplish their mission, children were not allowed to use their native language or practice their customs, and this was a sure means of thwarting the Indigenous culture and replacing it with the mainstream American culture. Research on how to effectively teach American Indian students has shown that it's imperative for educators to lead by

incorporating Native American culture, understanding Native American culture and their beliefs, showing concern, making students accountable, and requiring them to do the work, being fair and sincere, creating a positive environment, providing options or choices in assignments, giving reasons for what students are learning and relating the learning to the real world, pointing out success stories, and treating. (Sorkness & Kelting-Gibson, 2006, p. 10)

- *African American:* A person having origins in any of the Black racial groups of Africa.

African American children may use different dialects from the standard, and whether to accept or reject these dialects has been a societal predicament for many decades in this country (Smitherman, 1986). In 1954, *Brown v. Board of Education* was decided by the U.S. Supreme Court, making segregation (i.e., separating people based on race, ethnicity, gender, or religion) unconstitutional. However, even though the Supreme Court ruled against segregated schools, many districts and schools remained and still are de facto segregated (Lane et al., 2020). According to Cornell Law School (n.d.), *de facto segregation* describes a situation where school segregation continued regardless of legislation ruling that the segregation of students by race was not in accordance with the U.S. Constitution. Based on personal experience and in liaising with African American parents, El-Mekki (2017) published recommendations to adopt when teaching African American students. These are

having the right mindset, supporting students in developing a positive racial identity, having high expectations and high support, helping the students see themselves as contributors to society and as future leaders, serving holistically, learning the culture, helping African American students become skilled in channeling anger, having a communal outlook, and maintaining a strong sense of purpose. (El-Mekki, 2017, para. 3)

- *Hispanic:* A person of Cuban, Mexican, Puerto Rican, Cuban, South or Central American, or other Spanish culture or origin, regardless of race.

People who are Hispanic are now the largest minority group in the United States (U.S. Census Bureau, 2019). For this microculture, community and family needs are more important than individual needs. In addition, in comparison to White students, Hispanic students are more collectivistic in nature, as evidenced by being cooperative, not exhibiting competitiveness, and tolerating group members who do not do their work. Hispanic students are also documented to sometimes help their peers by allowing them to copy their work (Neuliep, 2020). According to Howe (1994), improving achievement for Hispanic students entails

> placing value on the students' languages and cultures, setting high expectations for the students, designing staff development to help teachers and other staff serve Hispanic students more effectively, designing counseling programs that give special attention to Hispanic students, encouraging parents to become involved in their children's education, and building a strong commitment among school staff members to empower these students through education. (p. 44)

- *Asian:* A person having origins in any of the original peoples of the Far East, Southeast Asia, or the Indian subcontinent including, for example, Cambodia, China, India, Japan, Korea, Malaysia, Pakistan, the Philippine Islands, Thailand, and Vietnam. (p. 8)

Asian Americans are among the fastest-growing ethnic groups in the United States. The term "Asian American" refers to a wide range of national and religious/cultural heritages, implying that even though there are similarities among different Asian subgroups, they differ in origins and history as well (Feng, 1994). The most prevalent stereotype of Asian students is that they are smarter than every other student, and the reality is these children are a diverse group and should not be viewed as all being the same. There are widely known and accepted recommendations for how teachers can successfully educate Asian students, and these are

> familiarizing themselves with the values, traditions, and customs of various cultures, learning the migratory conditions specific to each of their students' families, learning at least a few words of their Asian students' native languages, encouraging parents to help children maintain their native language at home, while the school helps the child attain proficiency in English, basing academic expectations on individual ability rather than on stereotypical beliefs, and alleviating the disconnection Asian children may experience between school and home. (Feng, 1994, p. 4)

- *Arab:* "A person with ancestries originating from Arabic-speaking countries or areas of the world" (Neuliep, 2020, p. 112).

Arab students in U.S. schools represent approximately 20 nations in the Middle East and Northern Africa and face challenges related to not only racial discrimination but also misinformation about their religious and cultural beliefs (American-Arab Anti-Discrimination Committee [AAADC],

2002). Sadly, regardless of increases in the number of Arab students in U.S. public schools, many schools still do not acknowledge Arab history and culture, let alone act against stereotypes, discrimination, and violence against Arab individuals (AAADC, 2002). It is essential for schools to provide safe and supportive school climates for these children because that's a basic human right. There are available recommendations for schools with Arab students, and these include

> representing Arabs accurately, completely, and fairly in the curriculum and school activities, ensuring that Arab students are treated equitably and without prejudice by teachers and peers, and that teachers respond to incidences of racism and discrimination strongly and quickly, with attention to both the perpetrators and the victims, correcting erroneous information when confronted with it, and not enforcing dress codes or showering requirements that violate the Muslim tradition of modesty or require Muslim students to engage in coed physical education classes. (Zehr, 1999, p. 10)

Exceptional Learners

Since 1975, legislation (P.L. 94-142, P.L. 105-17, Section 504 of Vocational Rehabilitation Act, and **Americans with Disabilities Act [ADA]**) has been passed to mandate that all students be educated in their **least restrictive environment (LRE)**, which means to educate with their peers to the maximum extent possible (Swafford & Giordano, 2017). On the continuum of services, the LRE is a full-time placement in the general education classroom, and that classroom may be the FCS classroom.

Students with exceptionalities are generally those students who perform cognitively above or below the age range of typically developing children. Students with exceptionalities may range from one with an intellectual disability to one that is gifted. This term may also include individuals that have various physical disabilities that make daily tasks difficult (e.g., cerebral palsy, spina bifida, etc.). Including students with exceptionalities and students from diverse cultures in the regular classroom provides all with opportunities to participate with peers and gain skills and self-esteem. The placement of students is determined by assessments and multidisciplinary team members: parents, educators, and the student (if over the age of 14) who attend an **individualized education plan (IEP)** meeting. The placement ranges from full time in a self-contained classroom to full-time placement in a general education classroom such as FCS with appropriate modifications and/or accommodations (Turnbull et al., 2006).

FCS content courses provide the opportunity to merge skills with real-life situations. In addition, the FCS classroom provides the perfect environment to showcase the diversity of family roles/traditions, food preparation, child-rearing practices, and other unique perspectives of family and culture.

Becoming Culturally Competent

In order for educators to create inclusive and equitable classroom environments, they need to be intentional. Educators should be empowered to be competent enough to design learning spaces that are welcoming and safe for every student. **Cultural competency** is an awareness of oppression faced by others and active involvement in social justice (Allen, 2005). It is important to be cognizant of the existing power relationship used by schools that students and families encounter day to day, as many individuals from marginalized populations (minorities) or with disabilities face oppression and discrimination. Educators who have been taught to appreciate diversity are more self-confident, have increased abilities, and move beyond judging students by superficial attributes such as skin, color, speech patterns, and exceptionality (Swafford & Dainty, 2009).

To have a culturally competent learning environment, FCS educators must know their students, identify factors that will help them be successful in the classroom, be aware of situations their students may face in everyday life, keep communication open, and explore hidden or implicit biases. **Hidden or implicit bias** is an unconscious bias that may be demonstrated in action or beliefs that result in stereotypes/prejudices or discriminating behavior. When educators identify and explore their own biases, they can monitor and ameliorate attitudes and behavior before they are demonstrated in the classroom. Make sure the policies of the school/classroom are not contributing to **institutional discrimination**, which is defined as embedded "normal" practices of an institution that are unfair to certain individuals or cultures. An example is when a student must miss school to serve as a translator for the family. Upon returning to school, the student is unable to make up missed work because of going beyond the number of absences that are deemed appropriate by the school in order to make up work. Incorporating and accepting a flexible attitude with high expectations will enhance the learning potential of all students (Rhem & Allison, 2006).

SPOTLIGHT: UNDERSTANDING BIAS: THE HIDDEN BIAS TEST

Hidden or Implicit Bias Test

Use the following link to evaluate hidden biases that you may have. Reflect on how these biases may impact your classroom environment and include ways to address your biases.

http://www.tolerance.org/activity/test-yourself-hidden-bias

Students of Promise

Respecting diversity requires that educators view all students with interest and openness and be flexible during instruction. However, in order for diverse learners to feel accepted, differences must be viewed as assets rather than deficits (Davis, 2006). As such, Blasi's (2002) study prepared individuals to support diversity by shifting the focus from deficiency to one of strength. The goal was for preservice educators to view students and families through a strength-based perspective and look for potential instead of deficiencies. This study used the term "of promise" when describing students and families living in poverty, belonging to a cultural/ethnic minority, a family having a nontraditional family structure, and a family who spoke a first language other than English. Using this strategy, the educator becomes aware of the importance of being nonjudgmental and accepting of all families while recognizing the strength of the families and culture.

SPOTLIGHT: QUINCEAÑERA

By Melinda Swafford

Lack of knowledge, stereotypical beliefs, and/or myths about someone or something different often leads to **prejudice** (a belief that some individuals are not equal to others because of some difference) or **discrimination** (an act of treating people unequally due to some difference). During my last few years as an FCS educator in a 7–12 school in a small rural community, many Hispanic families moved into the community. This was a drastic change to our 99.9% White community and school. One could hear rumblings of comments as some students were having difficulty welcoming and accepting the new students. I heard one student say, "Their food stinks!" In addition to a language barrier, students were facing discrimination due to **intersectionality** (multiple aspects that created disadvantages). Something had to be done to change this!

A colleague who taught music, Mrs. B, approached me and another teacher, Ms. K, to help her with a project. Mrs. B. had several female Hispanic students in her music class who were turning 15 soon. She wanted to have a quinceañera-type event at the school. After permission was granted by the administration, we set about educating the student body on the Latin American culture of quinceañera. The event was held in the school auditorium during the third block class, which was also the first lunch, to provide opportunities for more students who wanted to attend to be excused from their usual classes.

Mrs. B. planned the ceremony that included a guest speaker and cultural music and songs. The female students wore beautiful gowns, and chambelanes (boys of the quinceañera court) and damas (girls of the quinceañera court) were selected. Mrs. B. tried to make the event as authentic as possible. Ms. K taught dance in her strength and condition class, and those who wanted to participate could. My food and nutrition students prepared a reception that consisted of tamales, salsa, rice, and cake. After the speaker blessed the students, beautiful songs and music were provided by Mrs. B., and Ms. K's class performed a traditional dance and invited other students to join in and participate.

Afterward, all were dismissed to my FCS room for a reception. Our goal was to gain an understanding and appreciation of Latin American culture through this activity. The event was not as heavily attended by the White students as we would have liked. However, we noticed a sense of pride in the students who participated. In the school newspaper, one student wrote, "Thanks to everyone who shared in the event. It made the girls feel closer to home. Also thanks to the students that have let Latin American culture become a part of this school" (Domingo, 2001, p. 4).

Becoming Culturally Proficient

To become "culturally proficient" does not mean that one must understand everything about everyone's culture, but one must acknowledge how beliefs impact actions; building respect and accommodations for cultural aspects of students' lives formulates a positive belief system (Swafford & Dainty, 2009). Classroom activities that validate other cultures and disabilities help students gain respect and become informed learners about the world. Including content on how different cultures and individuals with disabilities embrace many topics, such as child-rearing practices, family interactions, food or food preparation techniques, finances, and family values will build cultural proficiency.

Research by Rehm and Allison (2006) indicated that FCS educators are aware of diversity in the classroom. However, most of the accommodations/modifications include grading or presentation of materials. If the climate of the classroom is not modified, students will imitate the attitude the teacher is modeling, so educators must be accepting of all students and recognize their strengths.

Mental and physical abilities are components of our macroculture. The language we use as well as syntax (word order) reflects our acceptance and respect for individuals with disabilities. One way to become culturally proficient is to incorporate **person-first language (PFL)** into your vernacular. PFL is associated mostly with individuals with disabilities, as it is a respectful way to put the person before the disability. "A person's self image is tied to words used about them" (Snow, 2016, para. 8). For example, instead of using the phrase *mentally retarded individual,* using the phrase student with a cognitive disability or student with an intellectual disability denotes that the person is an individual first before the disability (Snow, 2016). The term *mentally retarded* is very disrespectful and should never be used. PFL can also be used in other situations where the emphasis is put on the person, not the difference. An example of using PFL with the race/ethnicity microculture, is to state students who are Hispanic instead of Hispanic students. It may take a conscious effort to change your vernacular, but it will be noticed in the respectful way one interacts with others.

In contrast to PFL, we have individuals who prefer **identity-first language (IFL)**, which includes individuals who see a disability as part of who they are. Individuals who embrace this countermovement believe that disability is not a negative or derogatory word. In using this vernacular, one would say, "I am a disabled person." It is observed by those in the Deaf community and autistic community.

ACTIVITY 2.1: WEBSITE REVIEW

For more information, view the Disability is Natural website (https://disabilityisnatural.com). For information on identity first, view the web page "What Is Identify First Language" (https://ausometraining.com/identity-first-language/).

What Is Identity-First Language? | AUsome (ausometraining.com)

After viewing the websites, respond to the following questions: Do you prefer person-first or identity-first language? Why?

SPOTLIGHT: TIPS ON CREATING A CULTURALLY COMPETENT CLASSROOM CLIMATE (SWAFFORD & DAINTY, 2009)

1. Review curriculum and other resources, such as audiovisual, bulletin boards, and posters, to represent all genders in supportive and nurturing roles within the family.

2. To avoid invisibility, make sure each cultural group in your class, as well as individuals with exceptionalities, are depicted in a positive light (Banks & Banks, 1997).

3. Use language that respects all diversities. An example would be to use PFL by referring to the student first, such as "the student with Down syndrome" rather than "the Down syndrome student."

4. Discuss contributions of individuals who are minorities, such as Maya Angelou, John L. Lewis, Oprah Winfrey, Sonia Sotomayor, and Cesar Chavez.

5. Display articles and advertisements that discuss diverse cultures.

6. Treat each culture as a unique culture by not lumping together all minorities or exceptionalities. Do not assume that all students who speak Spanish speak the same dialect and can understand each other. For example, there are many dialects in Guatemala.

7. Encourage participation of all students, even if it requires the use of nods, hand signals, and visuals.

8. Use peer tutoring and collaborative activities to assist students.

9. Become aware of the technology that families are comfortable using for communication. Do families prefer email, text, or letters? Make sure these are translated into their respective language. Do families prefer face-to-face communication? If so, provide a translator if available.

Students with Exceptionalities and Legislation

Figure 2.3 provides a visual of the special education process. A parent, educator, or administrator may refer a learner for special education services. The school system has 60 calendar days to complete the referral process, which includes observation by educators, parental input, and screening

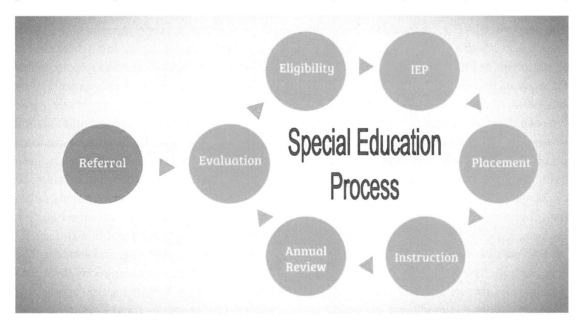

FIGURE 2.3 Special Education Process

and evaluation of the learner's current ability. An IEP meeting is held with the family of the learner, along with educators, administrators, and school psychologists. During this meeting, the learner's present level of performance, placement, academic goals, objectives, and related services will be determined, present level of performance, as well as any required instructional accommodations or modifications. Yearly, a meeting will be held to determine progress toward the learner's goals and objectives. At age 14 transitions for after high school will be addressed.

Under the **Individuals with Disabilities Act (IDEA)**, students with exceptionalities are provided with six principles in legislation: zero rejection, appropriate education, LRE, parent participation, nondiscriminatory evaluation, and procedural due process (Turnbull et al., 2006). *Zero rejection* is based on the 14th Amendment and requires that everyone should have equal educational opportunities and must be educated regardless of the type or extent of disability at no charge, known as **free appropriate public education (FAPE)**. Prior to the passage of the Education for All Handicapped Children Act of 1975, one million students were excluded from public education. Families were forced to find services outside public education, and when services were received, the educational needs of the students were not being met (Turnbull et al., 2015).

Appropriate education was included in the law to avoid placing students with disabilities in a segregated setting. Appropriate education provisions describe related services (speech, transportation), supplementary aides (technology), services (occupational and or physical therapy), and program modifications (opportunities to redo work, extra time, oral testing, small group, and/or peer tutoring). At the time of this writing, the latest data indicates that between 2018 and 2019, 7.1 million or 14% of children between the ages of 3 and 21 received special education services in public schools under IDEA (National Center for Education Statistics, 2020).

Inclusion

The purpose of LRE is to educate students with disabilities with age-appropriate peers to the maximum extent possible. IDEA favors **inclusion** but does not use the term *inclusion*; instead, it refers to education in the LRE with age-appropriate peers. Educators should make planned lessons accessible for students by planning appropriate accommodations and modifications for the students to be successful. **Accommodation** is when you do not change the curriculum, but you simply offer some type of aid or make a change to help the student overcome a disability. An example accommodation is when you have a student following a recipe that requires chopped onions. The student can use a pizza cutter to chop the onions instead of using a knife if using a knife is too difficult. The standard has not changed. A **modification** is when you change the curriculum—that is, change what is learned or change an expectation. If that same student uses onion flakes or frozen chopped onions rather than chopping fresh onions because for some reason they cannot chop onions, then a modification has been made because the curriculum has been altered when the psychomotor skill was deleted.

For inclusion to be successful, three things are necessary: desire, planning, and support. The educator must have the desire to create a sense of belonging for everyone in the classroom. It requires planning to make sure the content of the lesson is appropriate for everyone, which includes appropriate accommodations and modifications needed in the planning, implementation, and assessment of all lessons. Planning includes peer tutoring or cooperative groups so that students with difficulty in reading comprehension may be placed with students who read well. Use hand-over-hand accommodation when a student is first using a knife to cut, or use a pizza cutter instead of a knife to cut items in a recipe. Support is also necessary; this may mean an education assistant, use of peer tutoring, use of technology, and access to funds to purchase equipment needed by the student. When an educator has the desire to include individuals with exceptionalities, takes the time to plan, and is provided with Attending the IEP meeting provides the FCS educator with important knowledge of the student and the opportunity to plan the appropriate modifications/accommodations to help the student achieve course standards resources to support a culturally competent classroom, all students feel welcomed and succeed.

Response to Intervention

Response to intervention (RTI) became a part of special education during the 2004 reauthorization of IDEA. RTI is a tiered approach of academic intervention for students who struggle academically and/or behaviorally. The tiered approach includes high-quality instruction and screening for all students. Group-targeted and intensive interventions for students who struggle academically and behaviorally are implemented with progress noted at each level and decisions made for either continuation in the general education classroom or referral for special education interventions (Ehren, 2008).

The Office of Special Education Programs included notes in IDEA 2004 that school systems could use either the discrepancy model or RTI as an indicator of students with specific learning disabilities. Prior to 2004 school systems across the country could only use the discrepancy model to identify students with learning disabilities for special education services. The discrepancy model compares the student's IQ to academic achievement. Several problems are associated with the discrepancy model, as students are often identified late in the school year; students eligible for special education in one state may not be eligible in another state; and areas of concern (such as math, reading, writing) were not identified by the discrepancy model (Understood, n.d.).

According to research by Burns (2010), the three-level framework includes Tier 1, which consists of high-quality research-based instructional strategies for all learners. This tier will usually address the needs of most learners (usually 80%) using differentiated instruction strategies and other research-based strategies. However, for learners needing additional support (usually less than 20%), Tier 2 is implemented. This tier may include small group instruction. For learners who need more intense intervention and support (usually no more than 5%), Tier 3 is incorporated to provide additional resources and interventions, like one-on-one intervention (Burns, 2010). Differentiated instruction and research-based strategies will be addressed with more content in Chapter 8, "Instructional Strategies."

RTI in the FCS Classroom

RTI provides a more cohesive effort for student success rather than just identifying students who need special education services, as many students may not qualify for special education services but still need help for academic success (Ehren, 2008). To implement RTI in the FCS classroom, the educator will observe *all* students in reading, writing, and math early in the school year. The educator will identify various levels and targeted supports to help students that struggle in academics and/or behavior. The educator will note various strategies that improve content retention and application of content and skills and continue use or fade out as needed. Learners who do not improve with support are referred to special education services (Burns, 2010). See "Differentiated Instruction" in

TABLE 2.2   Examples of Modifications and Accommodations, Borrowed from Kessler (n.d.)

General Accommodations	General Modifications
Additional time	Outline instead of writing an essay
Restate information	Use alternative books/materials
Restate/review directions	Provide word banks
Adapt writing or working utensils	Video clips instead of reading
Use visuals	Simplify/reword language of test questions
Assistance with organization and decluttering	Lesson workload
Home-school communication logs, notebooks, or emails	Lessen length of exams
Peer notetaking/scribe	Lesson length of assignments
Large print	Pass/no pass option
Visual and verbal cues	Allow spell check
Recorded lectures	Allow calculator
Recorded books	Highlight important phrases and words
Reduce distractions	Modify time restraints
Routines	
Breaks	

Chapter 8 for specifics on targeted supports and interventions. See the Spotlight selection "Reflections of a Preservice Teacher During Residency/Student Teaching" by Kristen Giordano, MS, in Chapter 11 for targeted supports and interventions with instruction and assessments.

Nondiscriminatory evaluation provides for fair and unbiased evaluation that identifies the student's strengths and needs. For example, if a student is an ELL, then the student must be given the evaluation in their primary language and not in English.

Procedural due process provides options for settling the conflict between the school system and the family. Mediation (collaborative problem solving with an impartial mediator) is the first step. If that is not successful, a resolution session should be held between the IEP team and the local education association person with the power to make decisions, discuss disputes, and resolve conflicts. If that is not successful, the resolution session is followed by a due process hearing. This involves an impartial hearing officer who conducts a mini-trial between the school and family challenging each other's actions in providing the six principles of IDEA.

The Americans with Disabilities Act (ADA) is a civil rights legislation, passed in 1990, that prevents private employers, state and local governments, agencies, and unions from discriminating against individuals with disabilities in the areas of education and employment (Richey, 2000). This legislation also impacted the daily lives of individuals with disabilities in regard to access and services. In educational settings, ADA provided the addition of handrails, ramps, extension of the width of doorways to accommodate wheelchairs, accessible bathroom facilities, and lab facilities that are accessible for use by all individuals.

Educators must also make accommodations required by 504 plans. Passed in 1973, this legislation, **the Rehabilitation of 504**, was the first civil rights act to protect individuals with disabilities. This plan provides accommodation for students with exceptionalities that do not require an IEP. However, because of some specific conditions, the student needs accommodation to experience academic success in the general education classroom. An example might be a peanut-free environment for a student with a severe peanut allergy in the FCS food lab. Figure 2.4 demonstrates Culinary Art students providing a peanut free lab of cereal as a way to promote careers for kindergarten students

Career Technical Education Programs

Due to legislation, career technical education (CTE) and FCS programs of quality must meet the requirements of ADA, 504 plans, Perkins, and IDEA. These federal laws prevent discrimination in educational settings by providing inclusive programs. Inclusion began with the 14th Amendment, which protected the rights of citizens and provided equal protection under the law. Later, in 1954, the *Brown vs. Board of Education* decision noted that separate educational facilities were unconstitutional. As covered in Chapter 1, the passage of the legislation has included support for marginalized populations. In legislation such as the Vocational Education Act of 1963, funding was provided to serve individuals with disabilities in CTE courses. In Perkins II, Vocational Education Act of 1984, funding was designated to ensure that underserved individuals would have equal access to educational opportunities and work-based learning. This legislation provided funding to include individuals with disabilities, individuals living in poverty, and ELLs and eliminated gender

FIGURE 2.4 Virginia CTE Culinary Arts Students Host Career Exploration for Kindergarten Students

bias in CTE courses. Subsequent reauthorization of Perkins has continued to provide funding for individuals with disabilities and those who are at risk, students who are ELL, and students living in lower SES with career-to-work opportunities. This legislation also required a correlation between the student's IEP and the CTE courses

SPOTLIGHT: REVIEW TEACHING MATERIALS FOR BIAS

There are six biases that are commonly found in teaching materials: (1) linguistic bias, (2) stereotyping, (3) invisibility, (4) imbalance, (5) unreality, and (6) fragmentation (Banks & Banks, 1997). Furthermore, biases and stereotyping may be exhibited in the classroom through language, tone of voice, and images. Swafford and Dainty (2009) identified suggestions to help eliminate bias with classroom materials.

1. If the material contains biases, confront the bias with a classroom discussion rather than ignore it.
2. Supplement materials when the textbook is biased.
3. Intervene when students group by race/gender during cooperative group activities, and encourage and praise when diverse groups work together.
4. Become aware of verbal and nonverbal communication from all cultures in the class. Be cognizant of mixed messages or words that may mean something totally different in American culture.

Tips on Planning and Presenting Classroom Materials

When planning to meet the diverse needs of your students, it is very important to know your audience. The teacher must have knowledge of the stages of learning and of the various learning styles. They must also provide more than one mode of presenting information and use alternatives, such as pictures, translated materials, and physical modification of equipment. Focus on the strengths of the individual student.

1. Attend the IEP meeting and suggest appropriate accommodations and modifications to course standards if needed.
2. When using computer programs to translate, it is better to use isolated words and phrases. When whole paragraphs are translated, meaning may be lost, so it may help to consult bilingual professionals to promote accuracy, communication, and instruction.
3. Consider service-learning projects. Service-learning projects are helpful in changing the climate of the classroom to one that is focused on helping others. Service-learning projects require students to give to something beyond themselves, such as family, peers, and community. Students gain decision-making skills and increase problem-solving, collaboration, and communication skills. The project may be used in Family, Career, and Community Leaders of America STAR Events.

SUMMARY

Changes in demographics within our country and the education system have greatly impacted the student population and resulted in increased diversity within a typical CTE classroom. For social justice in education, FCS educators need to be prepared to work with students and families from different cultures, family structures, and various types of learners. Collectively, IDEA, ADA, and Perkins legislation and the professional organization of AAFCS provided the following for diverse students, as well as students with exceptionalities: equal opportunity, which is the same opportunities in life like everyone else; requires that students fully participate, are included in all aspects of their community, and are not discriminated against because of diversity; disability; independent living, which provides an opportunity to make choices about how to live life; and economic self-sufficiency, which provides opportunities to engage fully in income-producing work or unpaid work that contributes to household or community. Students will imitate the attitude the educator is modeling; therefore, an educator must be sure that the classroom environment is one where all students, regardless of their gender, culture, language ability, or exceptionality, are emotionally and physically safe. Students enrolled in FCS develop skills that enable them to meet the challenges of society, ultimately impacting quality of life.

KEY TERMS

Least restrictive environment (LRE)

Free appropriate education (FAPE)

Individuals with Disabilities Act (IDEA)

Individualized education plan (IEP)

Person-first language (PFL)

Prejudice

Disability

Procedural due process

Discrimination

Institutional discrimination

Microcultures

English language learners (ELLs)

Inclusion

Cultural competency

Intersectionality

Modification

Accommodation

Identity-first language (IFL)

The Rehabilitation of 504

Systematic discrimination

Hidden or implicit bias

Americans with Disabilities Act (ADA)

Response to Intervention (RTI)

QUESTIONS AND ACTIVITIES

1. Gather various children's literature that represent diverse economic backgrounds, such as *A Different Pond* by Bao Phi, *The Can Man* by Laura E. Williams, and *A Bike Like Sergio's* by Maribeth Boelts. Examine the texts for stereotypes and assumptions related to low-income families, immigrant families, and homeless families. Engage in a critical conversation using conversation stems (Appendix A) regarding economic diversity and hardships. Book suggestions are borrowed from Quast and Bazemore-Bertrand (2019).

2. Do I know my own biases? Have I made an effort to understand them? What changes can I make that are positively responsive to everyone?

3. After reading "Review Teaching Materials for Bias," select content that is often used in the FCS classroom to review. Note any bias toward diversity. Share with others in the class.

4. Read the following case study and respond to the following questions. You are a Caucasian woman teaching a class where students who are Latino are in the majority. While they are media savvy and on the surface quite acculturated, you learn through class discussions that students' families hold traditional views about the roles of men and women in the family. Do you feel comfortable addressing gender issues in this class? How do you address issues such as gender discrimination in the workplace and gender roles in the home while still respecting the norms and values of the students? How do you empower the female students without taking anything from the male students (Arnet, 2012)?

REFERENCES

Allen, K. R. (2005). Families facing the challenges of diversity. In P. C. McKenry & S. J. Price (Eds.), *Families and change: Coping with stressful events and transitions* (3rd ed., pp. 285–305). SAGE Publications.

American-Arab Anti-Discrimination Committee. (2002). *Arab American students in public schools.* https://www.adc.org/arab-american-students-in-public-schools/

Arnett, S. E. (2012). Diversity needs: Preparing family and consumer sciences teachers for the 21st-century classroom. *Journal of Family and Consumer Sciences Education, 30*(2), 66–71. http://www.natefacs.org/JFCSE/v30no2/v30no2ArnettDiv.pdf

Banks, J., & Banks, C. (Eds.). (1997). *Multicultural education issues and perspectives* (3rd ed.). Allyn and Bacon.

Blasi, M. W. (2002). An asset model: Preparing pre-service teachers to work with children and families "of promise." *Journal of Research in Childhood Education, 17*(1), 106–122.

Burns, M. (2010). Response-to-intervention research: Is the sum of the parts as great as the whole? RTI Action Network. http://www.rtinetwork.org/component/content/article/10/293-

Children's Defense Fund. (2020). *The state of America's children.* https://tinyurl.com/34rn8rjx

Cornell Law School. (n.d.). *De facto segregation.* https://www.law.cornell.edu/wex/de_facto_segregation

Couch, S., & Alexander, K. L. (2009). Professionalism: Ethical professional practice for teachers of family and consumer sciences. *Journal of Family and Consumer Sciences Education, 27*(National Teacher Standards 4), 60–76. https://www.natefacs.org/Pages/v27Standards4/v27Standards4Couch.pdf

Davis, B. M. (2006). *How to teach students who don't look like you: Culturally relevant teaching strategies.* Corwin Press.

Domingo, P. (2001, March). Quinceanera celebrated at MHS. *Cat Tales,* 1–4.

Ehren, B. J., (2008). *Response to intervention in secondary schools: Is it on your radar screen?* RTI Action Network. http://www.rtinetwork.org/about-us/advisory-council/ehren-barbara-j

El-Mekki, S. (2017). *9 things every educator should know when teaching black students.* Ed Post. https://tinyurl.com/eaut7wnk

Farnsworth, D., Clark, J. L., Green, K., López, M., Wysocki, A., & Kepner, K. (2004). *Diversity in the workplace: Benefits, challenges, and the required managerial tools.* IFSA Extension. https://tinyurl.com/4a2r3bke

Feng, J. (1994). *Asian-American children: What teachers should know* [ED369577]. ERIC. https://files.eric.ed.gov/fulltext/ED369577.pdf

Ferlazzo, L. (2012, March 12). *Dos & don'ts for teaching English-language learners.* Edutopia. https://tinyurl.com/3neuysdp

Fujiura, G. T., & Yamaki, K. (2000). Trends in demography of childhood poverty and disability. *Exceptional Children, 66,* 187–199. https://doi.org/10.1177/001440290006600204

Gonzalez, J. (2014, December 11). *12 ways to support English language learners in the mainstream classroom.* Cult of Pedagogy. https://tinyurl.com/y6h6md9j

Gurin, P., Dey, E. L., & Hurtado, S. (2002). Diversity and higher education: Theory and impact on educational outcomes. *Harvard Educational Review, 72*(3), 330–366. https://doi.org/10.17763/haer.72.3.01151786u134n051

Guyton, G. (2019, April 8). What do racism, diversity, and inclusion really mean? *Glen Guyton* (blog). https://tinyurl.com/162lot3a

Hall, L. E. (2005). *Dictionary of multicultural psychology: Issues, terms, and concepts.* SAGE Publications. http://dx.doi.org/10.4135/9781452204437

Harry, B. (2002). Trends and issues in serving culturally diverse families of children with disabilities. *Journal of Special Education, 36*(3), 131–140. https://doi.org/10.1177/00224669020360030301

Harry, B. (2008). Collaboration with culturally and linguistically diverse families; ideal versus reality. *Exceptional Children, 74,* 372–388. https://doi.org/10.1177/001440290807400306

Harry, B., Klinger, J. K., & Hart, J. (2005). African American families under fire: Ethnographic views of family strength. *Remedial and Special Education, 26*(2), 101–112. https://doi.org/10.1177/07419325050260020501

Hochschild, J. L. (2003). Social class in public schools. *Journal of Social Issues, 59*(4) 821–840. https://tinyurl.com/2knw6say

Howe, C. K. (1994). Improving the achievement of Hispanic students. *Educating for Diversity, 51*(8), 42–44. https://tinyurl.com/srm8sv4

Hu, S., & Kuh, G. D. (2003). Diversity experiences and college student learning and personal development. *Journal of College Student Development, 44*(3), 320–334. https.//doi.org/10.1353/csd.2003.0026

Kessler, E. (n.d.). *Examples of accommodations and modifications.* Smart Kids with Disabilities. https://tinyurl.com/pwra234

Lane, S. R., Palley, E. S., & Shdaimah, C. S. (2020). *Social welfare policy in a changing world.* SAGE Publications.

Lightbown, P. M., & Spada, N. (2011). *How languages are learned.* Oxford University Press.

Lynch, M. (2016). *The sobering history of Native American education in the 19th century.* The Edvocate. https://tinyurl.com/2yu7yyyo

Marion, M. (2015). A teacher's role in guiding young children. In M. Marion (Ed.), *Guidance of young children* (9th ed.). Pearson.

Misra, S., &, McMahon, G. (2006). Diversity in higher education: The three Rs. *Journal of Education for Business, 82*(1), 40–43. https://doi.org/10.3200/JOEB.82.1.40-43

Myers, V. (n.d). *Diversity and inclusion training.* https://www.vernamyers.com/

National Clearinghouse for English Language Acquisition. (n.d.). *What legal obligations do schools have to English Language Learners (ELL)?* https://tinyurl.com/6jenwe7h

National Center for Education Statistics. (2020). *Students with disabilities.* https://tinyurl.com/2pammva3

Neuliep, J. W. (2020). *Intercultural communication: A contextual approach* (8th ed.). SAGE Publications.

Newsom, K., Chancellor, L., & McClish, K. (2021). *Cultural diversity in family life education.* Cognella.

O'Boyle, T. (2020, June 20). *5 reasons why diversity is important in the 21st century.* Global Youth. https://tinyurl.com/1strj327

Office of Management and Business. (1997). Revisions to the standards for the classification of federal data on race and ethnicity. *Federal Register, 62*(210), 58782–58790. https://tinyurl.com/96zsmvf2

Papalia, D., Feldman, R., & Martorell, G. (2012). *Experience human development.* McGraw Hill.

Parish, S. L., Rose, R. A., & Andrews, M. E. (2010). TANFS's impact on low income mothers raising children with disabilities. *Exceptional Children, 76*, 234–253.

Purdue University. (2021). *Why is cultural diversity important?* Partnership International. https://tinyurl.com/p3v1xlun

Quast, E., & Bazemore-Bertrand, S. (2019). Exploring economic diversity and inequity through picture books. *The Reading Teacher, 73*(2), 219–222. https://doi.org/10.1002/trtr.1807

Rehm, M. L., & Allison, B. (2006). Positionality in teaching culturally diverse students: Implication for family and consumer science teacher education program. *Family and Consumer Sciences Research Journal, 34*(3), 260–275. https://doi.org/10.1177/1077727X05283593

Ricee, S. (2021, April 23). *What is DEI & EDI?—The complete guide.* Diversity for Social Impact. https://tinyurl.com/1sh2nzkj

Richey, D. D. (2000). Section I: Principles overview. In D. D. Richey & J. J. Wheeler (Eds.), *Inclusive early childhood education* (pp. 1–2). Delmar Thompson Learning.

Schaedig, D. (2020, August 24). *Self-fulfilling prophecy and the Pygmalion effect.* Simply Psychology. https://bit.ly/3n79Gc5

Segal, E. A. (2019, July 16). Why we need diversity. *Psychology Today.* https://tinyurl.com/4zn48e5y

Sherbin, L., & Rashid, R. (2017, February 1). *Diversity doesn't stick without inclusion.* Harvard Business Review. https://tinyurl.com/44n2crvz

Smitherman, G. (1986). *Talkin' and testifyin': The language of Black America.* Wayne State University Press.

Snow, K. (2016). *People first language.* Disability is Natural. https://www.disabilityisnatural.com/people-first-language.html

Sorkness, H. L., & Kelting-Gibson, L. (2006). *Effective teaching strategies for engaging native American students* [Conference session]. National Association of Native American Studies Conference Baton Rouge, LA, United States. https://tinyurl.com/4ast53ym

Swafford, M. D., & Dainty, H. T. (2009). Learning environment: Respecting diversity and exceptionality. *Journal of Family and Consumer Sciences Education, 27*(National Teacher Standards 4), 45–59. https://tinyurl.com/fjzsfbvh

Swafford, M., & Giordano, K. (2017). Universal design: Ensuring success for all FCS students. *Journal of Family and Consumer Sciences, 109*(4), 47–52.

Swafford, M., Wingate, K. O., Zagumny, L., & Richey, D. (2015). Families living in poverty: Perceptions of family-centered practices. *Journal of Early Intervention, 37*(2). https://doi.org/10.1177/1053815115602880

Turnbull, A. T., Turnbull, H. R., Erwin, E. J., Soodak, L. C., & Shoegren, K. A. (2006). Partnerships as archways. In *Families, professionals and exceptionality: Positive outcomes through partnerships and trust* (7th ed., pp. 113–134).). Pearson Merrill Prentice Hall.

U.S. Census Bureau. (2019). *National population by characteristics: 2010–2019*. U.S. Department of Commerce. https://tinyurl.com/1gosde27

U.S. Census Bureau. (2018, March 13). *Older people projected to outnumber children for first time in U.S. history*. U.S. Department of Commerce. https://tinyurl.com/4hlwtckm

van Onselen, G. (2012, June 6). Why difference is important. *Inside Politics*. https://tinyurl.com/iqg99qf4

Williams Shanks, T. R., & Danziger, S. K. (2016). Antipoverty policies and programs for children and families. In J. M. Jenson & M. W. Fraser (Eds.), *Social policy for children and families* (pp. 22–50). SAGE Publications.

Figure Credits

Adverse Childhood Experiences and Trauma-Informed Classroom Approach

Elizabeth Ramsey, PhD; Rufaro A. Chitiyo, PhD; and Melinda Swafford, PhD

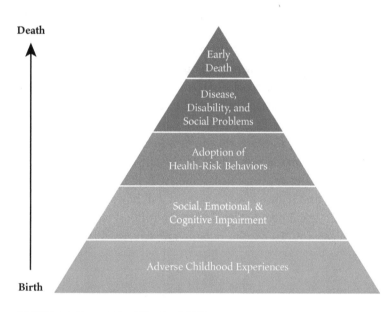

FIGURE 3.1 Cumulative Effects of ACEs

Chapter 3 Objectives

Upon completion of the chapter, the learner should be able to

- identify adverse childhood experiences (ACEs) and describe the impact that ACEs have on the developing brain;
- explain epigenetics and intergenerational transmission;
- identify various types of trauma;

- describe a trauma-informed classroom approach;
- identify various types of behaviors in children and adolescents who have experienced trauma and ACEs;
- analyze the impact of ACEs and trauma on individual behavior, as well as identify strategies to respond to that behavior; and
- develop strategies that build resiliency in children and adolescents.

Introduction

According to the Centers for Disease Control and Prevention (CDC, 2021b), **adverse childhood experiences (ACEs)** are defined as potentially traumatic events that people experience before the age of 18. The definition also encompasses any aspect of children's environments that threaten their ability to bond with caregivers, safety, and stability.

ACEs originated from a 1995 collaborative study conducted by the CDC and Kaiser Permanente in California. In the original study, ACEs referred to adversities that children faced in their home environments—namely, neglect, physical and emotional abuse (abuse), and household dysfunction (Center on the Developing Child at Harvard University, n.d.).

Understanding the impact that abuse, neglect, and household dysfunction can have on children under the age of 18 is pivotal, and learning how to build resiliency for children and adolescents is key to being an effective educator. The mission of family and consumer sciences (FCS) education is to improve quality of life. FCS professionals need to be well versed in ACEs and implementing a trauma-informed classroom, as FCS education can serve as prevention to the trauma and adverse conditions experienced by individuals and families. Statistics show that 68% of children have experienced a possible traumatic event prior to the age of 16 (Pappano, 2014), while 61% of survey adults in the United States report at least one ACE (CDC, 2021b). These statistics show that the average FCS middle and high school classroom will have students who have experienced trauma. FCS educators who teach occupational early childhood should include ACEs as part of the curriculum. Knowledge of ACEs can be beneficial when working with special populations as required by Perkins legislation. Additionally, some FCS professionals will become educators to the community, such as extension agents, and having a firm foundation in ACEs is important when working with individuals, families, and the community. On the other hand, creating a trauma-informed classroom is becoming a much-needed approach in today's educational environment because of the high incidence of ACEs. It is important to note that not all ACEs result in a traumatic response, but creating a trauma-informed classroom can ensure the support and success of all students.

Many states have included ACEs as part of the curriculum that FCS educators implement. Referring back to the current statistics of children experiencing trauma before the age of 16 mandates that high school students become well versed in ACEs as an ethical obligation of our profession when teaching in the career pathways of human sciences and education while working with children and families. Some states offer occupational early childhood endorsements that high school students can pursue as part of their plan of study that will make them more marketable. One such example is Tennessee, where students can obtain a child development associate endorsement, which puts them on the pathway to a promising career in early childhood education (Tennessee Department of Education, 2020). Additionally, in some states, high school students can receive dual credit with partnering universities in FCS programs and early childhood education programs, where they will become FCS professionals or early childhood educators. Examples include Alabama, Arizona, California, Florida, Tennessee, and Georgia.

This chapter will address trauma-informed responses that help build resiliency in children and adolescents, along with how to implement a trauma-informed classroom approach. Strategies and responses to use when working with children and adolescents who have experienced ACEs and trauma will be included.

Healthy Brain Development

Brain development is not the most visible domain of development. Stories abound of parents often looking at their newborn babies, assessing whether everything is intact, thereby in a way evaluating whether anything is "wrong." But how do you "see" whether the brain is healthy or not? While the reality is that no parent expects or looks forward (hopes) to having a child with disabilities (physical or otherwise), sometimes that's the hand they are dealt. This results in the family learning how to navigate life with this different reality.

While all these biological components are beyond people's control, adults taking care of children can control the environment however they want, which can directly impact brain development. Among other things, adults can provide safety and security for children in their care by not being abusive (in any way), among other things. Adults can also sometimes minimize the risk of children experiencing adversity as they grow (we say sometimes because in some instances, adversity is inevitable). ACEs can have a major impact on early brain development, which can have lasting effects on individuals throughout their life spans.

How Brains Are Built

A child's brain should be healthy in order for development to be considered "typical." We are using the word *typical* to imply what is expected for a child to go through when everything is developing as expected, based on the science of development. Healthy brains are built during pregnancy as the mother ingests the right nutrients like sufficient amounts of folic acid and protein and avoids exposure to toxins and infections such as tobacco, alcohol, Zika virus, and cytomegalovirus, among other things (CDC, 2021b; Hauser-Cram et al., 2014; Levine & Munsch, 2020; Mustard, 2006; Papalia & Martorell, 2015). In addition, routine health care while pregnant is among the protective factors for preventing premature birth and other complications known to affect a baby's brain (CDC, 2021b). Biologically speaking, brain development happens through a process known as neurulation (Alberta Family Wellness Initiative [AFWI], 2021). This implies that the brain's formation begins with an embryonic structure known as the neural tube. Within a few months, the embryonic brain cells multiply. In addition to that proliferation process, they also become more distinct in terms of cell type and move and land in their appropriate positions within the brain cavity. Immediately after that is when the cells start developing connections that compose the neural circuits of the brain (AFWI, 2021).

In addition to genetics, science has proven that people's experiences during their early years of life also have a huge impact on brain architecture (CDC, 2021b; Center on the Developing Child at Harvard University, 2021; Hauser-Cram et al., 2014; Levine & Munsch, 2020; Mustard, 2006; Papalia & Martorell, 2015; The Urban Child Institute [TUCI], 2010; Tierney & Nelson, 2009). Brain architecture basically means the process of how the brain develops and is the foundation of all that happens in the future. Later development and health, therefore, are predicated on what happens during the early years. This is because brain development begins in utero, and even though it doesn't end until adulthood, the first 8 years of life build the foundation for the future (Center on the Developing Child at Harvard University, 2021; Hauser-Cram et al., 2014; Levine & Munsch, 2020; Papalia & Martorell, 2015).

According to TUCI (2010), an ideal situation is when children have nurturing environments during their earliest years because such surroundings stimulate "optimal brain development and provide young children with a solid foundation on which their later skills and abilities will be built" (p. 60). These nurturing environments begin in the womb. According to Enlow et al. (2018), maternal trauma and high cortisol stress hormones while pregnant are associated with infant sadness and distress, demonstrating the impact of the prenatal environment. However, negative factors such as stress and exposure to toxins also affect brain development (AFWI, 2013; CDC, 2021b). When a building structure has a weak foundation, its quality and durability are compromised. The same applies to brain architecture. ACEs can negatively affect brain development, and the resulting negative effects can last into adulthood (Mustard, 2006).

AFWI (2013) created a video explaining the science behind the process of how brains are built. In their engaging video, the argument is that brains are not just born but are also built based on the experiences that we go through in life. This means genetics are not the only factor contributing to brain development. A good base for brain development involves positive interactions between a child and a caregiver. These positive experiences are what brain experts call "serve and return" interactions (AFWI, 2013). When a child "serves" something via communication or interaction, an adult caregiver should "return" the communication in a positive and engaging manner in order for the child to benefit from the exchange (AFWI, 2013). This echoes TUCI's (2010) proposition that a child's daily experiences are essential to brain development.

So, what happens when children are deprived of reciprocity during serve and return games? AFWI (n.d.) posited that when there are consistently no responses when children reach out, brain architecture is weakened over time. This also impairs health and the development of essential skills and abilities. According to Mustard (2006), experience also affects how synapses connect among the "neurons to establish pathways for the different hierarchies of brain function. These pathways govern or control our intellectual, emotional, psychological, physiological and physical responses to what we do every day" (p. 571). While caregivers cannot control everything in order to ensure their child's/children's optimal brain development, the authors suggest creating healthy environments for children in hopes that their experiences as they grow help develop healthy brains.

Types of Childhood Stress

It is inevitable to experience stress in life. Science has proven that children need to experience small doses of good stress as they grow (AFWI, 2013; Hauser-Cram et al., 2014; Levine & Munsch, 2020; Papalia & Martorell, 2015). Additionally, as children grow, they should learn how to manage and cope with stress in their lives. So what kinds of things can be stressful for children?

- Schoolwork or grades
- Juggling responsibilities, such as school and work or sports
- Problems with friends, bullying, or peer group pressures
- Changing schools, moving, or dealing with housing problems or homelessness
- Having negative thoughts about themselves
- Going through body changes, in both boys and girls
- Seeing parents go through a divorce or separation
- Money problems in the family
- Living in an unsafe home or neighborhood (MedlinePlus, 2021, para. 3)

When stress is present, there are three types of stress responses that children experience: positive, tolerable, and toxic. A **positive stress** response is also known as **eustress** and is defined as the stress stemming from brief, mild experiences mediated by the presence of a caring adult (Lumen Learning, n.d.). This type of stress is good for brain development. Examples include experiences such as meeting new people and making new friends. When children experience more intense adverse experiences, they go through a **tolerable stress** response, which is considered short-lived, and children can overcome such stress. Examples include death in the family and family disruptions such as divorce. **Toxic stress** is excessive stress that is chronic in nature and is above a child's coping capacity. Examples include physical or emotional abuse and caregiver substance abuse or mental illness.

Lasting Effects of ACEs

Based on the results of the original ACE study, it has been established and is now widely accepted that experiencing ACEs is linked to multiple negative effects later in life. These negative outcomes are categorized as either behavioral or physical/mental health in nature (see Figure 3.2). Life potential is impacted by ACEs, as academic achievement, graduation rates, and potential for success in careers will be negatively impacted. Under the behavioral category, the effects included smoking, alcohol and drug use, missing work, and lack of physical activity. Negative effects under the physical/mental health domain included depression, diabetes, severe obesity, STDs, suicide attempts, broken bones, stroke, lung disease, heart disease, and cancer (Felitti et al., 1998). According to Felitti et al. (1998), as the number of ACEs one experienced went up, so did the risk of experiencing negative long-term effects. Specifically, persons who had experienced four or more categories of childhood exposure, compared to those who had experienced none, had four- to twelvefold increased health risks for alcoholism, drug abuse, depression, and suicide attempt; a two- to fourfold increase in smoking, poor self-rated health, > or = 50 sexual intercourse partners, and sexually transmitted disease; and 1.4- to 1.6-fold increase in physical inactivity and severe obesity (Felitti et al., 1998, p. 245).

ACES can have lasting effects on....

Health (obesity, diabetes, depression, suicide attempts, STDs, heart disease, cancer, stroke, COPD, broken bones)

Behaviors (smoking, alcoholism, drug use)

Life Potential (graduation rates, academic achievement, lost time from work)

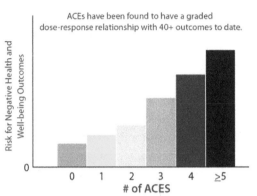

ACEs have been found to have a graded dose-response relationship with 40+ outcomes to date.

Risk for Negative Health and Well-being Outcomes

# of ACES

This pattern holds for the 40+ outcomes, but the exact risk values vary depending on the outcome.

FIGURE 3.2 Negative Public Health Outcomes from ACEs

As FCS professionals, we consider these findings a critical piece of information in our quest to understand who people are (those we serve, as well as those we work with), why they behave the way they do, and how they became who they are. We encourage you to venture into exploring ACEs studies that have been conducted in your state to get an idea and an understanding of the impact of ACEs in your community. For example, based on 2012 data, slightly more than half (52%) of Tennessee's population had at least one ACE, and 21% reported three or more ACEs (Tennessee Department of Health, 2015).

Attachment

One of the effects of experiencing trauma is that individuals may end up with attachment disorders. **Attachment**, a bond between individuals, is reciprocal in nature and critical for social and emotional development. Bowlby (1969, 1988) and Ainsworth (1989) stressed the importance of attachment to caregivers as a key in the social, emotional, and cognitive development of individuals. Furthermore, the type of attachment formed in childhood has long-term implications, not only in terms of a child's development but also may transition into adulthood, influencing employer/employee relationships and romantic relationships, as well as impacting adult caregiving styles for infants, children, and the elderly (Ainsworth, 1989; Bowlby, 1988).

Trauma experienced in the home and with caregivers can negatively impact the attachment of a child to a caregiver. A study conducted by Swafford and Jolley (2012) revealed participants with insecure or ambivalent attachments to a caregiver had difficulty in forming secure adult romantic relationships. FCS educators need an understanding of attachment for the promotion of child well-being to help in the prevention of serious and harmful outcomes.

SPOTLIGHT: BRUCE PERRY, MD, PHD

Dr. Bruce Perry is a childhood trauma expert researcher in children's mental health and neurosciences. His research on abuse, neglect, and trauma has impacted policies and programs worldwide. He is the author of *Born for Love: Why Empathy Is Essential and Endangered* and coauthored with Maia Szalavits the book *The Boy Who Was Raised as a Dog*. Dr. Perry recently coauthored with Oprah Winfrey *What Happened to You? Conversations on Trauma, Resilience and Healing* in 2021. Dr. Perry has served as a consultant for the U.S. government on traumatic events, including children involved in the Columbine High School shooting, Sandy Hook school shooting, Hurricane Katrina, the Oklahoma City bombing, and the Waco siege. He is the founder and senior fellow of the Child Trauma Academy in Houston, Texas (SXSW EDU, 2021, p.1).

ACTIVITY 3.1: SUMMARY AND REFLECTION

View the following Seven Slide Series video: *Threat Response Patterns*

 Perry, B. D., & The ChildTrauma Academy. (2013). 3: Threat Response Patterns [Video].
YouTube. https://www.youtube.com/watch?v=sr-OXkk3i8E&feature=youtu.be

 Summarize and reflect in a one-page paper the threat response patterns of the brain when exposed to trauma.

Epigenetics

Epigenetics is a relatively new field of study for researchers. It's rooted in molecular biology (Mitchell, 2019) and is described as the process of how the environment affects a child's genetic expression (Center on the Developing Child at Harvard University, 2018). According to the CDC (2020), "Epigenetic changes are reversible and do not change your DNA sequence, but they can change how your body reads a DNA sequence" (para. 1). Epigenetics has been credited as the answer to the long-standing nurture versus nature debate because it has proven that genetics are not set in stone. In other words, "genes are not destiny" (Mitchell, 2019, para. 1).

Researchers from Emory University found that animals can pass on traumatic experiences to their offspring, not by socialization but rather by inheritance (Szyf, 2014). In Szyf's (2014) research, mice were conditioned to a startle response using a mild electric foot shock upon the scent of cherry blossoms being released into the cage. The mice eventually demonstrated visible signs of anxiety upon smelling the scent of cherry blossoms absent the electric shock. Consequently, their offspring, even with no previous exposure to the smell of cherry blossoms, demonstrated similar responses of anxiety and fear as parents. Likewise, the response was the same for second-generation mice pups and mice pups conceived through in vitro fertilization, demonstrating that somehow the response to the smell was being genetically transmitted.

When it comes to development, epigenetics strengthens the argument that there is an interaction between one's genetics and the environment they are living in (Center on the Developing Child at Harvard University, 2018). The difference between genetics and epigenetics lies in the fact that genetics is the study of genes, whereas epigenetics emphasizes how genes are expressed based on what is transpiring in the environment (Psychology Today, n.d.). Although there is much to learn in this new field of study of epigenetics, it is worthy of mention when considering the impact of ACEs and trauma. As such, the National Scientific Council on the Developing Child (2010) strongly suggests the importance of society at large shifting our attention to not only young children's experiences but also their surroundings.

Environmental Factors Impacting Trauma

As discussed previously in this chapter, ACEs were originally identified by the landmark Kaiser Permanente study. Not all adversity experienced in childhood is categorized as ACEs. Likewise, not all ACEs result in traumatic stress. Some children may be deeply traumatized by, for example, their parent's divorce, while others fare well or even thrive when parents divorce. In another example, one refugee child fleeing their country may perceive their circumstances differently than another refugee. Trauma differs from adversity in the length of exposure and severity but also in response. Trauma can occur when there is prolonged exposure to adversity—weeks, months, or years (Jamieson, 2019)—yet it can also be an isolated event, such as surviving a tornado or car crash. Likewise, "not every child who experiences a traumatic event is traumatized by it" (Jamieson, 2019, para. 11).

When an event is dangerous, violent, or threatening and poses risk to a child's body or life, it is considered a **traumatic event** (National Child Traumatic Stress Network, 2021). A traumatic event can also occur when a child witnesses a loved one's life or security threatened. Young children are especially vulnerable to trauma, as they completely rely on their caregivers for their safety and security (National Child Traumatic Stress Network, 2021). Traumatic experiences can leave behind reminders that are connected to the original experience that can persist throughout the years. Reminders linger in everyday lived experiences, such as holidays, situations, people, or feelings.

Types of Trauma

According to the National Child Traumatic Stress Network (n.d.), **trauma** occurs when a child feels intensely threatened by an event that they have witnessed or experienced. A variety of events are

TABLE 3.1   **Types of Trauma**

Bullying	Intimate partner violence	Refugee trauma
Community violence	Medical trauma	Sexual abuse
Complex trauma (neglect/abuse)	Early childhood trauma (birth–6 years)	Sex trafficking
Disasters	Physical abuse	Terrorism and violence
Traumatic Grief		

National Child Traumatic Stress Network (n.d.)

considered trauma as identified by the National Child Traumatic Stress Network, an affiliate of the Substance Abuse and Mental Health Services Administration.

Typically, most adults and families work hard to keep children and adolescents safe; however, danger, disaster, and accidents still happen within or outside of the family.

ACTIVITY 3.2: TRAUMA: CAUSE, EFFECTS, AND NEEDED RESOURCES

Choose two types of trauma from the list to explore further. Define the trauma and identify its effects. Develop resources that would help build resilience in the individual and family.

Individual Responses to Trauma

Why is it that not all children who experience trauma suffer from trauma symptoms? Several factors play into whether or not a child experiences symptoms, such as the severity of the event, closeness to the event, caregivers' response, former history of trauma, and community and family factors (National Child Traumatic Stress Network, 2021). Children and adolescents who experience traumatic events can develop symptoms and responses that affect their daily living.

Responses to trauma can last anywhere from a few days to a few months; over time, as a person processes the adversity, they begin to feel better, yet certain memories or events can trigger a response even long after a person has processed an event. Children are more likely to be traumatized if they are already under heavy stress, have been traumatized, or have recently experienced loss (Robinson et al., 2020).

Symptoms from trauma vary according to response but can be physical and/or emotional. Physical symptoms can include insomnia, easily startled, heartbeat racing, agitation, hypervigilance/edginess, muscle tension, changed eating habits, and achiness (Lake Behavioral Hospital, 2021; Robinson et al., 2020). Emotional symptoms can vary, including cognitive changes such as nightmares, flashbacks, intrusive thoughts, mood swings, difficulty concentrating, and difficulty remembering (Lake Behavioral Hospital, 2021). Emotional symptoms are also revealed in behavior patterns such as avoiding people involved with the trauma and withdrawal (Lake Behavioral Hospital, 2021). Psychological symptoms of trauma may include anxiety/panic attacks, obsessions/compulsions, fear, irritability, anger, depression, guilt, and shame (Lake Behavioral Hospital, 2021).

Intergenerational Transmission of Trauma

An individual who has experienced trauma and has not reconciled the trauma may use ineffective coping strategies to manage conflict or other stressful situations. These strategies and emotional tensions may be passed down from generation to generation. **Bowen's intergenerational model** is used to help FCS professionals understand how experiences in the family of origin can influence future generations' development and patterns of interaction within the family, as well as with those outside the family (Price et al., 2017).

Differentiation is a key concept in this model and refers to both the individual and the family. Individual differentiation is the ability to be autonomous and express individuality while still being connected to the family. Differentiation within the family refers to patterns of interaction within the family that affect the development of self and how individuality is tolerated (Price et al., 2017).

Differentiation can range from a high level to a low level for both individuals and families. A high level of differentiation in a family would respect the rights and privacy of members and encourage others to think and act independently. Individuals who are highly differentiated are sensitive, empathetic, and respectful of others.

Individuals who have low levels of differentiation view individuality as being disloyal and a threat to the family. Families who have low levels of differentiation may become emotionally enmeshed or even disengaged and often solve problems in the family using destructive strategies that are harmful (Price et al., 2017).

Using this model as a premise for trauma, individuals from low-differentiated families manage unresolved trauma in ways that are destructive to the self and to future generations of the family (Anderson & Sabatelli, 2007). Three strategies that individuals and families of low differentiation use to solve problems are conflict, overfunctioning or underfunctioning, and family projection (Anderson & Sabatelli, 2007). In the **conflict strategy**, individuals use anger, yelling, and fault finding to maintain a sense of self. This conflict strategy prevents a close bonding of the person to another individual, therefore maintaining a sense of self. Using the **underfunctioning strategy,** the individual takes on a passive and childlike demeanor, which results in not making decisions that may be in conflict with another individual. In contrast, using the **overfunctioning strategy**, the individual takes on a dominant demeanor and does not compromise with others. **Family projection strategy** involves the parent "projecting" their unresolved emotional attachments or conflicts onto the children, which leads to recurrent patterns of behavior in future generations. As an example, a parent who was reared in an authoritarian home uses the same strategies of anger and fault finding to parent their child. Another example is often when children are sexually abused, they may become perpetrators and sexually abuse others.

It is vital that FCS professionals are aware of trauma and how unresolved experiences can impact the individual and future generations of the individual's family. The FCS curriculum provides the learner with content on human development, relationships, family resources, parenting, self-efficacy, and coping strategies; furthermore, when teaching this content, educators will develop a rapport with the learner of caring and trust that will foster the growth. This results in FCS educators becoming the caring adult who provides a caring responsive relationship and that promotes resiliency (Swafford & Dainty, 2009).

Trauma-Informed Care Approach

When implementing a trauma-informed approach in any organization, including school systems, all people on all levels in the organization should have a basic understanding of trauma and its effects on communities, organizations, individuals, and families (SAMHSA, 2014). Along with a basic understanding of trauma, workforce individuals, faculty, and staff need to be trained to recognize the signs and symptoms of trauma, respond in appropriate ways, and avoid retraumatization (SAMHSA, 2014). There are six principles to a trauma-informed approach as identified by SAMHSA (2014): "safety; trustworthiness and transparency; peer support; collaboration and mutuality; empowerment, voice, and choice; cultural, historical, and gender issues" (p. 10).

Concerning safety, it is important that all individuals who are served by an organization or school system feel physically and psychologically safe. Transparency in all matters should be the goal of the administration, along with building trust among the individuals they serve. Peer support is essential for individual recovery. Peers can be defined as friends, other trauma survivors, or even close family members if the child is young. Peer support groups are beneficial for survivors of trauma in the school system and other organizations. Leveling power, building relationships, and shared decision making help build collaboration and mutuality. Recognizing and building on individual strengths helps to empower people, along with giving them a voice and choice. Considering that many trauma survivors have experienced a loss of choice or voice, and even coercive treatment, offering them a choice and allowing their voice to be heard and valued is an important strategy. Lastly, it is vital that organizations and school systems avoid any stereotypes and biases and address historical trauma.

Behaviors in Children and Adolescents with Trauma

When working with children who have experienced ACEs and/or trauma, the behavior that you witness is best thought of as "the tip of the iceberg" (Tennessee Department of Education, 2019). In other words, when viewing an iceberg, you only see the tip of the iceberg—the behavior—but you do not see what lies underneath: the trauma that resulted in the behavior (see Figure 3.3).

The following chart (Table 3.2) was borrowed from the Tennessee Department of Education (2019). Understanding that the behavior comes from a student's best attempt at coping with trauma, we become better at understanding why students respond the way they do. Notice the chart is laid out in the flight, fight, or freeze response pattern because when the body is exposed to repetitive toxic stress, the limbic system—specifically the amygdala, the part of the brain responsible for emotional response and instinctive behaviors—takes over. Oftentimes, individuals who have experienced repetitive toxic stress remain in a flight, fight, or freeze

FIGURE 3.3 Tip of the Iceberg

TABLE 3.2   **Common Behaviors in Students With Trauma**

Flight	Fight	Freeze
Withdrawal	Acting out	Numbness
Running out of the classroom	Aggression	Refusal to answer
Daydreaming	Refusal and defiance	Refusal to get needs met
Appearance of sleeping	Silliness	Giving a blank look
Avoidance of others	Hyperactivity	Inability to move or act
Hiding or wandering	Argumentative	Answering "I don't know"

Tennessee Department of Education (2019)

pattern because the repetitive activation of the amygdala can disrupt brain architecture and result in cognitive impairment.

As educators, what can we do to help these students? The answer lies in implementing a trauma-informed care approach.

SPOTLIGHT: JIMMY'S STORY
By Elizabeth Ramsey

I worked with a little boy, Jimmy, in a middle school who had been severely physically abused and neglected by his birth mother. I did not know his entire back story, but pieces of his story became clearer throughout the course of the academic year. I learned that as a toddler he had been severely beaten by his mother for a potty-training accident and that he was removed from the home. He was later reunited with mom and currently lives with her and her boyfriend. I became concerned that Jimmy may be neglected because when meeting with mom, I suspected drug use/abuse. She was thin, missing teeth (indicative of methamphetamine abuse), and her hair was always extremely greasy. Jimmy was troubled to say the least. He was aggressive, violent, and destructive. His handwriting was equivalent to a first grader, and his reading level was second-grade level, even though he was in fifth grade. He destroyed anything he could get his hands on, including books and journals, pencils, Chromebooks, and so on. I remember him taking a pencil and digging a hole in his journal and textbooks. He would pop several of the keys off the keyboard of the Chromebook. All of his teachers tracked his behavior because it was so extreme. I took every moment I could to build a loving, trusting relationship with Jimmy, along with catching him making great choices and praising him. Because of his behavior, we met with mom and developed a behavior plan moving forward. We wrote a behavior plan with goals and strategies to help Jimmy. With my background in FCS, trauma, and ACEs, I knew the behavior that Jimmy displayed was only the tip of the iceberg. I fought for Jimmy to be included in my Social Health class because I knew he needed to learn life skills on learning how to solve problems with friends, manage his anger and emotions, and self-regulate. I advocated for empathy talk to be added to his behavior plan because Jimmy had a difficult time empathizing with other people. For example, when talking with him after being aggressive with classmates and friends, he had a difficult time understanding other people's perspectives. I met with his mom one on one and shared tips and strategies that she could implement at home. I tried everything I knew to keep Jimmy in school and in the classroom while keeping those around him safe. One day, Jimmy was in another teacher's classroom where he inappropriately spanked a fellow female student's bottom. That day, Jimmy was suspended indefinitely. He ended up at a reform school. This was not the outcome that I wanted for Jimmy, but with his previous behavior record, the principal made the decision to send him to reform school.

Principles of a Trauma-Informed School

As discussed previously in the chapter, trauma in children is prevalent throughout the United States. When working with individuals and students who have trauma in their background, there are guiding principles that should be implemented (Sporleder & Forbes, 2016; Tennessee Department of Education, 2019).

First, realize that the stress the student is experiencing is coming from outside. With this in mind, it is not about you as an educator, and it is best not to take it personally. Second, it is best not to try to solve the problem in the heat of the moment. Designate a place in your classroom or just outside of your classroom where the student can de-escalate. Wait until the student has de-escalated and emotionally regulated before trying to solve the issue. Third, the emotions and issues you are witnessing are usually not about the issue at hand, but go much deeper—think "tip of the iceberg." It is important to ask yourself what is truly driving the behavior that you are seeing; therefore, be the one who asks open-ended questions, listens, and values your student's voice. Be willing to explore the underlying issues in the student's life. Fourth, the behavior displayed is not a behavior issue; it's a brain issue. Your goal should be to help students build self-regulation, not simply learn how to behave. Build self-regulation exercises into your classroom to help students learn to self-regulate. Lastly, the root word of discipline means "to teach" (Keim & Jacobson, 2011); it does not mean to punish. Discipline should always occur within the context of relationships. Consequences should not only keep students in school but also build trust and safety between students and caring adults.

The following concepts should guide you when forming your trauma-informed classroom (Sporleder & Forbes, 2016; Tennessee Department of Education, 2019):

1. Trauma leaves an individual feeling unsafe; therefore, structure safety into your classroom.
2. Trauma leaves individuals feeling helpless; therefore, offering students choices will lead to empowerment.
3. Trauma leaves individuals in need of strong and sustaining relationships; therefore, offer opportunities for collaboration and building relationships.
4. Trauma leaves individuals in a heightened state of caution and instability; therefore, structure for predictability and trustworthiness.

SPOTLIGHT: RICKY
By Elizabeth Ramsey

I was working with a middle school student, Ricky, who had trauma in his background. One of his issues was lying—he told big stories that I could sense were not true. He wanted to be liked by the other students and wanted their approval as well as mine. His habit of telling lies actually worked to his disadvantage. The other students could sense that he was lying and ended up rejecting him, which in turn caused fights between him and the other kids. Unfortunately, his fights often escalated into a physical nature. One day, I pulled him aside after he had told me a big story and gently explained that I noticed some of his stories were difficult to believe. I shared with him that I liked him. In fact, I told him that he had so many nice qualities about his personality, naming a few—like he was very outgoing and easy to talk to. I told him that he did not need to impress me by telling me big stories—that I liked him just the way he was. I noticed after our conversation that he felt more accepted by me; his lies began to minimize; the stories he told seemed more plausible.

Resilience

Resiliency is often described as the process of rising above adversity (Swafford & Dainty, 2009). Resilient individuals adapt by connecting with supportive individuals who have high expectations, as well as by providing learners who have experienced trauma opportunities to be actively involved in their environment. This supportive environment helps the learner face the hardships to adapt to become an emotionally healthy adult with a productive life (Swafford & Dainty, 2009). Trauma-informed classrooms foster resiliency in those who have faced trauma by providing a safe environment, where positive attributes of the individual are recognized. The individual also has opportunities to be actively engaged in the environment with appropriate activities as well as develop a meaningful relationship with a caring, responsive adult. If the adult is not a family member, they can be an educator, pastor, or coach.

Responding Versus Reacting

The following chart (Table 3.3) was borrowed from Forbes (2012). To create a trauma-informed classroom, it is necessary to identify challenging moments with students as opportunities. Think of these challenging moments as opportunities to build trusting, nurturing relationships, along with moments to help your students feel safe. Students will notice how we respond to their needs and feelings in the way that we respond. Notice the suggested trauma-informed responses. Sending those loving, enduring messages will soothe a student who has experienced trauma.

TABLE 3.3   Responding Versus Reacting

In the left-hand column are some of the traditional reactions matched up with a new trauma-informed response in the right-hand column.

Traditional Reactions	Trauma-Informed Responses
"Go to the principal's office."	"I'm here. You're not in trouble."
"Stop crying."	"It's okay to feel."
"Stop acting like a baby."	"That really set you back, didn't it?"
"Detention is waiting for you."	"Sit with me."
"Don't you talk to an adult like that!"	"You're allowed to have a voice. Let's talk together."
"You're old enough to handle this on your own."	"Let's handle this together."
"Stop whining."	"I want to understand you better. If I know how you feel, I'll be able to help you better. Use your voice so I can really understand."
"It's not that difficult."	"I need to know how hard this is for you."
"You should have never acted like that."	"Sometimes life just gets too big, doesn't it?"
"Act your age."	"This is too big to keep to yourself."
"I can't help you with this issue. I've got 30 other children in this class."	"We'll get through this together. Every single student in this class is important."
"I'm calling your parents. Wait until they find out."	"Let's get everyone involved to support you. You're not in trouble. I want your parents involved so we can all find a way to make this better."
"Nobody is going to like you if you keep misbehaving."	"I know you want to be well-liked, so let's make that happen."
"You need to take ownership."	"I'm sorry this is so hard."

Taken from *Help for Billy: A Beyond Consequences Approach to Helping Challenging Children in the Classroom*, Forbes (2012)

SPOTLIGHT: COREY

By Elizabeth Ramsey

I was teaching social health in middle school, and one of my students, Corey, was placed in my classroom because he was having a difficult time getting along with other students. One of his teachers expressed concern about him because he was not meeting deadlines or turning in home-work, but she was also concerned because he was constantly accusing other children of bullying him, being mean to him, and lashing out at other students. She suspected that he was not truly being bullied but was quick to accuse others of bullying him when in reality, it wasn't happening. This was a big accusation to make because bullying is not tolerated, and it concerned me.

I began to find out about Corey through the course of study. The first unit of social health was about identifying different types of families. I found this unit to be a great way for me to get to

(Continued)

know my students, as we identified our own families as we learned. Corey told me about his family. He was living with a single father and his older brother. Later on, one of our units covered substance abuse, and he disclosed that his mother left when he was a baby and was currently in jail because of her drug use. Not to mention, in the unit about mentors and role models, Corey disclosed some information about his older brother, and it sounded like his older brother was unduly harsh with him. Slowly, I put the pieces of the puzzle together about Corey's life. He was abandoned by his mother who was addicted to drugs, was raised by a single father, and was picked on by his older brother. Needless to say, Corey's relationships with other students were strained.

One Friday, we were playing a game of duck, duck, goose because we always did fun activities on Fridays—I called them "Fun Fridays." We put our newly learned skills to the test on these Fridays, but the children never knew that was my intention; they just had fun. Corey had a meltdown playing the game. Honestly, I had never seen anything like it. He got so upset with everyone playing. He started accusing everyone of making him lose and ganging up on him. He was crying and yelling uncontrollably. I knew right away that he was feeling threatened and more than likely triggered by something that had happened in this harmless game.

I helped him walk to the hall and sit down in a spot that we had identified as a peaceful spot. I explained to him that he was not in trouble, that I cared about him, and when he was ready, that I was here for him. I told him to take all the time he needed. I periodically checked in with him and asked if he was ready to talk to me. As I recall, he must have turned me down around three times, but I did not take that personally. I hung in there with him, reminding him that I cared for him and that I was here for him. Corey eventually talked to me. I told him that I could see he was really upset and hurt and asked if he could tell me about that. When he did, he described how everyone was against him and hated him. As he talked, I listened. Little by little, I started reminding him of my care for him and how the other students cared about him too. It turned out that one of the children tagged him out, and instead of simply taking this as part of the game, he took it personally. We talked about that. I asked him if he could consider that his friend was just playing by the rules and that he wasn't truly against him. Corey slowly came around. One of the phrases that we used frequently in that class was "water off a duck's back." I asked him, "Can this be water off a duck's back?" He agreed it could be.

He had begun to slowly pull himself together over the course of our talk, but his face was beet red from crying so hard. I offered him a choice because so many children who have experienced trauma feel like they have no choices. I asked him if he would like to go to the bathroom to refresh before coming back to class. I also put my trust in him by telling him to take all the time he needed and to come back to class when he was ready. Most teachers would be reluctant to tell a child who has a previous record of discipline issues to take all the time they need in the bathroom, but I knew he needed to feel trusted. He agreed that he would like a moment to freshen up in the bathroom. Before he left me, I hugged him and reminded him that I was in it for the long haul with him, that I loved him and cared about him, and that I liked him. He only took a few minutes that day in the bathroom and came right back to class with a smile on his face. From that point forward, Corey and I had a very special relationship, and many times if he was struggling, he ended up coming to my classroom for help.

Give Emotional Space

How do you give someone emotional space? More specifically, how do you give a student emotional space in school? The answer is pretty simple, according to the trauma-informed care approach (Tennessee Department of Education, 2019). First of all, be willing to accept the student without trying to solve the issue. Notice in Corey's story how emotional space was offered to him throughout the encounter with time to think and be alone, my acceptance of him, and time to refresh. Second, ask questions so that you understand what is going on in your student. Remember in Corey's story how he was asked to tell the teacher why he was so upset? If you take the time to ask and truly show concern, students will talk to you. Next, allow the student to be upset. This is an important step, and many times it can be difficult because people can be uncomfortable with negative feelings, but embrace them. Allow your students' space to feel. Lastly, be empathetic to your students. This does not necessarily mean that you agree with your students, but be empathetic to their feelings. Notice in Corey's story how the teacher confirmed his feelings—yes, he was sad and upset, and he needed space and time to work through them.

Trauma-Informed Classroom Strategies

The following chart (Table 3.4) was borrowed from the Tennessee Department of Education (2019) and provides goals and strategies for implementing a trauma-informed classroom in a secondary education setting.

TABLE 3.4 Trauma-Informed Classroom Strategies

Goal	Secondary Educational Strategy
Build relationship	Connect with the student Assign a mentor to students in need Have a special lunch with the principal
Build self-esteem	Affirmations
Create a calm classroom	Warm lighting and increased natural light White noise Animals Decrease clutter and wall hangings
Create a "family" atmosphere in the classroom	Welcome each student by using their name Chart with "school hierarchy"
Focus on breathing	Meditation Gonoodle.com Pinwheels
Focus on safety	Safe zone in classroom Mantras In-school suspension room
Focus on regulation versus dysregulation	Teach brain science and impact of trauma on brain Knitting and/or coloring books Phone or text home Listen to music

TABLE 3.4   **Trauma-Informed Classroom Strategies**

Goal	Secondary Educational Strategy
Provide movement opportunities	Taped pacing area Rocking and/or running Walk, talk, regulate Gonoodle.com
Provide purpose	Before school check–in
Provide nourishment	Have snacks and water at all times
Provide structure	Be consistent Keep daily schedule visible Create traditions
Support transitioning	Be present in hallways
Teach emotional expression	Teach basic feeling words Teach character analysis
Teach how to identify stress	Use a stress indicator form Identify visceral reactions to stress
Teach social skills	Teach social-emotional learning Group sessions with guidance counselor Use autism resources

SPOTLIGHT: MORNING MEETING/CLASSROOM MEETING

One strategy that can help build the concepts of trauma-informed care into the classroom is the use of a morning meeting or classroom meeting every day. The essential components of a morning/ classroom meeting are as follows:

1. **Greeting.** Greet each student by name. Many times, this can be done when checking attendance. Ask students to respond to you with a greeting as well. This is usually very telling of the day your students are having, whether they give you a verbal greeting or just a wave or a nod of their head.

2. **Write It and Share It, If Desired.** Keep cards in a basket for each student to pick up on their way into class titled shout out, concern, apology, or news. Students take a moment to choose what topic they want to write about. Give them an opportunity to share if they desire. Many times, problems are solved, emotions are shared, and this time can be very cathartic for students.

3. **Music.** Including an upbeat song or music video after sharing time can help people who have experienced trauma cope with trauma (Garrido et al., 2015). When using music with students, sometimes students will begin singing or dancing. Some will choose to simply sit and listen. Either way, it is a few minutes well spent.

4. **Positive Ending Message.** This can be an inspirational quote, a meme, or any type of message that you would like to include.

Restorative Circles

Another strategy for the trauma-informed classroom is the use of restorative circles, which is a technique where every person has an equal opportunity to share and listen. Restorative circles can be beneficial, especially in schools, because they give students the opportunity to resolve conflict by listening and sharing in a safe space. There are three different types of restorative circles (Women Wonder Writers, 2021):

1. **Sequential Circle.** This type of restorative circle begins with one person sharing and moves in a clockwise or counterclockwise fashion to where everyone has an opportunity to share. As each student shares, no one else is allowed to interrupt. This type of circle is great for a daily check-in, simple mindfulness exercises, or setting goals. You, as the classroom teacher, facilitate the circle, posing a question, statement, or idea.

2. Fishbowl Circles. This type of restorative circle is best used when you have several people, but not everyone needs to share. Fishbowl circles are best implemented with a talking piece—the person holding the talking piece is the person who talks. Examples of talking pieces are a small stuffed animal or a small ball. The fishbowl circle was used with Jimmy, whose story can be found earlier in this chapter. Jimmy would frequently chase, push, and hit other students on the playground. One day, the teacher conducted a fishbowl with Jimmy and the other students involved. The students shared how they felt about the way Jimmy interacted with them on the playground—how they felt afraid, hurt, and overwhelmed when he pushed, hit, and was aggressive with them. Jimmy also had an opportunity to share how he was trying to play the game of chase. Jimmy had a difficult time empathizing with his friends, but all in all, the experience benefited the students. Jimmy had a better understanding of how to play with his classmates. Fishbowls can also be implemented with a sequential circle inside with active participants in the sequential circle and observers seated in the fishbowl outside of the sequential circle. The outside observers may have occasional input, but for the most part, they are considered observers.

3. **Real Justice Circles.** This type of circle is recommended for outside of the classroom and is often used in youth courts. This circle includes the victim, victim supporter, offender, and offender supporter. A facilitator is used to ask questions to each participant, and the participants speak one at a time.

SUMMARY

Both genetics and people's experiences during their early years of life also have a huge impact brain architecture. Statistics show that 68% of children have experienced a possible traumatic event prior to the age of 16. Children and adolescents who experience traumatic events can develop both physical and emotional responses that affect their daily living. ACEs should be a part of the FCS preservice educator's program of study. FCS professionals need to be well versed in implementing trauma-informed care as an FCS educator in an early childhood program or in a middle and high school FCS program. Trauma-informed classrooms foster resiliency in those who have faced trauma by providing a safe environment where positive attributes of the individual are recognized.

KEY TERMS

Bowen's intergenerational model

Positive stress

Adverse childhood experiences (ACEs)

Toxic stress

Traumatic event

Trauma

Tolerable stress

Differentiation

Resiliency

Epigenetics

Underfunctioning strategy

Conflict strategy

Overfunctioning strategy

Attachment

Family projection strategy

QUESTIONS AND ACTIVITIES

1. After reading the section on multigenerational transmission, summarize examples of the three strategies that are used by poorly differentiated individuals.
2. After reading the section on types of trauma, define each type and provide an example.
3. Research attachment theory. Summarize the types of attachments between child and adult and how each impacts the child/caregiver relationship.
4. Design a set of classroom rules needed to implement restorative circles. Describe how you will explain the rules to the students.
5. Create an infographic differentiating between healthy and unhealthy brain development. Please include at least seven items that can impact healthy development and seven items that can impact unhealthy development. Please be as creative as possible. Free infographic templates can be accessed through Canva, PicMonkey, Venngage, or Piktochart. You may use other templates as desired.
6. Research ways to build resilience in individuals online. Create a 3- to 5-minute video clip in which you identify and briefly describe at least seven supports (individual, family, community, or institutional) that build resilience in individuals.

REFERENCES

Ainsworth, M. D. S. (1989). Attachment beyond infancy. *American Psychologist, 44,* 709–716.

Alberta Family Wellness Initiative. (n.d.). *Serve and return.* https://www.albertafamilywellness.org/what-we-know/serve-and-return

Alberta Family Wellness Initiative. (2013). *How brains are built: Introducing the brain story.* https://www.albertafamilywellness.org/resources/video/how-brains-are-built-core-story-of-brain-development

Alberta Family Wellness Initiative. (2021). *Brain architecture.* https://www.albertafamilywellness.org/what-we-know/brain-architecture

Anderson S. A., & Sabatelli, R. M. (2007). *Intergenerational models in family interaction: A multigenerational developmental perspective* (5th ed.). Pearson.

Bowlby, J. (1969). *Attachment and loss: Vol. 1. Attachment.* Basic Books.

Bowlby, J. (1988). *A secure base: Parent-child attachment and healthy human development.* Basic Books.

Center on the Developing Child at Harvard University. (2018). *What is epigenetics and how and how does it relate to child development?* https://developingchild.harvard.edu/resources/what-is-epigenetics-and-how-does-it-relate-to-child-development/

Center on the Developing Child at Harvard University. (2021). *Brain architecture.* https://developingchild.harvard.edu/science/key-concepts/brain-architecture/

Center on the Developing Child at Harvard University. (n.d.). *What are ACEs and how do they relate to toxic stress?* https://developingchild.harvard.edu/resources/aces-and-toxic-stress-frequently-asked-questions/#

Centers for Disease Control and Prevention. (2020). *What is epigenetics?* https://www.cdc.gov/genomics/disease/epigenetics.htm

Centers for Disease Control and Prevention. (2021a). *Early brain development and health.* https://www.cdc.gov/ncbddd/childdevelopment/early-brain-development.html

Centers for Disease Control and Prevention. (2021b). *Preventing adverse childhood experiences.* https://www.cdc.gov/violenceprevention/aces/fastfact.html

Enlow, M. B., Devick, K. L., Brunst, K. J., Lipton, L. R., Coull, B. A., & Wright, R. J. (2018). Maternal lifetime trauma exposure, prenatal cortisol, and infant negative affectivity. *National Center for Biotechnology Information (NCBI) Health and Human Services (HHS) Public Access.* https://www.ncbi.nlm.nih.gov/pmc/articles/PMC5624542/

Felitti, V. J., Anda, R. F., Nordenberg, D., Williamson, D. F., Spitz, A. M., Edwards, V., Koss, M. P., & Marks, J. S. (1998). Relationship of childhood abuse and household dysfunction to many of the leading causes of death in adults: The adverse childhood experiences (ACE) study. *American Journal of Preventive Medicine, 14*(4), 245–258. https://doi.org/10.1016/S0749-3797(98)00017-8

Forbes, H. (2012). *Help for Billy: A beyond consequences approach to helping challenging children in the classroom.* Beyond Consequences Institute, LLC.

Garrido, S., Baker, F. A., Davidson, J. W., Moore, G., & Wasserman, S. (2015). Music and trauma: The relationship between music, personality, and coping style. *Frontiers in Psychology, 6*(977). https://doi.org/10.3389/fpsyg.2015.00977

Hauser-Cram, P., Nugent, K. K., Thies, K. M., & Travers, J. F. (2014). *The development of children and adolescents.* Wiley.

Jamieson, K. (2019). *The power of language: ACEs and trauma.* The Center for Childhood Counseling. https://www.centerforchildcounseling.org/the-power-of-language-aces-and-trauma/

Keim, R. E., & Jacobson, A. L. (Eds.). (2011). *Wisdom for parents: Key ideas from parent educators.* de Sitter Publication.

Lake Behavioral Hospital. (2021). *Recognizing the signs and symptoms of emotional & psychological trauma.* https://www.lakebehavioralhospital.com/recognizing-the-signs-and-symptoms-of-emotional-psychological-trauma/

Levine, L. E., & Munsch, J. (2020). *Child development: From infancy to adolescence.* SAGE Publications.

Lumen Learning. (n.d.). *Childhood stress and development.* https://courses.lumenlearning.com/wm-lifespandevelopment/chapter/childhood-stress-and-development/

MedlinePlus. (2021). *Stress in childhood.* https://medlineplus.gov/ency/article/002059.htm

Mitchell, K. (2019). *Epigenetics: What impact does it have on our psychology?* The Conversation. https://the-conversation.com/epigenetics-what-impact-does-it-have-on-our-psychology-109516

Mustard, J. F. (2006). Experience-based brain development: Scientific underpinnings of the importance of early child development in a global world. *Paediatric Child Health, 11*(9), 571–572. https://doi.org/10.1093/pch/11.9.571

National Child Traumatic Stress Network. (n.d.). *Trauma types.* Retrieved May 26, 2021, from https://www.nctsn.org/what-is-child-trauma/trauma-types

National Child Traumatic Stress Network. (2021). *About child trauma. https://www.nctsn.org/what-is-child-trauma/about-child-trauma*

National Scientific Council on the Developing Child. (2010). *Early experiences can alter gene expression and affect long-term development: Working paper No. 10.* https://46y5eh11fhgw3ve3ytpwxt9r-wpengine.netdna-ssl.com/wp-content/uploads/2010/05/Early-Experiences-Can-Alter-Gene-Expression-and-Affect-Long-Term-Development.pdf

Papalia, D. E., & Martorell, G. A. (2015). *Experience human development.* McGraw Hill.

Pappano, L. (2014, May 14). *"Trauma sensitive" schools—Harvard education letter.* https://traumasensitive-schools.org/trauma-sensitive-schools/

Perry, B. D., & The ChildTrauma Academy. (2013) *3: Threat response patterns* [Video]. YouTube. https://www.youtube.com/watch?v=sr-OXkk3i8E&feature=youtu.be

Price, C. A., Bush, K. R., & Price. S. J. (Eds.) (2017). *Families and change: Coping with stressful events and transitions* (5th ed.). SAGE Publications.

Psychology Today. (n.d.). *Epigenetics.* https://www.psychologytoday.com/us/basics/epigenetics

Robinson, L., Smith, M., & Segal, J. (2020). *Emotional and psychological trauma.* Help Guide. https://www.helpguide.org/articles/ptsd-trauma/coping-with-emotional-and-psychological-trauma.htm

Sporleder, J., & Forbes, H. (2016). *The trauma-informed school.* Beyond Consequences Institute.

Substance Abuse and Mental Health Services Administration. (2014). *SAMHSA's concept of trauma and guidance for a trauma-Informed approach.* https://ncsacw.samhsa.gov/userfiles/files/SAMHSA_Trauma.pdf

Swafford, M., & Jolley, L. A. (2012). Exploring FCS role in promoting secure relationships in families. *Journal of Family and Consumer Sciences, 104*(4), 34–39.

Swafford, M. D., & Dainty, H. T. (2009). Learning environment: Respecting diversity and exceptionality. *Journal of Family and Consumer Sciences Education, 27* (National Teacher Standards 4), 45–59. http://www.natefacs.org/JFCSE/v27Standards4/v27Standards4Swafford.pdf

SXSW EDU. (2021, March 9–11). *Keynote session. Dr. Bruce Perry.* Oprah Winfrey & Dr. Bruce Perry keynote announced for SXSW EDU Online 2021. https://www.carrolup.info/oprah-winfrey-dr-bruce-perry-in-conversation-sxsw-edu-2021/

Szyf, M. (2014). Lamarck revisited: Epigenetic inheritance of ancestral odor fear conditioning. *Nature Neuroscience, 17*(1), 2–4. https://doi.org/10.1038/nn.3603

Tennessee Department of Education. (2019). *Building strong brains: Strategies for educators, training of trainers.*

Tennessee Department of Education. (2020, November). *Child development associate (CDA)*. https://www. tn.gov/content/dam/tn/education/ccte/eps/credentials/cte_sic_ChildDevelopmentAssociate.pdf

Tennessee Department of Health. (2015). *Adverse Childhood Experiences in Tennessee*. https://www.tn.gov/ content/dam/tn/health/documents/Tennessee_ACE_Final_Report_with_Authorization.pdf

The Urban Child Institute. (2010). *Early experiences affect a child's cognitive and brain development*. http:// www.urbanchildinstitute.org/sites/all/files/databooks/TUCI_Data_Book_V_2010.06_education. pdf

Tierney, A. L., & Nelson, C. L. (2009). Brain development and the role of experience in the early years. *Zero Three, 30*(2), 9–13.

Women Wonder Writers. (2021). What are restorative circles and how to conduct them. *The Write of Your Life*. https://thewriteofyourlife.org/what-are-restorative-circles/

Figure Credits

Learning Theories and Educational Psychology

Elizabeth Ramsey, PhD, and Melinda Swafford, PhD

FIGURE 4.1 Theory Explains Behavior

Chapter 4 Objectives

Upon completion of this chapter, the learner will be able to

- define the learning process,
- define educational psychology,
- summarize major components of selected learning theories,
- analyze the relationship of theories to teaching and learning, and
- discuss which educational psychology perspectives they relate to most as a preservice educator.

Introduction

Providing a comparative overview of major learning theories allows the family and consumer sciences (FCS) preservice educator to formulate a philosophy of practice. *Theories* are a set of principles that explain facts or an event (Merriam-Webster, n.d.). Learning theories provide the educator with an understanding of how knowledge is acquired, processed, and retrained. FCS professional educators need to understand the teaching and learning process in order to plan meaningful opportunities for learners. "Any and all theories are based on limited information; they are conjectures and assertions based on empirical research, and all scientists, including learning scientists—are constantly interrogating their theories. Moreover, there are times when one needs multiple theories" (Wilson & Peterson, 2006, p. 3). For example, in an occupational early childhood education program, if children have not developed the skills of listening, observing, participating, talking, and problem solving, then they may have difficulty functioning in a developmentally appropriate classroom without accommodations as they may have difficulty sharing, turn taking, and following directions. (Warash et al., 2008). This chapter will cover how knowledge is acquired, processed, and obtained during the learning process. Learning is influenced by environmental factors, and knowledge of theories is essential when planning appropriate instructional methodologies.

The Learning Process

In the past, the learning process involved a traditional model where a teacher served as the purveyor of information and learners were sitting in rows in a classroom (Sequeira, 2017). In this passive role of education, an educator hoped that learners would take notes, process the presented content, and retain the information to use later.

The current learning process recognizes that not all individuals learn at the same pace, or in the same manner, and past experiences of the learner impact learning. Also, active learning strategies result in students who are attentive and active in the learning process. Educators must use a variety of teaching strategies that embrace the learning process. Learning is influenced by environmental factors. "Teaching is a set of events, outside the learners, which are designed to support the internal process of learning. … Learning is internal to learners. You cannot motivate others if you are not self-motivated" (Sequeira, 2017, p. 3).

Each learner demonstrates a preference for acquiring knowledge. Yet learning styles research, which is popular and used by many educators, lacks validity (Chick, 2010; Newton & Miah, 2017). Furthermore, Chick (2010) explains that the popularity of learning style inventories is because people enjoy them, and they can serve as a way to categorize people. Although not valid, learning styles assessments were useful in the educator's understanding of the need to use a variety of instructional strategies, resources, and the learning environment (Li et al., 2016).

Furthermore, learning style inventories can serve as a form of metacognition (Chick, 2010). **Metacognition** is an awareness of how one thinks and learns (Chick, 2013). Practices of metacognition are not to be taught individually but should be incorporated into the context of the lesson (Pintrich, 2002). When incorporating practices of metacognition into the lesson, the educator can model the process of thinking through to solve a problem. Also, the educator could encourage open discussion of different strategies to solve a problem. This works well with FCS career clusters of human services. Learners participating in the discourse may identify their own areas of weakness and strengths in metacognition. Once this is identified, the learner can comprehend ways to expand strengths to overcome weaknesses. "Students who know about the different kinds of strategies for learning, thinking, and problem-solving will be more likely to use them" (Pintrich, 2002, p. 222). Through this awareness, a learner will identify how to transfer learning to new tasks (Chick, 2013).

Research by Pintrich (2002) indicates the more awareness learners have of metacognition and how they learn, the easier it is for them to learn. To promote metacognition with teaching instructions, the educator should incorporate preassessments so learners can identify what they already know. This can be accomplished with a concept mapping exercise at the beginning of the lesson or learning segment. In addition, reflective activities are also metacognition strategies, as reflection allows learners to gain an understanding of why a concept was difficult or which strategies were successful (Chick, 2013). This could be used as closure for the lesson. Using practices of metacognition within FCS content promotes thinking about thinking.

Three Stages of Learning

Research by Lewis and Doorlag (2006) identifies three stages of learning: acquisition, maintenance, and generalization. An educator must comprehend these stages in order to plan relevant and engaging lessons that address the three stages of learning. These concepts can be easily included in a general lesson plan.

In the **acquisition** stage, the learner is acquiring knowledge or initial learning of concepts. Acquisition of knowledge may occur during a pretest, the set, and/or the body of the lesson. During the set, the educator may survey the learners to determine if this is new knowledge or how much is previously known on the topic. During instruction, in the body of the lesson, the educator provides content on the topic. During this time of instruction, it is important to correct misconceptions that learners may previously have of the content.

In the **maintenance** stage, the educator is building on the new knowledge. Concepts are maintained and recalled, and knowledge is demonstrated by viewing, listening, and discussing the concepts in various ways during instruction. Maintenance may occur during instruction or during assessments. In the final stage, **generalization**, a student can apply the maintained knowledge learned to new situations with case studies and other higher order thinking activities. This may occur during assessment or during the closure of the lesson.

SPOTLIGHT: EXAMPLE OF THREE STAGES OF LEARNING

After a pretest in a lifespan development course, the educator realizes that many 10th-grade students believe that conception occurs in the uterus. However, after instruction, students learn that conception occurs in the fallopian tube. This is new knowledge or the acquisition stage of learning.

(Continued)

The educator corrected errors and misconceptions believed by many of the learners. In the maintenance stage, the educator plans instruction, presenting information in the text by incorporating a PowerPoint, 3D model, visual chart, and a video clip. Learners answer questions that the educator poses in the class and draw diagrams of the correct placement of conception. In the final stage, generalization, the application of the learned content is applied to a new situation concerning contraception. Since learners have the correct knowledge and understanding of where conception occurs, students will understand how a tubal ligation can prevent conception.

Educational Psychology

Educational psychology is the process of how individuals learn, problems associated with learning, teaching strategies, and evaluation of learners on assessments (Merriam-Webster, n.d.). There are different perspectives in the field of educational psychology that address these factors. In this text, we are referring to them as learning theories. We do need both an understanding of education's psychological perspectives and a philosophy of education when preparing to become effective educators (Devine & Tesar, 2015). Educational psychology impacts how an individual learns and how a learning environment may promote or impede learning. During our interactions with learners and fellow educators, the teaching strategies we select to use and our assessments of learning are dependent upon the educational psychological perspectives we embrace.

Learning Theories

Learning theories are a set of principles that provide a basis for how individuals learn. "Selection of theories depends on an assessment of the situation, identification of the targeted population, an understanding of the behavior to be addressed or change to be made, and determination of outcomes that are strategic, measurable, achievable, relevant and timely" (Braun et al., 2014, p. 2). Understanding learning theory allows the educator to plan content to achieve the desired outcomes.

There are many educational theories to research. For this chapter, learning theories are classified into the categories of constructivism, cognitivism, humanism, and behaviorism. However, one may find an overlap of theorists within the four categories. Furthermore, researchers in education recognize that more than one theory will be used in all levels of education (see Figure 4.1). For example, the complexity of teaching in early childhood is not an either/or situation. "It requires enacting a continuum of ideology with no theory practiced in isolation" (Warash et al., 2008, p. 441). Moreover, the authors included Freud's theory in this chapter, as his psychoanalytical theory serves as the foundation for many other theories (Wheeler & Richey, 2005).

Constructivism

Educators who embrace the learning theory of constructivism believe that individuals construct their own knowledge of the world through experiences and reflection on these experiences. In other words, constructivist theorists believe that learning occurs not by sitting in a class, listening to a lecture (a passive role for the learner) but through experience, reflection, and doing (an active role for the learner), which results in new learning. Since individuals are unique, each individual's learning experience is unique (Stevens-Fulbrook, 2019). Instructional strategies that support this theory include problem-based learning, cooperative groups, research, and projects. Notable individuals that embrace the constructivist thought of learning include John Dewey, Jean Piaget, Lev Vygotsky, and Jerome Bruner (Odom, 2016).

Vygotsky

Lev Vygotsky believed that learning is a collaborative process involving social interaction as a key part of the learning process. His early work with young children documented that learning was enhanced when children engaged in activities they enjoy and worked in social settings with other children (Wheeler & Richey, 2005). Vygotsky is noted for two concepts: zone of proximal development and scaffolding. The **zone of proximal development** occurs when a learner collaborates with someone who provides support as they complete an unfamiliar task (Marion, 2014). **Scaffolding** occurs by building upon previous knowledge with the assistance of others for prompts and feedback.

Dewey

John Dewey, a strong supporter of student-centered learning and collaborative learning, used an experimental philosophy, **collaborative learning**, which posits that children should learn by doing. He believed the role of the educator was to observe children for their interests, provide background information, and place children in groups to tackle the concept (Janse, 2019). He believed that for learning to occur, children must link the current content to prior experiences. He has influenced many in the field of education (Janse, 2019). Dewey agreed with Piaget that the environment influenced learning in children. Furthermore, he agreed with Vygotsky that children learn best in a social situation with others who might provide support.

In the classroom, educators who adopt the constructivist philosophy serve as facilitators of learning. A facilitator of learning has a student-centered classroom that encourages learners to engage in critical thinking and problem-based learning. Educators, who are facilitators of learning, serve as consultants, coaches, and guides in the classroom, while the learner actively engages with the content that results in higher order thinking (Odom, 2016).

Cognitivism

Cognitive learning theorists believe that learning is not dependent upon stimuli or reinforcements from the environment but that learning occurs when an individual internally processes new content in the brain. Learners process information by **schema**, or mental representation of an object, and relate new information to the existing schemas. Notable theorists who embrace cognitivism include Jean Piaget, Lev Vygotsky, Benjamin Bloom, Jerome Bruner, Abraham Maslow, Erik Erikson, David Kolbe, and Howard Gardner (Stevens-Fulbrook, 2019).

Bruner

Bruner also believes that learning is enhanced when the material is of interest to the learner. He made significant contributions to cognitive learning theories in children and is associated with the establishment of the Head Start Program. Bruner believed in active learning. He is also responsible for the term *scaffolding* (building upon prior knowledge). He proposed a **spiral curriculum**, an educational approach in which content is reviewed at intervals with more complex content added at each interval. For example, basic knowledge is presented at the first meeting; during the second meeting, a review of basic material occurs for reinforcement plus the addition of content at a more complex level each time. Bruner believed the role of the educator is to engage the learner in active dialogue, and through scaffolding, the educator helps translate information into a format that fits the learner's current state of understanding.

Bloom

In 1956, Benjamin Bloom proposed that objectives could be categorized into areas specific to learning and ranked in a hierarchical arrangement of cognitive processes from easy to more difficult. The subdivisions referred to as "Bloom's Taxonomy" included knowledge, understanding, application, analysis, synthesis, and evaluation (Stevens-Fulbrook, 2019). Furthermore, he categorized learning into three domains: cognitive, affective, and psychomotor. The cognitive domain represents knowledge, the affective domain represents values and feelings, and the psychomotor represents skills. In 2001, Bloom's former student and research partner revised Bloom's Taxonomy to include action verbs, not nouns, to make it easier to use when writing objectives (Stevens-Fulbrook, 2019). See Figure 4.2 for the revised version of Bloom's Taxonomy.

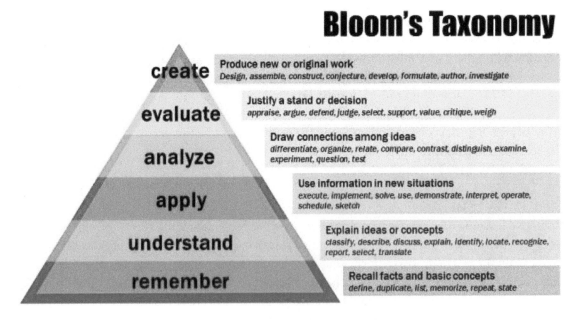

Bloom's Taxonomy

create — Produce new or original work
Design, assemble, construct, conjecture, develop, formulate, author, investigate

evaluate — Justify a stand or decision
appraise, argue, defend, judge, select, support, value, critique, weigh

analyze — Draw connections among ideas
differentiate, organize, relate, compare, contrast, distinguish, examine, experiment, question, test

apply — Use information in new situations
execute, implement, solve, use, demonstrate, interpret, operate, schedule, sketch

understand — Explain ideas or concepts
classify, describe, discuss, explain, identify, locate, recognize, report, select, translate

remember — Recall facts and basic concepts
define, duplicate, list, memorize, repeat, state

FIGURE 4.2 Revised Bloom's Taxonomy

Piaget

Jean Piaget's (Figure 4.3) developmental theory can be classified as cognitive constructivist, as Piaget believed that learning occurred in stages where the learner constructed knowledge by seeking balance in life, or equilibrium. Piaget's theory involves the term *schema*, which means a mental pattern that children use to understand their environment (Stevens-Fulbrook, 2019). Learning occurs by the adaption and assimilation of experiences/knowledge from the environment into new cognitive structures within the child's brain (Regents of the University of California, 2016).

FIGURE 4.3 Jean Piaget

In Piaget's theory, there are four stages of cognitive development. Stage 1 is the sensorimotor stage, which begins at birth and goes to age 2. During this stage, the child explores their environment with their senses. Object permanence (the beginning of memory) is also developed during this time. In the preoperational stage, from age 2 through age 7, the child is able to think symbolically. Symbols, objects, and words are important to a child's environment. Children begin to imitate. Children at this stage are also egocentric and have difficulty with empathy and the viewpoints of others (Stevens-Fulbrook, 2019). During the concrete operational stage, children begin to think logically and in concrete terms. This stage begins around age 7 and goes to age 11. In the final stage of cognitive development, formal operations, children can think abstractly and use deductive reasoning (Stevens-Fulbrook, 2019). This stage begins at age 11 and goes to adulthood.

Piaget's theory has been used as a foundation for the education of young children. "Piaget's theory and developmental stages are major components of Developmentally Appropriate Practice (DAP)" (Warash et al., 2008, p. 443) as children construct knowledge from active engagement in the environment. The research-based principles of DAP recognize that the developmental domains (cognitive, social-emotional, and physical) are related and interdependent and that development occurs in an orderly manner with new knowledge and skills, which build upon previous knowledge and skills through play (Wheeler & Richey, 2005). See the Spotlight on DAP and Activity 4.1.

SPOTLIGHT: DAP

Preservice teachers must be able to recognize DAP along with connecting practices to theory. This assignment was created to help students recognize DAP and connect activities to theories. First, explore the "NAEYC Developmentally Appropriate Practice Position Statement" (2020) found online in downloadable form (https://www.naeyc.org/resources/position-statements/dap/contents). This PDF can be downloaded in either English or Spanish. Each of the following position statements

(Continued)

is thoroughly explained in the online document. The following list is taken from the National Association for the Education of Young Children's (NAEYC, 2020) position statement on DAP:

1. "Development and learning are dynamic processes that reflect the complex interplay between a child's biological characteristics and the environment, each shaping the other as well as future patterns of growth" (NAEYC, 2020, p. 8).

2. "All domains of child development—physical development, cognitive development, social and emotional development, and linguistic development (including bilingual or multilingual development), as well as approaches to learning—are important; each domain both supports and is supported by the others" (NAEYC, 2020, p. 9).

3. "Play promotes joyful learning that fosters self-regulation, language, cognitive and social competencies as well as content knowledge across disciplines. Play is essential for all children, birth through age 8" (NAEYC, 2020, p. 9).

4. "Although general progressions of development and learning can be identified, variations due to cultural contexts, experiences, and individual differences must also be considered" (NAEYC, 2020, p. 10).

5. "Children are active learners from birth, constantly taking in and organizing information to create meaning through their relationships, their interactions with their environment, and their overall experiences" (NAEYC, 2020, p. 11).

6. "Children's motivation to learn is increased when their learning environment fosters their sense of belonging, purpose, and agency. Curricula and teaching methods build on each child's assets by connecting their experiences in the school or learning environment to their home and community settings" (NAEYC, 2020, p. 11).

7. "Children learn in an integrated fashion that cuts across academic disciplines or subject areas. Because the foundations of subject-area knowledge are established in early childhood, educators need subject-area knowledge, an understanding of the learning progressions within each subject area, and pedagogical knowledge about teaching each subject area's content effectively" (NAEYC, 2020, p. 12).

8. "Development and learning advance when children are challenged to achieve at a level just beyond their current mastery and when they have many opportunities to reflect on and practice newly acquired skills" (NAEYC, 2020, p. 12).

9. "Used responsibly and intentionally, technology and interactive media can be valuable tools for supporting children's development and learning" (NAEYC, 2020, p. 13).

Kolb

David Kolb's learning theory states that experience is critical to the construction of knowledge. He defined learning as a process where knowledge is created through the reshaping of experience (Kurt, 2020). His learning style model theory is represented by a four-stage learning cycle. For learning to occur, the individual must progress through all four stages. The first stage is a concrete experience with the concepts. This is followed by the second stage of observation and reflection on

---

ACTIVITY 4.1: APPLICATION OF CHILD DEVELOPMENT THEORY ACTIVITY

After becoming familiar with DAP, complete the following:

Create an activity that would be developmentally appropriate for preschool or kindergarten.

For example:

Upper Case/Lower Case Letter Dig

- Materials: Plastic tub full of sand or rice, upper case and/or lower case plastic letters, and plastic shovels

- Instructions: Children will work in small groups of three or four. Give each child a plastic shovel. Ask them to dig the letters out of the sand or rice and work together to arrange them into the alphabet

- Variations: Children can create upper case alphabet, lower case alphabet, or both. For younger children, they could construct their names instead of constructing the alphabet. Older children could construct sight words.

- After creating a DAP activity, connect the activity to a theory. Explain what theory or theorist you are using and how it connects to the activity. Connect the activity to a state standard and justify your reasoning.

---

the concrete experience. The third stage is analysis and generalization of the concepts. In his final stage, the learner tests hypotheses of the concept to use in other situations (McLeod, 2017). Kolbe believes that each stage is supportive of and feeds into the next stage. The learner may enter the cycle at any point; however, effective learning occurs when a learner participates in all four stages (McLeod, 2017). Kolb's experiential learning theory works well with CTE courses, as most programs of study have aspects of experiential learning in each course.

Gardner

Howard Gardner, a cognitive psychologist, studied under Erikson and Breuner at Harvard University. He believes that intelligence is the ability to solve a problem or make a product (Stevens-Fulbrook, 2019). Gardner believed that individuals have a blend of multiple types of intelligence (Smith, 2008). His theory provided content so that educators would reflect on their teaching and expand from lectures to incorporate a variety of strategies (Smith, 2008). Gardner stated, "It's not how smart you are that matters, what really counts is how you are smart" (Inspiring quotes.us, 2021). Gardner saw past the standardized intelligence test and considered that there are several different ways in which intelligence is expressed and measured.

Humanism

A humanistic learning theory is a person-centered theory, with learning being self-directed through observing and exploring (Purswell, 2019). The focus of this theory is the personal growth of the individual (Johnson, 2012). The major emphasis of this theory is placed on the process of learning

TABLE 4.1   Multiple Intelligences Theory

Linguistic intelligence	The ability to learn and use language in written and spoken forms to express oneself
Mathematical intelligence	The ability to solve problems logically, to solve mathematical problems, and to perform scientific investigations
Musical intelligence	Having skill in appreciation, composition, and performance of musical patterns, including the ability to recognize tone, pitch, and rhythm
Bodily-kinesthetic intelligence	Using mental abilities to coordinate body movements to solve problems
Spatial intelligence	Recognizing and using patterns in a wide or confined space
Interpersonal intelligence	Understanding the desires, motivations, and intentions of other people
Intrapersonal intelligence	Understanding your fears, feelings, and motivations
Naturalist intelligence	The ability to perceive, recognize, and order features from the environment

and then on the outcome (Stevens-Fulbrook, 2019). Major theorists include Abraham Maslow, Erik Erickson, Carl Rogers, and David Kolb, who believe the goal of education is to promote development and self-actualization (Purswell, 2019). "Additionally, humanistic theorists hold a phenomenological view of humans in that they believe each person's view of the world is reality for that person and that learning is motivated by personal need based on one's internal frame of reference" (Purswell, 2019, p. 359).

Erikson

Erik Erikson (Figure 4.4) was born in Germany in 1902 and was greatly influenced by Freud (Cherry, 2020). Erik Erikson expanded on Freud's beliefs and developed the theory of psychosocial development (Table 4.2), which is an eight-stage theory that considers social and cultural influence during development. In Erikson's theory, each stage of development involves a psychological challenge, known as a crisis, that must be resolved to maintain healthy development (Papalia et al., 2021).

Each stage or crisis as identified in Erikson's theory needs successful resolution in order for the individual to develop the quality at each stage (Cherry, 2020). For example, consider elementary age and middle school children: They are in the crisis of industry versus isolation. Educators and parents need to offer opportunities for children to be industrious, to work diligently, and to be successful. It is important to offer this age group activity that they can master and feel successful at. For children or students who struggle with mastery, it is important to recognize their struggle and modify activities or assignments as needed so that they can be successful—this is DAP. In addition to DAP, Erik Erikson's theory supports the importance

FIGURE 4.4 Erik Erikson

TABLE 4.2 Erikson's Psychosocial Stages of Development

Crisis	Age Range	Virtue
Trust versus mistrust	Birth to 18 months	Hope
Autonomy versus shame or doubt	18 months–3 years	Will
Initiative versus guilt	3–6 years	Purpose
Industry versus inferiority	6 years–puberty	Skill
Identity versus isolation	Puberty to young adulthood	Fidelity
Intimacy versus isolation	Young adulthood	Love
Generativity versus stagnation	Middle adulthood	Care
Integrity versus despair	Late adulthood	Wisdom

of play in children, as it offers children the opportunity to master emotional development (Sluss, 2015). Children need opportunities to play because while playing, they solve problems, use their imaginations, create games, and learn how to thrive socially. They exert their autonomy, take initiative, and are industrious while playing.

Maslow

Abraham Maslow's motivational theory of hierarchy of needs is one of the most referenced theories of human behavior and is known by those in the education field, as well as in other professions (Henwood, et al., 2015). In this theory, individual needs are categorized in hierarchical ranking from basic physiological needs to individuals' achieving self-actualization. His theory posits that individuals' growth is dependent on basic needs being met before one can move on to meeting higher level needs such as love. Figure 4.5 illustrates that an individual must satisfy the needs of

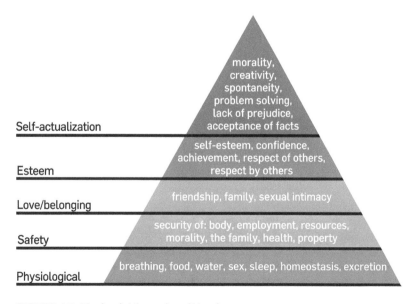

FIGURE 4.5 Maslow's Hierarchy of Needs

shelter, food, safety, love, and belonging before the individual prioritizes needs of self-esteem, respect for others, and self-improvement (Maslow, 1943). In education, faculty, administrators, and lawmakers have since recognized the importance of basic needs being met prior to learning. Programs that offer free or reduced-price breakfast and lunch are an example of meeting a child's basic needs in order for a child to succeed academically. Another example in education is creating a welcoming and loving classroom environment, as this fulfills the social belonging tier of Maslow's hierarchy of needs.

Rogers

Carl Rogers developed his theory in the 1980s. He believed that learning involves the entire individual—both cognitive and affective elements of heart and brain. Rogers believed in two types of learning: rote, which he believed does not last, and experiential learning, which he believed occurs in everyday life and has meaning. For learning to occur, educators should serve as facilitators of instruction rather than the distributors of knowledge and provide experiential learning with real and practical problems. Effective educators build relationships with the learners and possess three characteristics of realness, trust, and empathy (Stevens-Fulbrook, 2019).

Behaviorism

Individuals who embrace this theory believe that behavior is learned through an individual's environment that includes stimuli and responses or consequences. Students learn through practice and positive experiences. Learning is also impacted by an individual's history and influences through interaction with others (Wheeler & Richey, 2005). Behaviorism involves repeated actions, verbal feedback, and other reinforcements for learning to occur (Stevens-Fulbrook, 2019), as learning can be observed by a change in behavior. Notable theorists include Ivan Pavlov, Edward Thorndike, B. F. Skinner, and John Watson (Wheeler & Richey, 2005). Pavlov's research focused on respondent conditioning. Thorndike's research was on consequences. Watson's research, which brought an emphasis on environmental events and the responses from those events, also coined the term *behaviorism*, and Skinner expanded the work of Watson and Pavlov to humans; his research focus was operant conditioning in behavior modification (Wheeler & Richey, 2005).

Reinforcement and feedback are terms associated with behavioral theories. **Reinforcement** "is a consequence that follows a behavior that strengthens the behavior" (Wheeler & Richey, 2005, p. 148) to construct more helpful skills and/or competencies.

Feedback is information from an individual regarding performance or behavior. Reinforcement and feedback are vehicles for making changes in behavior or learning (see Table 4.3). Two types of feedback include specific or unspecific. Specific feedback praise is related directly to an event. For example, "Thank you for sitting quietly while I paid this bill." "I am so proud of you for not running in the hall." Make sure to relate the feedback directly to the event. Give praise as soon as possible after the event. Finally, reward small steps contingent on the behavior, and you may also include suggestions for a change. Unspecific praise is given independently of anything the individual has done. For example, "I love you." "You are great!" Specific praise is more preferred than unspecific praise.

TABLE 4.3 **Types of Reinforcement and Feedback**

Positive reinforcement	Adding something to increase the likelihood the behavior will continue
Vicarious reinforcement	Praising others' behavior to promote others to imitate the behavior
Negative reinforcement	Removal of an adverse stimulus when the desired behavior is achieved
Specific feedback	Related directly to the event
Unspecific feedback	Given independently, not tied to an event, and has less meaning to the individual
Ignoring behavior	Only use when the function is for attention

Positive reinforcement's purpose is to increase the likelihood that the behavior will continue by adding something. Tangible tokens can also be included with positive reinforcements. Examples of **tokens** include stickers; gestures, such as thumbs up, high five, or fist bump; or food (which can be controversial). However, it is important to fade out the tangible tokens and allow the social and emotional feeling to be the reward to take the place of the object.

Vicarious reinforcement is praising someone else's behavior to change the behavior of another. For example, "I like the way John cleans up his work area," or "Thank you, Maria, for sitting quietly during the oral presentations." The principle behind vicarious reinforcement is that others will emulate the behavior that was recognized with positive reinforcement.

Premack's principle is defined as engaging in a highly preferred activity as a result of performing a less preferred activity. It is also referred to as the "grandma principle." For example, "If you do this … you will get this…" Preferred activities vary as much as the individual. I used this principle as a form of behavior management in my FCS classroom. I told the students if we got on tasks and completed the assignment correctly, I would give them some free time to talk before dismissal.

Negative reinforcement is the removal of a stimulus that is aversive to the individual to strengthen the behavior (Wheeler & Richey, 2005). For example, the seat belt alarm stops when a person buckles up in an automobile. The smoke alarm stops when the presence of smoke is removed from the home. Ignoring behavior is also a type of reinforcement. It is effective when children and students want attention. However, do not use this when someone is being harmful to another person or destroying an object. Negative reinforcement is often confused with punishment; however, negative reinforcement does not reduce the behavior as punishment may. It relies on the principle that people will stop the behavior to avoid the stimulus. Unlike negative reinforcement, punishment is a negative consequence set in place by a caregiver or person in authority in an attempt to reduce the likelihood of a behavior. See Chapter 7 for more information on Positive Behavior Interventions and Supports (PBIS) and applied behavior analysis in the learning environment and as classroom management strategies.

Social Learning Theory

Alfred Bandura's social learning theory states that individuals learn by observing others. Furthermore, the environment and those within the environment influence an individual's learning. This theory merges cognitive and behavior theories (Wheeler & Richey, 2005). Modeling and imitation are key concepts of the theory, as learning occurs during the imitation of models. **Modeling** is learning that occurs through observation. **Imitation** is different from modeling; when the child performs the behaviors learned via the modeling, imitation has occurred (Marion, 2014).

Psychoanalytic Theory

The psychoanalytic theory was founded by an Austrian neuroscientist, Sigmund Freud, whose ideas were later expanded upon by Erik Erikson. The psychoanalytic theory is foundational when educating children and adolescents because it considers the environment of the child/adolescent and the importance of relationships and human interaction. Also, understanding this theory is the basis for implementing DAP.

Sigmund Freud

Sigmund Freud's contribution to early psychology and developmental theory is profound. Although many of his ideas are reputed today, some of his ideas are still accepted, and his theory remains the foundation for other theorists (Wheeler & Richey, 2005). Sigmund Freud conducted his research on predominantly White, upper-class females. Additionally, many of his subjects were reported to experience mental illness. With this said, his work is not considered generalizable to the general population, yet his work serves as a foundation for the study of psychology and human development today. His theory, called the psychosexual theory of development, identifies three parts of the personality: the id, which operates on the pleasure principle and governs newborn behavior; the ego, which operates under the reality principle, develops in early life, and represents reason; and the superego, which develops later in childhood or adolescence and includes the conscience. In Freud's theory of psychosexual development, as the stages of personality development, the zones of gratification shift from the mouth, to the anus, and lastly to the genitals. Freud identified that early experiences shape later functioning in life and that adult behavior is preceded by childhood (Papalia et al., 2021). Freud's theory relates to education in that he believes that development is influenced by biology and the environment.

How Theories Relate to Teaching and Learning

Effective FCS educators incorporate learning theories as they plan and deliver FCS content, as well as assess learners' acquisition of content. Piaget's cognitive development knowledge of the stages informs the educator of the developmental level of the learner, as knowledge of this theory impacts what the educator will plan and how the educator will present the content (Stevens-Fulbrook, 2019). Knowledge of Maslow's theory will enhance the educator's ability to recognize if the basic needs of the learners are met in order to motivate the learners to have the prerequisite to acquire content needed to improve quality of life.

Bloom's Taxonomy is used when educators write objectives when planning lessons. This theory provides an avenue for educators to plan effectively so learners build upon their prior understanding. Use of other cognitive theories in the classroom can be found throughout the lesson plan, such as in the set, a review of previous knowledge or skills needed for the new content, use of graphic organizers for learners to see how content is connected, as well as during formative and summative assessments.

Examples of the constructivist theory are found in the classroom when educators have learners participate in collaborative groups, research projects, problem-based learning, and other creative projects. The humanist theory is present throughout the FCS classroom, as the content is to improve the quality of life for individuals and families, therefore benefiting individual growth and development.

SUMMARY

Understanding learning theories is essential when planning appropriate lessons that incorporate various instructional methodologies to enhance learning. Major theories include constructivists who believe learners create or construct knowledge out of experiences. Behaviorists believe that learning occurs through the reinforcement of behavior. Cognitivists believe that individuals learn by assimilating content from the environment. Humanists believe that learning occurs through observation, and it is self-directed. Finally, Freud's psychoanalytic theory serves as the foundation for many learning theories.

KEY TERMS

Metacognition	Imitation
Acquisition	Shema
Maintenance	Collaborative learning
Generalization	Reinforcements
Scaffolding	Feedback
Zone of proximal development	Tokens
Spiral curriculum	Premack's principle
Modeling	Vicarious reinforcement

QUESTIONS AND ACTIVITIES

1. Select a concept in an FCS program of study course standard; describe how one can apply Lewis and Doorlag's (2006) three stages of learning to cover the content.
2. Describe how aspects of behaviorist theories are incorporated into the FCS classroom.
3. Most of our learners in the FCS classroom will be in Erikson's identity versus inferiority stage. How will you incorporate this into the FCS learning environment?
4. Describe why an educator must know Maslow's theory.

5. Analyze how an educator can incorporate constructivism in the classroom without using a lab.

6. Summarize aspects of cognitivism that can be incorporated into the FCS classroom or by an extension agent.

REFERENCES

Braun, B., McCoy, T., & Finkbeiner, N. (2014). *Extension education theoretical framework with criterion-referenced assessment tools.* University of Maryland Extension.

Cherry, K. (2020). *History and biographies: Biography of Erik Erikson (1902–1994).* Very Well Mind. https://www.verywellmind.com/erik-erikson-biography-1902-1994-2795538

Chick, N. (2010). *Learning styles.* Vanderbilt University Center for Teaching. https://cft.vanderbilt.edu/guides-sub-pages/learning-styles-preferences

Chick, N. (2013). *Metacognition.* Vanderbilt University Center for Teaching. https://cft.vanderbilt.edu/guides-sub-pages/metacognition/

Devine, N., & Tesar, M. (2015). Philosophy and pedagogy of educational psychology. *Knowledge Cultures, 3*(2), 11–17.

Henwood, B. F., Derejko, K. S., Couture, J., & Padgett, D. K. (2015). Maslow and mental health recovery: A comparative study of homeless programs for adults with serious mental illness. *Administration and Policy in Mental Health, 42*(2), 220–228. https://doi.org/10.1007/s10488-014-0542-8

Inspiring quotes.us. (2021). *It's not how smart you are that matters, what really counts is how you are smart.* https://www.inspiringquotes.us/quotes/5JXS_jluTaeqp

Janse, B. (2019). *John Dewey theory.* ToolsHero. https://www.toolshero.com/change-management/john-dewey-theory/

Johnson, A. P. (2012). *Humanistic and holistic learning theory.* www.opdt-johnson.com/ch_9_humanistic_holistic__1_.pdf

Kurt, S. (2020) *Kolb's experiential learning theory & learning styles.* Educational Technology. https://educationaltechnology.net/kolbs-experiential-learning-theory-learning-styles/

Lewis, R., & Doorlag, D. (2006). *Teaching special students in general education classrooms.* Pearson/Merrill/Prentice Hall.

Li, Y., Medwell, J., Wray, D., Wang, L., & Liu, X. (2016). Learning styles: A review of validity and usefulness. *Journal of Education and Training Studies, 4*(10). https://doi.org/10.11114/jets.v4i10.1680

Marion, M. (2014). *Guidance of young children* (19th ed.). Pearson.

Maslow, A. H. (1943). A theory of human motivation. *Psychological Review, 50*(4), 370–396.

McLeod, S. A. (2017). *Kolb—learning styles.* Simply Psychology. https://www.simplypsychology.org/learning-kolb.html

Merriam-Webster. (n.d.). Theory. In *Merriam-Webster.com dictionary.* Retrieved August 26, 2021, from https://www.merriam-webster.com/dictionary/theory

National Association for the Education of Young Children. (2020). NAEYC position statement: Developmentally appropriate practice. https://www.naeyc.org/sites/default/files/globally-shared/downloads/PDFs/resources/position-statements/dap-statement_0.pdf

Newton, P. M., & Miah, M. (2017). Evidence-based higher education—is the learning styles 'myth' important? *Frontiers in Psychology, 8*, 444. https://doi.org/10.3389/fpsyg.2017.00444

Odom, S. L. (2016). The role of theory in early childhood special education and early intervention. In B. Reichow, B. Boyd, E. Barton, & S. Odom (Eds.), *Handbook of early childhood special education* (pp. 21–36). Springer.

Papalia, D. E., Feldman, R. D., & Martorell, G. (2021). *Experience human development.* McGraw-Hill.

Pintrich, P. (2002). The role of metacognitive knowledge in learning, teaching, and assessing. *Theory into Practice, 41*(4), 219–255. https://doi.org/10,1207/s15430421tip4_3

Purswell, K. E. (2019). Humanistic learning theory in counselor education. *The Professional Counselor, 9*(4), 358–368. https://doi.org/10.15241/kep.9.4.35

Regents of the University of California. (2016). *Overview of learning theories.* Graduate Student Instructor Teaching & Resource Center, Graduate Division, UC Berkeley.

Sequeira, A. H. (2017). *Introduction to concepts of teaching and learning.* National Institute of Technology Karnataka.

Sluss, D. J. (2015). *Supporting play in early childhood.* Cengage Learning.

Smith, M. K. (2008) Howard Gardner and multiple intelligences. In *The Encyclopedia of Pedagogy and Informal Education.* https://www.infed.org/mobi/howard-gardner-multiple-intelligences-and-education.

Stevens-Fulbrook, P. (2019). 15 learning theories in education: A complete summary. Retrieved August 25, 2021, from https://www.educationcorner.com/learning-theories-in-education/

Warash, B., Curtis, R., & Hursh, D. (2008). Skinner meets Piaget on the Reggio playground: Practical synthesis of applied behavior analysis and developmentally appropriate practice orientations. *Journal of Research in Childhood Education, 22*(4), 441–453.

Wheeler, J. J., & Richey, D. D. (2005). Understanding behavior in children and youth. In J. J. Wheeler & D. D. Richey (Eds.), *Behavior management: Principles and practices of positive behavior support* (pp. 1–34). Pearson.

Wilson, S. M., & Peterson, P. L. (2006). *Theories of learning and teaching: What do they mean for educators?* NEA Working Papers.

Figure Credits

Curriculum, Standards, and Philosophy of Education

Melinda Swafford, PhD; Elizabeth Ramsey, PhD; and Kayleigh Beasley, MA

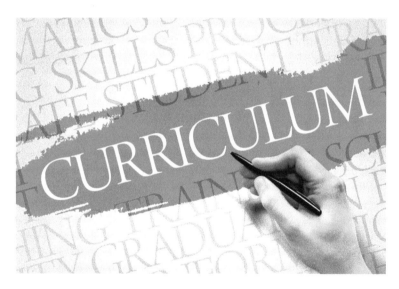

FIGURE 5.1 Curriculum

Chapter 5 Objectives

Upon completion of this chapter, the learner will be able to

- define pedagogy,
- describe traits of a quality educator,
- analyze how they will apply these traits in their professional experience,
- identify the units of instruction included in curriculum planning,
- summarize how and why standards were developed,

- identify the family and consumer sciences (FCS) programs of study and the courses within the 16 national career clusters that represent the learner's specific state,
- identify three philosophies that impact educational thought in FCS content courses,
- analyze the impact of ones' educational philosophy on teaching, and
- create a personal philosophy of education.

Introduction

McGregor (2020) stated that family and consumer sciences (FCS) textbooks that prepare students to become educators often lack chapters on curriculum mapping/development, module/learning segment planning, and developing a personal educational philosophy. We agree with McGregor that these concepts are foundational to developing an effective FCS educator. Like McGregor, we believe this content is imperative to prepare preservice teachers to become FCS educators. We included these concepts to make this text comprehensive. This chapter includes a focus on curriculum development by using **course standards** that are included in the various courses in the programs of study. Lesson plans and learning segments will be covered in detail in Chapter 6. This chapter will also include a brief overview of educational philosophies, as well as describe the need for developing a personal philosophy of education.

As covered in Chapter 1, FCS education courses are classified as career technical education (CTE) courses. CTE programs and courses vary among the states. However, quality programs currently receive funding by Perkins V legislation and have these common features: Programs are connected to a career cluster; each cluster has a **program of study** that includes a series of courses; and each course has course standards that serve as a guide to the educator when planning so students may gain skills and master content.

What Is Pedagogy?

Pedagogy is the science or art of teaching that involves the planning and the practice of educating others (Merriam-Webster, n.d.). Pedagogy also includes such decisions as promoting a student-centered versus a teacher-centered learning environment and selecting appropriate teaching strategies, assessments, and classroom management styles.

Effective Educators

Historically, Dewey (1933) highlighted three characteristics of effective teaching: open-mindedness, wholeheartedness, and intellectual responsibility, which are still relevant today. An open-minded, wholehearted educator is free from prejudices, has an enthusiasm for teaching and students, and possesses the intellect to develop teaching strategies that are engaging for the learner. Furthermore, research by Grant and Gillette (2006) emphasized that the ability to develop a curriculum that is relevant to the student is essential. Meeting the student's educational and social needs regardless of "where, who, or what" the educator will teach is a quality of an effective educator.

In reflecting upon these statements, pedagogy is not only about the materials used in teaching but also about the relationship with the learner, the learning environment, and the process used to engage the learner. When planning instruction, one main function is to know your learner. Get to know your students' learning styles and specific learning needs, and align these concepts with the goals for your class. This will help in forming a respectful relationship between educator and learner and result in lessons that are engaging and relevant to the learner. Consequently, the skills of reflection, such as the assessment of student learning, identification of problems, and a reflection of how you perform as an educator, are helpful in teaching any grade level or content.

ACTIVITY 5.1: APPLICATION OF SEVEN PRINCIPLES OF GOOD PRACTICE IN TEACHING

Chickering and Gamson (1987) published a framework based on research for over 50 years on evaluating teaching in higher education entitled "Seven Principles of Good Practice in Undergraduate Education" (Graham et al., 2001). This framework is based on traditional face-to-face teaching. We feel it can easily be adapted by the FCS educator for use in the FCS classroom.

"Seven Principles for Good Practice in Undergraduate Education" (Graham et al., 2001):

1. Encourage contact between students and faculty.
2. Encourage cooperation among students.
3. Encourage active learning.
4. Give rich, rapid feedback.
5. Emphasize time on task.
6. Communicate high expectations.
7. Respect diverse talents and ways of learning.

After reading "Seven Principles for Good Practice in Undergraduate Education," discuss how you will apply each of these principles as an FCS educator.

National Board Certification

Teachers must possess the following qualities to receive national board certification. Educators must have a commitment to students and have an understanding of the learning process. Educators must know their specific content well and how to teach the concepts. It is important that educators manage the learning environment and reflect on their educational practice. And, finally, educators should work collaboratively with others in the learning community to advocate, evaluate, and develop a school community that meets student needs (National Board for Professional Teaching Standards, 2014). We feel these qualities should be embraced by all FCS educators.

ACTIVITY 5.2: REFLECTION ON KNOWLEDGE BASE OF TEACHING

Most teacher preparation programs include courses that will prepare one to be a quality educator. McGregor (2020) states that the knowledge base for teaching should be included in quality FCS teacher education programs. These bases are content, curricula, philosophical, general pedagogical, learners, educational context, and pedagogical content. How will you as a preservice FCS educator be prepared to obtain the aforementioned qualities? Table 5.1 summarizes the meaning of these concepts.

TABLE 5.1   Knowledge Base for Teaching

Content:	Foundation of the subject matter
Curricula:	Curriculum development theory, resources, materials
Philosophical:	Goal and purpose of education
General pedagogical:	Strategies and assessments
Learners:	Individual learning needs and learning styles
Educational context:	Financial support, laws, educational research
Pedagogical content:	Educator's expertise in human development, the learning environment and educational ethics

Curriculum

Curriculum is the planned experiences provided for students under the direction of an educator. "Curriculum provides structure for management of teaching and learning as well as staff development. Without a curriculum's structure, there is chaos" (Squires, 2005, p. 7). These planned experiences have input from professional organizations, the state department of education, the state school board, the county board of education, and the local community/school. "Curriculum development involves the selection of objectives, content, learning experiences as well as organizing and evaluating these experiences to determine the extent to which they are effective in achieving stated objectives" (Adirika, 2020, p. 324).

Two educational researchers in curriculum development are Ralph Tyler (Werhan et al., 2004) and Hilda Taba (Adirika, 2020). Tyler's framework for curriculum planning is considered a classic, as it is the inspiration for other models. He identified four essential concepts for curriculum development: what should be taught, what instructional strategies should be used, how learning experiences should be organized, and how learning should be evaluated (Grier, 2005). Tyler's model is a student-centered approach. A **student-centered approach** is defined as the use of strategies where students are actively engaged and interact with the content of the lesson. Furthermore, the lesson considers the unique needs, goals, and culture of the students (The Glossary of Education Reform, 2014). This is in contrast to a **teacher-centered approach** when the educator is the most active person in the room, with students learning in a passive manner. We will cover these concepts in more detail in Chapter 8.

Taba's curriculum model also has an interactive focus but considers environmental factors that may impact curriculum, such as school culture, school goals, and resources, as well as student needs (Adirika, 2020). Taba's model includes the following when planning the curriculum: determine needs, plan content to meet needs, plan objectives, determine instructional strategies to teach objectives, consider materials needed to fit instructional strategies, and evaluate student outcomes. The authors feel these two curriculum models represent FCS curriculum planning well.

McGregor (2019) urges urges that the FCS curriculum should provide contradictory notions of preconceived ideas of what "lay people" think about the purpose of the FCS profession. Furthermore, McGregor urges the profession to put forth a conceptual change to socialize preservice FCS educators and others to accept that the FCS curriculum and mission support family capacity building by teaching others to make wise decisions and use available resources (Swafford & Giordano, 2017). FCS university programs and professionals need to advocate for FCS professional identity whenever possible, beginning with FCS preservice educators (McGregor, 2019).

FCS Curriculum Development

National Standards

FCS curriculum is a standards-based curriculum. What are the standards? Standards are part of outcome-based education reforms beginning in the 1980s with A Nation at Risk and were still included in the No Child Left Behind reforms in the 2000s (Barton, 2010). Standards designate what students should know and be able to perform after instruction (Hamilton et al., 2008). In the 1990s, the reauthorization of the Perkins Act, known as Perkins II, required CTE courses to have standards as a measure of student performance.

In 1998, to ensure the broad range of content of FCS was addressed by educators, national standards for FCS education were developed (Heatherly, 1998) by the National Association of State Administrators of Family and Consumer Sciences (NASAFACS), currently known as LeadFCS Education (LeadFCS Education, n.d.). The National FCS standards are available in a comprehensive PDF document available on the NASAFACS website. The document includes the rationale for FCS education, including the vision and mission of the discipline, along with a historical perspective. These standards are broken down into 16 areas of study in FCS content. Nine of these content standards are focused on specific careers in housing, interiors, furnishings, textiles, and apparel. The other seven standards focus on comprehensive life-span development, parenting/child guidance, family studies/relations, nutrition/food preparation, wellness, and consumer economics (LeadFCS Education, n.d.). The national standards are outcome-based and grouped by areas of study, not courses. Each area of study was summarized through a comprehensive standard. The areas of study's comprehensive standard topics follow:

- Life roles and responsibility in family, community, and work
- Management practices related to human, economic, and environmental resources globally

- Knowledge, skills, and practices in early childhood, education, and services
- Knowledge, skills, and practices in facilities management and maintenance; family and its significance in the well-being of individuals and society
- Knowledge, skills, and practices in family and human services; knowledge, skills, and practices in food production and services
- Knowledge, skills, and practices in food science, food technology, dietetics, and nutrition; knowledge, skills, and practices in hospitality, tourism, and recreation
- Knowledge, skills, and practices for housing and interior design; human growth and development
- Relationships in family, workplace, and community; nutrition and wellness for individuals and family well-being; parenting roles and responsibilities on strengthening the well-being of the family, individuals, and society
- Knowledge, skills, and practices in careers in textiles and apparel (National Association of Teacher Educators for Family and Consumer Sciences, 2020)

All in all, the national standards are laid out in a systematic way, easy to understand, clearly written, and clearly labeled by area of study. Standards are included in an easily accessible document that justified the need for the areas of study to better the lives of individuals, families, and communities. The standards seem to advocate for themselves in the justification that content areas contribute to improving individuals, families, and society. Furthermore, these standards contribute to the notion that "FCS is anything more than technical skills for cooking and sewing" (McGregor, 2019, p. 28).

The national approach to standards differs from each state that has its own standards. Likewise, individual state departments of education have developed their own standards to cover the courses offered in their CTE programs of study. Because the field of FCS is a vast field, it is important to understand the differences and similarities in the national standards and state standards.

State Standards

State standards fall under the umbrella of CTE. In FCS education, as in other CTE courses, there are both state and national standards. Each set of standards is nestled under a career cluster, followed by a program of study. This approach ensures that states can keep a piece of the Perkins Act proverbial pie.

How do standards relate to the curriculum? According to Squires (2005), standards are not curriculum; however, curriculum is based on standards. Therefore, standards and curriculum should be linked. Standards are considered the learning goals of instruction. Each state collaborated with stakeholders to develop state standards that reflect the national standards. Examples of stakeholders usually include educators in higher education, state public educators in the field, the state board of education professionals, and industry leaders. FCS is embedded within several career clusters, and each state identifies them in various ways. By completing the following activities, the preservice FCS educator's understanding of the differences in FCS programs across the United States will be enhanced.

Career Clusters and Programs of Study

Career Clusters

Career clusters are careers that are categorized by common features. Currently, there are 16 national career clusters. See Table 5.2 for the categories of national career clusters. Of the 16 career clusters, six are embedded FCS content; however, FCS content does not represent the entire cluster, as there are other contents represented from outside of FCS content areas. These six career clusters are architecture and construction, agriculture, arts, audio/visual technology and communication, human services, education and training, and hospitality.

CTE National Career Clusters

In 2006, the Carl Perkins Vocational and Technical Education Act was reauthorized. It drastically changed how CTE was implemented. It required every program to have a focus on "career preparation" in order to receive funding from the Perkins Act (Education Commission of the States, n.d.). In other words, the CTE programs must teach not only academic skills but also transferable and adaptive skills for the workforce (Education Commission of the States, n.d.).

The U.S. Department of Education adopted 16 different career clusters, which take in both labor market needs and educational needs (Education Commission of the States, n.d.). The national career clusters include agriculture, food, and natural resources; architecture and construction; audio/visual technology; communication, business management, and administration; education and training; finance, government, and public administration; health science; hospitality and tourism; human services; information technology; law, public safety, corrections, and security; manufacturing and marketing; science; technology; engineering and mathematics; and transportation, distribution, and logistics

Programs of Study

CTE curriculum planning is a complex process that involves four connecting units of instruction: career cluster, course, learning segments, and lessons. Programs of study are a sequence of courses that align with a particular career path (Kamin, 2018). The authors of this text have experience in professional practice in Tennessee; therefore, the course standards and programs of study from

---

TABLE 5.2   National Career Clusters

Agriculture, Food, and Natural Resources	Government and Public Administration	Manufacturing
Architecture and Construction	Health Science	Marketing
Arts, Audio/Visual, Technology, and Communications	Hospitality and Tourism Human Services	Science, Technology, Engineering, and Mathematics
Education and Training	Information Technology	Transportation, Distribution, and Logistics
Finance	Law, Public Safety, Corrections, and Security	

Tennessee are used as examples in this text. However, activities are included that encourage learners to use their specific state to complete the activities (see Activity 5.1).

Current programs of study in Tennessee that contain FCS content include culinary arts, fashion design, interior design, teaching as a profession, human and social health, nutrition/dietetics, the middle school program of social health, and early childhood education and careers. These course sequences are developed within the department of CTE on the state level with input from industry stakeholders, FCS educators, and FCS content career professionals. The sequence of courses begins with a course that is broad in content, followed by subsequent courses that narrow in focus toward the specific career. Often, the final course is a work-based learning opportunity or practicum. Taking two courses in a program of study qualifies a student to become a CTE **concentrator** (Kamin, 2018). More than half the students taking CTE courses are concentrators (The National Center for Education Statistics, 2009). Students who take all courses in a program of study are called a **completer**.

SPOTLIGHT: HUMAN SERVICES CAREER CLUSTER

The career cluster of human services in the state of Tennessee (Tennessee Department of Education, 2018a) has a program of study called human and social sciences, which includes the following program of studies: (a) human and social sciences and (b) dietetics and nutrition. Like the other programs of study, there are four classes offered under each program of study, and the standards were written specifically for each course. The sequences of courses start with a broad overview and lead to more focused content needed for career readiness. In the state of Tennessee, these courses include Introduction to Human Studies, Life-Span Development, and Family Studies, with a final practicum course being a practicum in human services.

ACTIVITY 5.3: EXPLORE YOUR STATE WEBSITE

Explore your state education website and locate the CTE web page. Identify the FCS courses in the career clusters. Note: Some states will use the name family and consumer sciences, while other states have family and consumer sciences embedded within each cluster. How does your state identify FCS within the career clusters? Identify each program of study that falls under each career cluster within the FCS Ed content and the required courses in the plan of study. Create an infographic including career clusters and plans of study information for each of the areas above. Free infographic templates can be accessed through Canva, PicMonkey, Venngage, or Piktochart. You may use other templates as desired.

SPOTLIGHT: CURRICULUM DEVELOPMENT

To further explain FCS curriculum development, Werhan et al. (2004) revealed the importance of considering student wants/needs, current societal needs, and recommendations from experts in the field. These tasks can be accomplished through a student survey, gathering input from advisory council members, research, and national standards to gain recommendations from experts in the field.

An example of the connecting units in Tennessee includes the following: In Teaching as a Profession I (TAP 1) within the education and training career cluster, course Standard 13 requires students to identify technology applications that can be used in the classroom and explain how technology can enhance and inhibit learning (Tennessee Department of Education, 2018b). To meet the requirements of this standard while also being mindful of students' interests and wants and needs, the teacher could develop a lesson that allows students to determine which applications would be most meaningful in their own instruction, given the specific subject and grade level they want to teach. By requiring students to justify their selection of applications, the students must consider possible positive and negative outcomes of using each application. To further engage the students in the current topic of effectively integrating technology in the classroom, the teacher could also consider hosting a class debate that requires teams of students to find and present research that indicates the positive or negative impacts that technology has on students in the classroom. By using debate, the teacher is requiring students to take ownership of their research and learning rather than simply providing the information in a way that might be passively received by the students.

Another example of effective curriculum development in the TAP program could be found with Standard 8 of TAP 2. Standard 8 covers differentiating instruction to meet the diverse learning needs of students (Tennessee Department of Education, 2018c). With eight differences included in the standard (e.g., socioeconomic status, gender, religion, etc.), each student would differentiate their instruction differently depending on the subject and grade level they intend to teach. Therefore, the teacher should structure the lesson in a way that would allow students to develop their own plans to differentiate their instruction to meet the diverse needs of their classroom. For instance, a student teaching an elementary class that covers all subjects at a simplified learning level would differentiate their instruction quite differently than a social studies teacher at the secondary level. So while the common goal of the standard remains the same for all students within the TAP class, achieving the goal will look different for each student because they will be differentiating their instruction in ways that are most meaningful to their class. Each of these units will be explained in more detail in Chapter 6.

Educational Psychology and Educational Philosophy: Do We Need to Consider Both?

A common assignment in most teacher preparation programs is to write one's own philosophy of education. A *philosophy of education* is a set of personal beliefs regarding how an educator believes that students learn, as well as how students should be taught. The act of self-reflection and mindfulness may enhance the ability of a preservice educator to identify the values and traits of an effective teacher when composing a philosophy of education. Why is it important to have a philosophy of education? McGregor (2012) states educational philosophy provides the foundation of one's own teaching philosophy: "Philosophy plays a profound role in our practice as a mission-oriented profession focused on practical, perennial problems that span generations" (p. 1).

In Chapter 4, content on **educational psychology** was included with learning theories. Educational psychology is concerned with human development and behavior in an educational setting. It includes concepts of how individuals learn, problems associated with learning, teaching strategies, and evaluation and aptitude of learners on standardized assessments (Merriam-Webster, n.d.). Whereas educational philosophy is one's perspective of educational practices. What purpose do these concepts serve in preparing students to be educators of FCS? Why should these concepts be included in a textbook on FCS pedagogy?

Philosophy of Education

To teach, one must know the content; however, it is just as important to know how to teach the content using the profession's principles of ethical practice. "Without a professional philosophy, practitioners cannot really know what is motivating them to make such large decisions" (McGregor, 2012, p. 1). Couch and Alexander (2009) state that FCS professionals "must recognize the moral nature of our work and accept the responsibility to help individuals develop the capacity to address the moral issues they encounter in their own lives" (p. 70). Ultimately, ethical professional practice is about how we fulfill our responsibilities to those we serve, as we translate the content to improve our teaching practices.

Our philosophy as educators impacts our classroom management style and our interactions with students and peers. When considering the FCS body of knowledge, will your classroom promote capacity building of your students? Do you respect and embrace diversity and support an inclusive educational setting? Will you embrace the theories of life-span development and human ecosystems when planning? Will the content of your lessons bring awareness of the impact of global interdependence and the importance of resource sustainability and wellness?

When composing a personal **philosophy of education**, include thoughts on the purpose of education, the roles of the educator beliefs about how students learn, and thoughts on how to implement those beliefs into action in a classroom. Will you have a teacher-directed learning environment or a student-centered one and be a **facilitator of learning**? Will you include accommodations for diversity when you plan, teach, and engage students in the content? Our philosophy will dictate why we teach the content and why we promote the mission of the profession. Do we select a strategy to influence lifelong learning, or do we select a strategy to emphasize the real-world connection to the content?

ACTIVITY 5.4: PHILOSOPHY OF EDUCATION PERSPECTIVES

The following are brief summaries of a few general educational philosophy perspectives that educators may study as they prepare to write their own personal philosophy of education. Research each one for more details on how these perspectives may support your personal philosophy of education.

Progressivism

Educators who embrace progressivism believe that learning occurs through real-world experiences with others, and ideas are tested by active experimentation. The student-centered philosophy maintains a focus on the whole child. This philosophy values the scientific method of teaching, such as how one comes to know, and includes shared decision making in groups (Lynch, 2016a). This philosophy believes that schools should improve the way of life for citizens through experiencing freedom and democracy in schools. Curriculum is derived from student interests. Individuals who embrace this philosophy include John Dewey, Jean Piaget, and Jerome Bruner.

Perennialism

Educators who embrace perennialism believe that individuals should be engaged in learning that has stood the test of time. They view knowledge as enduring and view principles of existence as constant. Educators who embrace the principles of perennialism will avoid fads in education and focus on the basics. This teacher-centered philosophy is focused on teaching values associated with reason and critical thinking (Lynch, 2016a). Major followers of this philosophy were Robert Maynard-Hutchins and Mortimer Adler.

Essentialist

This philosophy puts emphasis on the intellectual and moral standards that schools should teach. Educators who embrace this philosophy believe that individuals should learn traditional basic academics of STEM. It is a teacher-centered philosophy where educators are the authority in the classroom, teaching content mastery progressively from less complex to more complex (Lynch, 2016b). Essentialists include William Badgley, Arthur Bestor, and E. D. Hirsch.

Postmodernism

Postmodernism challenges basic assumptions of modern education, and it is based on the foundation of Karl Marx. This philosophy strives for social justice in a society that is not dominated by others in power but encourages individual expression (Siegel, 2020). Those who embrace this philosophy do not believe in absolute truth but believe that truth changes with events (Lynch, 2016c). This philosophy uses a radical reappraisal of modern assumptions about culture, identity, history, or language (Lynch, 2016b). Postmodernists include Jacques Derrida and Michel Foucault.

Humanism

This student-centered philosophy believes in the idea of enhancing individual development. Educators emphasize a learning environment that supports emotional well-being and self-fulfillment. Students should be actively involved in all levels of their education and make decisions and input on what they will learn. Modern-day individuals who embrace this philosophy include Abraham Maslow, Carl Rogers, and Alfred Adler.

SUMMARY

In this chapter, several researchers in education have documented the qualities of effective educators. FCS educators should reflect on putting these suggestions into practice. Pedagogy (the art of teaching) and curriculum (the planned experiences that an educator provides for the learners) are both essential components of FCS education. Changes in Perkins legislation have resulted in CTE programs being divided into 16 career clusters. These clusters contain programs of study, which include course standards that prepare students for productive careers and lifelong well-being. The courses in the career clusters begin with a broad overview of the basic content, and each additional course focuses on more specific content and culminates with "hands-on"/practicum experience. Several philosophies of education were covered in this chapter. To enhance preservice FCS educators with the development of effective qualities, one should develop a personal philosophy of education.

KEY TERMS

Career clusters

Curriculum

Pedagogy

Facilitator of learning

Concentrator

Teacher-centered approach

Program of study

Student-centered approach

Educational psychology

Philosophy of education

Course standards

Completer

QUESTIONS AND ACTIVITIES

1. Define curriculum. What are the units of instruction used in curriculum planning?
2. Describe the components of pedagogy.
3. Discuss factors that contributed to the development of standards.
4. Explore the national FCS standards and compare them to your state FCS standards. You may find the national standards at LeadFCS (http://www.leadfcsed.org/national-standards.html). Write an essay describing the similarities and differences between your state's FCS standards and the national standards.
5. After reviewing the state and national standards, discuss how the standards are contributing to or refuting the "lay person's" perception of FCS mission and curriculum.
6. Conduct additional research on the educational psychological perspectives listed in the chapter. Identify techniques that support your values as an educator.
7. Compose your personal philosophy of education. When writing a philosophy of education, select one of the educational philosophies that best suits your style of teaching. Think about the following: why you want to teach, who you plan to teach, how you will teach, and what you will teach.

REFERENCES

Adirika, B. (2020). Examining models of curriculum development and processes: Implications for African educational heritage and review. *Social Sciences and Humanities Journal, 6,* 324–342.

Bales, B. L. (2007). Teacher education reform in the United States and the theoretical constructs of stakeholder mediation. *International Journal of Education Policy and Leadership, 3*(6), 1–13.

Barton, P. E. (2010). National education standards: To be or not to be? *Educational Leadership, 67*(7), 22–29.

Chickering, A., & Gamson, Z. (1987). Seven principles of good practice in undergraduate education. *AAHE Bulletin, 39,* 3–7.

Couch, S., & Alexander, K. L. (2009). Professionalism: Ethical professional practice for teachers of family and consumer sciences. *Journal of Family and Consumer Sciences Education, 27*(National Teacher Standards 4), 60–76. http://www.natefacs.org/JFCSE/v27Standards4/v27Standards4Couch.pdf

Dewey, J. (1933). *How we think: A restatement of the relation of reflective thinking to the educative process.* DC Heath and Company.

Education Commission of the States. (n.d.). *Individual state profile.* http://ecs.force.com/mbdata/mbprofall?Rep=CTA

Grant, C. A., & Gillette, M. (2006). A candid talk to teacher educators about effectively preparing teachers who can teach everyone's children. *Journal of Teacher Education, 57*(3), 292–300.

Grier, A. S. (2005). Integrating needs assessment into career and technical curriculum development. *Journal of Industrial Teacher Education, 42*(1). https://scholar.lib.vt.edu/ejournals/JITE/v47n1

Graham, C., Cagiltay, K., Lim, B., Craner, J., & Duffy, T. (2001). Seven principles of effective teaching: A practical lens for evaluating online courses. *The Technology Source.* April/May, 1–5.

Hamilton, L. S., Stecher, K. M., & Yuan, K. (2008). *Standards-based reform in the United States: History, research, and future directions.* RAND Corporation.

Heatherly, J. (1998). New standards, new era for FACS. *Techniques: Making Education & Career Connections, 73,* 46.

Kamin, S. J. (2018, May 29). *Career and technical education issue brief: Current trends and results.* UCONN. https://education.uconn.edu/2018/05/29/career-and-technical-education-issue-brief-current-trends-and-results/

LeadFCS Education. (n.d.). *FCS national standards.* www.leadfcsed.org/national-standards.html

Lynch, M. (2016a). *Philosophies of education: 2 types of teacher-centered philosophies.* The Advocate. https://www.theedadvocate.org/philosophies-education-2-types-teacher-centered-philosophies

Lynch, M. (2016b). *Philosophies of education: 3 types of student-centered philosophies.* The Advocate. https://www.theedadvocate.org/philosophies-education-3-types-student-centered-philosophies/

Lynch, M. (2016c). *Understanding the 4 main schools of philosophy: Principles of postmodernism.* The Advocate. https://www.theedadvocate.org/understanding-4-main-schools-philosophy-principle-postmodernism/

McGregor, S. (2012). The role of philosophy in home economics. *Kappa Omicron Nu FORUM, 19*(1). https://www.kon.org/archives/forum/19-1/mcgregor2.html

McGregor, S. L. T. (2019). Conceptual change during the professional socialization process, process. *Journal of Family and Consumer Sciences Education, 36*(1), 21–33.

McGregor, S. L. T. (2020). University-level methods courses for family and consumer sciences teacher education. *Journal of Family and Consumer Sciences Education, 37*(1), 27–41.

Merriam Webster. (n.d.). Pedagogy. In *Merriam-Webster.com dictionary*. Retrieved January 11, 2022, from https://www.merriam-webster.com/dictionary/pedagogy

Merriam-Webster. (n.d.). Educational psychology. In *Merriam-Webster.com dictionary*. Retrieved January 11, 2022, from https://www.merriam-webster.com/dictionary/educational%20psychology

National Association of Teacher Educators for Family and Consumer Sciences. (2020). *National standards.* Resources. Retrieved March 1, 2022 from https://www.natefacs.org/Docs/2020/FCS%20TeacherEducationStandards-Competencies%20NATEFACS-2020.pdf

National Board for Professional Teaching Standards. (2014). *Career technical education standards for teachers of students ages 11–18* (2nd ed.). http://www.boardcertifiedteachers.org/

National Center for Education Statistics. (2009). *Tables: Secondary/high school.* https://nces.ed.gov/surveys/ctes/tables/h123.asp

Siegel, H. (2020). Philosophy of education. In *Encyclopedia Britannica*. Retrieved February 27, 2021, from https://www.britannica.com/topic/philosophy-of-education.

Squires, D. (2005). *Aligning and balancing the standards-based curriculum.* Corwin Press.

Swafford, M., & Giordano, K. (2017). Universal design: Ensuring success for all FCS students. *Journal of Family and Consumer Sciences, 109*(4), 47–52.

Tennessee Department of Education. (2018a, January 26). *Human services.* https://www.tn.gov/education/career-and-technical-education/career-clusters/cte-cluster-human-services.html

Tennessee Department of Education. (2018b, January 26). *Teaching as a profession I (TAP I).* https://www.tn.gov/content/dam/tn/education/ccte/edu/cte_std_edu_tap_1.pdf

Tennessee Department of Education. (2018c, January 26). *Teaching as a profession II (TAP II).* https://www.tn.gov/content/dam/tn/education/ccte/edu/cte_std_edu_tap_2.pdf

The Glossary of Education Reform. (2014). *Student-centered learning.* https://www.edglossary.org/student-centered-learning/

Werhan, C. R., Buckland, S. S., & Vollmer, J. L. (2004). Finding a place for tradition in the curriculum: A case study for sewing the Ohio family and consumer sciences classroom. *Journal of Family and Consumer Sciences Education, 22*(1), 43–57.

Figure Credit

Fig. 5.1: Copyright © 2015 Depositphotos/dizanna.

Planning Lessons

Melinda Swafford, PhD; Elizabeth Ramsey, PhD; and Kayleigh Beasley, MS

FIGURE 6.1 "By Failing to Prepare, You Are Preparing to Fail." Benjamin Franklin (Michael, n.d.)

Chapter 6 Objectives

Upon completion of the chapter, the learner should be able to

- identify points to consider before actual planning;
- describe the importance of planning;
- identify the components of a well-written objective;
- evaluate a lesson plan for continuity in standards, objectives, academic language, and assessment;

- analyze objectives or learner outcomes for measurability, fluency, and practicality;
- describe the purpose of a set and compose an example; and
- describe the purpose of the closure and compose an example.

Introduction

During the program of study in family and consumer sciences (FCS) education, a preservice student will compose many lesson plans before becoming a licensed educator. Lesson planning is often viewed as time-consuming; however, planning becomes easier with practice. This practice will engrain the planning process so that as a seasoned teacher, you will be able to plan quickly, without the need of writing down each step. The purpose of this chapter is to provide a detailed focus on lesson planning. This includes points to consider prior to writing a lesson plan, components included in a lesson plan, detailed information on writing goals/central focus and measurable objectives, writing a set, and writing a closure. For the purpose of demonstrating writing a lesson plan, the authors have used a Tennessee state standard as an example through the text in each spotlight, as well as a Tennessee teacher education program template. This lesson plan template meets the requirements of edTPA, the national teacher evaluation program used by 41 states in our country in 2017 (edTPA, 2020). We recommend that you compare your state or teacher education program lesson plan template to the one in this chapter to make needed changes.

What Is the Purpose of Planning?

The purpose of a lesson plan is to help educators with organization skills so that the learning needs of the students are recognized and content is fully covered. For a preservice or new educator, the development of effective and engaging lessons takes time, effort, and commitment. Planning involves determining the intended learning outcomes, assessments, content, and instructional tasks required to effectively teach a lesson. It is often a task that new or preservice teachers do not enjoy. However, it is extremely important and central in educating learners (Montgomery, 2019). There are several benefits for preservice and new educators to use a written plan. Lesson planning includes not only what the learner will learn but also the process of how they will learn it. Lesson plans serve as a document of what has been taught, allow the instructor to remember what occurs next (when student questions interrupt the flow of the lesson), and allow one to remember adjustments and last-minute changes.

Writing lesson plans and learning segments is a tedious and time-consuming process. Usually, the final 2 years in an educational program of study will be devoted to the development and fine-tuning of lesson plans. The purpose of this strong focus on writing lesson plans is to enhance the ability of the preservice educator to immediately identify objectives, strategies, and assessments that will support course standards. During the teacher education program, practice will make perfect. Therefore, the focus of many upper division courses will require numerous lesson plans. With that said, on a weekly basis, writing such detailed lesson plans is unnecessary for the classroom teacher in many school systems. However, the types of lesson plans discussed in this chapter are typically reserved for preservice teachers for assessment purposes during student teaching/residency, as well as educators working in the field who are being assessed by the administration for state purposes.

Prior Knowledge

It is important to consider prior knowledge, experiences, interests, and learning styles of the learner. Students' prior knowledge and needs can be assessed by pretests, concept mapping activities, and surveys. Students also bring their own prior knowledge and experiences or lack of experience and knowledge to each stage. Therefore, for learning to occur, the student must find meaning in what is being taught, and the teacher must understand how best to motivate the student to learn. Learning problems can occur at any stage. Ultimately, the content must have relevance to the learner. This may require the FCS educator to "think outside the box" when planning relevant instructional strategies that recognize and respect the unique characteristics of learners.

The use of a **concept map**, a visual display of ideas, will link concepts of the lesson together. It is also a good way to assess students' prior knowledge. Concept maps can be in any form from a Venn diagram, other forms of graphic organizers, a table, or a T-chart. See Figure 6.2 for an example.

In Figure 6.2, the phrase "movement across the plasma membrane" is the main topic of the lesson. Words and short phrases that extend from the main topic may be generated in a variety of ways (educator posing questions to students, review of content after a video clip, or summarizing a piece of text) to pique the interest of the learner. Furthermore, concept mapping can serve as an interesting vehicle for introducing a lesson or a learning segment.

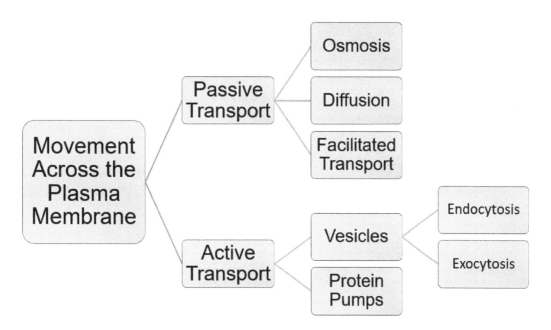

FIGURE 6.2 Concept Map an appropriate concepts map for a lesson on nutrient absorption

Learning Segments/Unit Plans

Determine the length of instructional time. "Learning segment" is a term used by edTPA for the unit plan. A learning segment is a set of lessons that include standards, objectives, and assessments that connect key concepts, goals, or central ideas from one lesson to the next. The set of lessons contains a consistent central concept taught over a period of time. The time frame can range from a few days to a week or more. It is simply a means of ensuring continuity and that each lesson is linked to the next by a central concept. When planning learning segments, standards do not have to be taught in the consecutive order that they are listed on the state website. In addition, a learning segment can contain one or more standards. Curricular mapping or pacing guides are vehicles to show the connection of key concepts when planning learning segments.

Components of the Lesson Plan

A well-written lesson plan should be so detailed that someone else could use it to teach the lesson. Components in a lesson plan vary across subject matter, and usually, each school system or district has a required format. Many preservice educators are taught to plan using a format that contains the following: an introduction to the lesson, a review of prior materials, presentation of new material, application of new material, assessment of learners on new materials, and closure of the lesson (Montgomery, 2019). Depending on your university, you will be provided with a recommended template to use for edTPA. See Figure 6.3 for the edTPA lesson plan format that was created by the Tennessee Technological University College of Education. This lesson plan format will be used for this text. It includes additional information required by Pearson edTPA, such as course standard(s), a central focus, goals or broadly stated learner outcomes, objectives/learner outcomes, and academic language. Also included in the lesson plan format is the instructional body/teaching activities, which include supervised and independent practice; evaluation/assessment, including both formative and summative; a list of materials/media included in the lesson; modifications for the learners; safety and management; and closure. More detailed information on the components of strategies, assessments, and use of technology included in lesson plans is presented in Chapters 8–11.

The completed lesson plan is available in Appendix C.

Backward Design

When planning, educators should begin with the end in mind. This is often referred to as a backward design (Wiggins & McTighe, 2005). To begin the planning process using the backward design, think of this question: "What do I want my learners to know?" See Table 6.1.

Backward design in planning includes three stages.

TABLE 6.1   Stages in Backward Design (Wiggins & McTighe, 2005)

Stage 1	Identify desired results	Review state and national standards
Stage 2	Determine acceptable evidence	Develop assessments and rubrics
Stage 3	Plan learning experience and instruction	Determine resources and experiences

Lesson Title:	Grade/Level:

Curriculum Standards	**Central Focus Question/Big Idea/Goal**
State Curriculum Standards (Include the number and text of the standard. If only a portion is being addressed, then only list the relevant parts.)	*What question(s), big idea(s), and/or goals drive your instruction?*

Lesson Objective(s)

Objectives are measurable.

Vocabulary/ Academic Language (Language Function)

What opportunities will you provide for students to practice content language/vocabulary and develop fluency?

Assessment/Evaluation

Formative (Informal): *How will students demonstrate understanding of lesson objective(s)? How will you monitor and/or give feedback?*

Summative (Formal): *What evidence will you collect and how will it document student learning/mastery of lesson objective(s)?*

Set/Motivator: *How to engage student interest in the content of the lesson? Use knowledge of students' academic, social, and cultural characteristics.*

Instructional Procedures/Learning Tasks: *Provide specific details of lesson content and delivery.*

Questions and/or activities for higher order thinking: *These cannot be answered by yes or no.*

Closure: *Verbalize or demonstrate learning or skill one more time. May state future learning.*

Material/Resources: *What do you need for this lesson?*
Adaptations to Meet Individual Needs: *How will you adapt the instruction to meet the needs of individual students?*

Management/Safety Issues: *Are there any management and/or safety issues that need to be considered when teaching this lesson?*

FIGURE 6.3 edTPA Lesson Plan Template
Created by Tennessee Technological University (2021)

Central Focus/Goal

The next step is to support the course standard by developing a central focus/goal. This is followed by educators writing measurable objectives that support the course standards and central focus. Instruction is determined by the central focus/goal and objectives, which are determined by the course standard. All three concepts should be in alignment with each other.

SPOTLIGHT: GOAL/CENTRAL FOCUS FOR STANDARD 12 OF TEACHING AS A PROFESSION (TAP) I

TAP I Standard 12:

Create an annotated visual representation of the key indicators, diagnostic tests, and most important features of effective instruction for students diagnosed with:

a. Intellectual disabilities

b. Developmental disabilities

c. Learning disabilities

d. Emotional/behavioral disorders

e. Autism spectrum disorders

f. Communication disorders

g. Hearing loss or deafness

h. Low vision or blindness

i. Attention Deficit Hyperactivity Disorder (ADHD) (TDOE, 2018)

When reviewing a standard, first determine the content and skills that are expected to be learned and determine how (if specified) mastery of the standard should be demonstrated. With the example of the standard given, "key indicators, diagnostic tests, and ... effective instruction" are listed as content that is to be learned in connection with each diagnosis listed. It is also inferred that a basic understanding of each diagnosis listed is needed as well. Demonstration of mastery for this standard is specified as it asks students to "create an annotated visual representation" (TDOE, 2018). With this information, a goal/central focus for this lesson could be: "After the lesson, the learner will (TLW) present an annotated graphic detailing the key indicators, diagnostics tests, and appropriate instruction for each of the given diagnoses, meeting 85% of the requirements included in the grading rubric."

Writing Objectives

The learner outcome is an objective that supports a course standard. The objective drive instruction, as it serves as the basis for all instructional decisions. In addition to determining what content or skills should be taught, objectives also include at what level and what types of learning experiences will be used (see Table 6.1).

There are three parts to an objective. A is the audience, who can be defined as the learner; B is the behavior that the learner will do as a result of the instruction; C is the condition or criteria that impact how the behavior will occur. Using the format of ABC when writing objectives ensures that the objective will be clearly written as to what will occur during the lesson (Youatt & Hitch, 2001). This will be helpful when completing edTPA during residency/student teaching or during your evaluations by a clinical supervisor or principal.

Bloom's Taxonomy

Bloom's Taxonomy was developed in the 1950s by Benjamin Bloom and collaborators to illustrate a continuum of six types of cognitive thinking. Bloom's hierarchical framework has been used for almost 50 years by educators to develop cognitive objectives (Armstrong, 2010). Since it is hierarchical, each level should be addressed and met before moving to the next level. The original levels included knowledge, comprehension, application, analysis, synthesis, and evaluation.

Bloom's Taxonomy was revised in 2001 to change the names of the categories from nouns to verbs (Armstrong, 2010; see Figure 6.4). Educators use this version of Bloom's Taxonomy to write measurable objectives and assess learning as an ongoing process (formative assessments). Furthermore, this version of Bloom's Taxonomy can be used by educators to plan activities that allow students to progress up the hierarchy (Persuad, 2021).

Objectives can be classified into three categories: **Cognitive** objectives emphasize comprehension, synthesis, defining, analysis, and evaluation; **affective** objectives emphasize feeling and/or the degree of acceptance or rejection of a concept; **psychomotor** objectives emphasize action, skill development, and movement of the learner (Youatt & Hitch, 2001). It is common for FCS educators to use all three types of objectives when planning instruction.

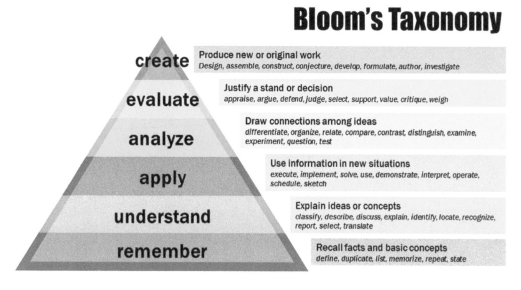

FIGURE 6.4 Revised Bloom's Taxonomy

TABLE 6.2   **Examples of Objectives**

Type of Objective	Example
Cognitive:	After completing the WebQuest on MyPlate, TLW categorize various food items into the correct food groups.
Psychomotor:	Given a set of blocks in various shapes, TLW (children aged 2) build a tower of six blocks.
Affective:	After hearing the panel speak on child guidance strategies, TLW list the benefits of not using corporal punishment on children.

ACTIVITY 6.1: IDENTIFY COMPONENTS IN OBJECTIVES

Identify the ABC components of the objectives written in Table 6.1.
    A = Audience B = Behavior C = Condition

Well-written objectives must be measurable, be written with fluent wording, and be realistically achieved through instruction. Measurable objectives contain action verbs (see Table 6.2). When in doubt if a verb is appropriate, ask yourself, "How will this be measured?"

TABLE 6.3   **Words to Avoid in Writing Objectives**

Know	Replace with define or identify
Understand	Replace with discuss or analyze
Learn	Replace with demonstrate or apply

SPOTLIGHT: WRITING OBJECTIVES FOR STANDARD 12 IN TAP 1

TAP I Standard 12:
    Create an annotated visual representation of the key indicators, diagnostic tests, and most important features of effective instruction for students diagnosed with:

    a.   Intellectual disabilities

    b.   Developmental disabilities

    c.   Learning disabilities

    d.   Emotional/behavioral disorders

    e.   Autism spectrum disorders

    f.   Communication disorders

    g.   Hearing loss or deafness

    h.   Low vision or blindness

    i.   Attention Deficit Hyperactivity Disorder (ADHD) (TDOE, 2018)

Reflecting on the information used to build the goal for standard 12 in TAP 1, sequential learning objectives can also be developed. Working in reverse order, creating the visual representation will be included in the final objective, as it requires the highest level of thinking. Prior to that, it is evident that the key indicators, diagnostic tests, and effective instruction would have to be analyzed before they could be illustrated. However, before then, students must first be familiar with each of the diagnoses listed. Therefore, appropriate objectives that correlate with standard 12 include:

Objective 1:

To begin the lesson, TLW define each of the listed diagnoses found in the course standard.

Objective 2:

After reviewing the characteristics of the listed diagnoses, TLW correlate key indicators, diagnostic tests, and effective instruction for each of the given diagnoses.

Objective 3:

After researching the key indicators, diagnostic tests, and effective instruction for the listed diagnoses, TLW create a visual representation of the information for each of the given diagnoses.

Academic Language

Academic language is the language of the discipline that educators and learners use orally and by writing when participating in activities that show understanding of content (Leland Stanford Junior College, 2019). Academic language is composed of four language demands: vocabulary, discourse, syntax, and functions. **Language vocabulary** includes terms needed to fully understand the content and terms with specific meaning in the content. An example of vocabulary in FCS content is the term *grading*. In clothing, construction grading means trimming the seam allowance down to get rid of bulk in the seam. In education, grading means the act of assigning a grade to completed work.

    Language **discourse** is how the learner and educator will use the language of the discipline during the lesson to illustrate concepts (Pearson, 2017). Will the learner be required to discuss, respond to questions, write a paragraph, and so on? **Language syntax** is word order. In academic language, this includes the way the words and phrases are organized. Are the words in a table, a food label, or in a graphic organizer? **Language function** includes the active verbs in the learning outcomes/ objectives. For example, will the learner summarize, write, organize, or evaluate?

During residency, candidates will be required to complete and submit an edTPA portfolio with three to five lesson plans in a learning segment (Pearson, 2017). A trained evaluator from Pearson will evaluate the submitted lesson plans. See the Spotlight on language demand for examples of how language demands are incorporated into the lesson for Standard 12 in TAP 1.

SPOTLIGHT: EXAMPLES OF LANGUAGE DEMAND FOR STANDARD 12 IN TAP 1

TAP I Standard 12:

Create an annotated visual representation of the key indicators, diagnostic tests, and most important features of effective instruction for students diagnosed with:

a.   Intellectual disabilities

b.   Developmental disabilities

c.   Learning disabilities

d.   Emotional/behavioral disorders

e.   Autism spectrum disorders

f.   Communication disorders

g.   Hearing loss or deafness

h.   Low vision or blindness

i.   Attention Deficit Hyperactivity Disorder (ADHD) (TDOE, 2018)

When considering Standard 12 in TAP 1 (see Spotlight for the language demand of vocabulary), it is somewhat apparent that each of the diagnoses would need to be defined in order to grasp the lesson. However, if students do not know the word "annotated," then they cannot accurately interpret what the standard is asking them to do. In this case, the word "annotated" should be defined and considered part of the academic vocabulary for the lesson. Furthermore, "key indicators" might seem like relatively simple terminology, but if the students do not grasp what might qualify as a "key indicator," then they will struggle in completing the requirements of the standard. To determine the student's familiarity with this wording, the teacher could ask students to provide examples of words or phrases that have synonymous meanings with "key indicators," and based on the students' responses, the teacher could determine if further explanation is needed before proceeding with the lesson.

Example of Language Discourse. Throughout this lesson, the educator will engage the learner to orally use academic language discourse when posing questions during formative assessments, while monitoring learners in independent work, and when providing feedback on learner responses. Learners will use discourse when composing the visual representation and during the presentation of the content to the class members.

Example of Language Function. The language function for this lesson requires learners to define, research, analyze, and synthesize information. For instance, at the beginning of the lesson, the students have to define the various types of disabilities to distinguish one from the other. By conducting research, students are analyzing the content in order to learn more about each of the diagnoses. And finally, students synthesize the content as they bring everything together in their annotated visuals.

Example of Language Syntax. After conducting research and during synthesis of the content for presentation, the learners will use syntax as they complete annotated infographic, which requires them to identify key factors of the diagnoses in a presentation with content and visuals. Infographics have a header, a body, and a footer; many include statistics and a visual theme for clarification and interest.

Assessment

Assessment is an information-gathering process that is used to provide accountability for instruction. The purpose of assessment is to monitor student progress, evaluate student achievement, make instructional decisions about learner outcomes, and evaluate programs. Educators who pay attention to the data collected will be able to provide effective learning experiences for learners.

Assessments can be categorized into two types: formative and summative. **Formative assessments** are used to find out how instruction is progressing so that the educator can decide how to proceed. This type of assessment allows one to monitor the progress of the students and adjust instruction accordingly (reteach or move forward). Examples often used are questions, think-pair-share activities, observation, closure activities, paper-and-pencil activities, checklists, and other exercises that are ungraded. See Spotlight for formative assessment in the example lesson plan.

SPOTLIGHT: FORMATIVE ASSESSMENT FOR STANDARD 12 TAP 1

TAP I Standard 12:

Create an annotated visual representation of the key indicators, diagnostic tests, and most important features of effective instruction for students diagnosed with:

a. Intellectual disabilities

b. Developmental disabilities

c. Learning disabilities

d. Emotional/behavioral disorders

e. Autism spectrum disorders

f. Communication disorders

(Continued)

g. Hearing loss or deafness

h. Low vision or blindness

i. Attention Deficit Hyperactivity Disorder (ADHD) (TDOE, 2018)

For the TAP 1 lesson on special populations, the following formative assessments are used. By prompting a think-pair-share activity at the beginning of the lesson, students share existing knowledge about each of the diagnoses, which allows the teacher to gauge the students' prior knowledge and therefore know how to proceed. Asking questions of higher order thinking throughout the lesson also ensures that students are finding and comprehending the information needed for the content of their graphics. And finally, basic observation of the sources students are reviewing, notes being taken, and small-group discussions taking place guides the teacher in providing any additional assistance that the students might need.

Summative Assessment

Summative assessments are evaluations that are intended for the purpose of assigning a grade. There is no plan to reteach the topic based on the assessment results, but instead, the teacher considers the instruction for the particular topic to be complete. Students will be assessed and evaluated for their mastery of the material, and then the class will move on to the next topic. Types of summative assessments include project rubrics, true/false, matching, multiple-choice, discussion questions, and essays.

Plan appropriate assessments to evaluate student learning. There needs to be a direct relationship between the objective and assessment as to what will be measured and how (see Table 6.4). In other words, the assessment needs to reflect the objectives. If the objective is to discuss, then the assessment would not be a true/false or a multiple-choice question. A written response would be appropriate for an objective that uses the verb "discuss." See the Spotlight on lesson plan summative assessments.

TABLE 6.4 **Appropriate Assessments for objectives**

Objective	Assessment
TLW demonstrate	The appropriate assessment would require a psychomotor or an application activity to assess this objective.
TLW analyze	An appropriate assessment would require an activity that requires evaluation.
TLW identify	An appropriate assessment would require an activity that requires the learner to recall concepts.

SPOTLIGHT: SUMMATIVE ASSESSMENT FOR STANDARD 12 TAP 1

TAP I Standard 12:

Create an annotated visual representation of the key indicators, diagnostic tests, and most important features of effective instruction for students diagnosed with:

a. Intellectual disabilities

b. Developmental disabilities

c. Learning disabilities

d. Emotional/behavioral disorders

e. Autism spectrum disorders

f. Communication disorders

g. Hearing loss or deafness

h. Low vision or blindness

i. Attention Deficit Hyperactivity Disorder (ADHD) (TDOE, 2018)

Standard 12 in TAP 1 specifies that students are to create an annotated visual that illustrates what they have learned in regard to the listed diagnoses. However, for students to successfully complete this summative assessment, a detailed scoring rubric would have to be provided by the teacher. The scoring criteria in the rubric need to reflect the learning outcomes mentioned in the learning objectives. So within the rubric, there should be grading criteria related to the students' definitions or descriptions of each diagnosis and criteria for the organized breakdown and synthesis of information on the key indicators, diagnostic testing, and effective instructional methods for each diagnosis. The teacher could also consider incorporating scoring criteria on things such as the quality of research, interpretation of information, and the appeal of the visual, which could clarify the level of expectation for the student's work while still relating to the desired student outcomes. See Table 6.3 for more examples that illustrate appropriate assessments for the objectives.

Instructional Strategies

Instructional strategies include all materials and activities used by educators to engage learners in standards, objectives, and content. Strategies often vary according to the needs of the learner, grade level, class size, available resources, and the subject matter being taught. It is important that instructional strategies motivate the learner and provide opportunities for supervised and independent practice with the content.

Well-developed instructional strategies include a **set**, which is defined as an introduction or an overview of the lesson. A set includes three components: a motivator, an overview of the objectives and topic to be covered, and a link to previous lessons. The purpose of a motivator is to capture the interest of the entire group of learners. This can be done by posing a question, a simple survey, or a short audio or video clip. Next, the educator will simply state the standards and objectives of the lesson, as well as provide a quick reference to past learning. During the residency observation of many preservice teachers, calling on students in the class to read the standard and objectives as well as pose a question on how this current lesson ties into the previous lesson will keep learners engaged. See the Spotlight for instructional strategies for the example lesson plan.

SPOTLIGHT: SET FOR STANDARD 12 TAP 1

TAP I Standard 12:

Create an annotated visual representation of the key indicators, diagnostic tests, and most important features of effective instruction for students diagnosed with:

a.   Intellectual disabilities

b.   Developmental disabilities

c.   Learning disabilities

d.   Emotional/behavioral disorders

e.   Autism spectrum disorders

f.   Communication disorders

g.   Hearing loss or deafness

h.   Low vision or blindness

i.   Attention Deficit Hyperactivity Disorder (ADHD) (TDOE, 2018)

Motivator. The teacher will (TTW) provide a sample piece of text that represents the difficulty of reading for students with dyslexia (various samples can be found online). TTW call on students to take turns reading the text. After reading the passage, TTW ask the class to explain how they felt attempting to read the jumbled text aloud. TTW ask how this impacted their ability to comprehend what they were reading. After discussion, TTW explain that knowing how to identify and then obtain the appropriate diagnosis for various disabilities is key to planning appropriate instruction for students with specific learning needs.

Overview. TTW call on students to read Standard 12 and the learning objectives for the lesson. TTW provide a basic preview of what will be done to meet the objectives and the anticipated time line for completing each part of the lesson.

Review. TTW ask students to recall the steps of the admission, review, and dismissal process; the purpose of individualized education programs (IEPs); and basic aspects of a least restrictive environment (LRE), all studied in Standard 11. TTW ask students how this prior knowledge might be used as they learn more about meeting the needs of various special populations listed in Standard 12.

Supervised and Independent Practice

The next part of the lesson includes supervised and independent practice. This has been referred to as "I do, we do, and you do." The "I do" is the part where the educator presents content. This is a great time for educators to pose various types of questions that can either be posed to the entire class or the educator may call on individual learners. The "we do" provides opportunities for learners to practice with the content. Both "I do" and "we do" are part of formative assessments, as well as instructional strategies. This is usually followed by "you do," which provides the learner with opportunities to engage in the content independently. This is also referred to as independent practice and can be a part of closure and summative assessment. See the Spotlight below for examples of practice in the lesson plan. More details on various types of instructional strategies will be included in Chapter 8 of this text.

SPOTLIGHT: SUPERVISED PRACTICE FOR STANDARD 12 IN TAP I

TAP I Standard 12:

Create an annotated visual representation of the key indicators, diagnostic tests, and most important features of effective instruction for students diagnosed with:

a. Intellectual disabilities

b. Developmental disabilities

c. Learning disabilities

d. Emotional/behavioral disorders

e. Autism spectrum disorders

f. Communication disorders

g. Hearing loss or deafness

h. Low vision or blindness

i. Attention Deficit Hyperactivity Disorder (ADHD) (TDOE, 2018)

To transition to the **supervised practice** portion of the lesson over Standard 12 in TAP 1, the teacher would prompt students to engage in the think-pair-share activity previously mentioned with formative assessment. From there, the teacher would use the smartboard to demonstrate how to find more information on each diagnosis by researching credible resources online; this could be considered the "I do" portion of the lesson. After that, students would be divided into groups to conduct their own research on their assigned diagnoses. Following the research, each group would be expected to share their findings and sources with the class. The group work would count as the "we do" portion of the lesson. And finally, following all group presentations, the **independent practice** portion of the lesson would consist of students working individually as they complete their annotated visuals mentioned for the summative assessment; this would be the "you do" portion of the lesson.

Closure

The purpose of **closure** is to pull together the major concepts of the lesson. Since it occurs at the end of the lesson, it provides the educator an additional opportunity to recap the lesson and provide an additional opportunity for assessment. Closure can be accomplished in several ways: by completing a written activity, learners responding orally to a series of questions posed by the educator, observing learners completing a performance activity (such as in a lab), or learners reflecting or drawing conclusions. See the Spotlight below for examples of closure in the lesson plan. Closure also provides an opportunity to set the stage for future learning. For example, "Tomorrow we will begin presentations of visuals on various disabilities."

SPOTLIGHT: CLOSURE FOR STANDARD 12 IN TAP 1.

TAP I Standard 12:

Create an annotated visual representation of the key indicators, diagnostic tests, and most important features of effective instruction for students diagnosed with:

a.   Intellectual disabilities

b.   Developmental disabilities

c.   Learning disabilities

d.   Emotional/behavioral disorders

e.   Autism spectrum disorders

f.   Communication disorders

g.   Hearing loss or deafness

h.   Low vision or blindness

i.   Attention Deficit Hyperactivity Disorder (ADHD) (TDOE, 2018)

To wrap up the lesson on Standard 12 in TAP 1, the teacher would likely want to follow up with students after they complete their annotated visuals. Since they have already demonstrated their level of mastery through their work, this does not have to be overly elaborate. The teacher could ask the class basic questions such as, "What was the most challenging part of this assignment?" or "How will you use what you learned throughout this lesson in your lesson planning moving forward?" or "Why is it critical for teachers to recognize the key indicators of these disabilities at a young age?" Posing such questions would help reinforce the purpose of the lesson, making it relevant to the students as they recognize the significance of learning this content as future teachers. For instance, the teacher should explain that in TAP 2, the students will be in alternate placements in other classrooms where there will likely be varying student needs. By using the content learned in this lesson, the TAP students should have better insight into the types of instruction and adaptations that could be used to meet these needs in their alternate placements.

Materials and Media

Materials and media are resources used to teach a lesson. These resources vary and are dependent on the topic of the lesson and how the lesson is assessed. This section of the lesson plan is mostly for the benefit of the educator as they identify the materials, media, and resources used to teach the lesson. Listing the materials, media, and other resources may help ensure that the educator does not forget the materials or equipment needed to ensure the successful presentation of the lesson.

SPOTLIGHT: MATERIALS AND MEDIA FOR STANDARD 12 TAP 1

TAP I Standard 12:

Create an annotated visual representation of the key indicators, diagnostic tests, and most important features of effective instruction for students diagnosed with:

a.   Intellectual disabilities

b.   Developmental disabilities

c.   Learning disabilities

d.   Emotional/behavioral disorders

e.   Autism spectrum disorders

f.   Communication disorders

g.   Hearing loss or deafness

h.   Low vision or blindness

i.   Attention Deficit Hyperactivity Disorder (ADHD) (TDOE, 2018)

For instance, based on the examples provided for the lesson over Standard 12 in TAP 1, the technology equipment needed would include a teacher station and smartboard, as well as student devices such as laptops or Chromebooks for their research. Having a printer would also be convenient if students want to print things for the annotated visuals or perhaps create and print the entire visual using computer software. Other materials needed might include poster boards or trifold displays, markers, scissors, glue, and any other craft supply that students might want to use for the visuals. Resources for the lesson would definitely include the reading sample to represent dyslexia for the motivator of the lesson as well as the instructions and rubric for the annotated visuals. Other teacher-made resources that could be used for the lesson might include a slide deck presentation with general information and/or a preview of the lesson, including the standard and objectives, or the teacher might choose to provide samples of previous students' work or handouts with information over the different diagnoses. Lastly, the teacher might choose to provide suggested online resources for the students to use during their research. Ultimately, it is the teacher's responsibility to provide all materials and resources necessary for the students to successfully complete the tasks of the lesson, but the teacher could also provide additional resources as they see fit.

Modifications for Learners

Legislation such as the Individuals with Disabilities Education Act, Section 504 of Vocational Rehabilitation Act of 1973, and the American with Disability Act was implemented to ensure that all learners receive an appropriate education in the LRE, which means that students should be educated with their peers to the maximum extent possible (Swafford & Giordano, 2017).

Additionally, inclusion, a term that describes LRE, is not included in legislation documents, nor is universal design, which means creating an environment for all individuals. Yet awareness and the ability to ensure that you are meeting the needs of your learners are essential to making educational opportunities accessible for all learners (Lewis et al., 2006). This includes learners who are academically gifted, as well as students with disabilities and those from diverse and ethnic groups with limited proficiency in English (Swafford & Dainty, 2009). A student with a disability may have an IEP, which may require accommodations and/or modifications, such as extra time, peer tutoring, one-on-one instruction, and reteaching. See Chapter 2 for more information on students with diverse needs such as English language learners, 504, and the IEP process. See Chapter 8 for more details on differentiated instruction and response to intervention.

Differentiated instruction uses the same curriculum for all learners but modifies the learning task and outcome while providing accommodations. Accommodations or modifications can occur in planning, during instruction, and during assessment (Broemmel et al., 2016, pp. 66–81; Watts-Taffe et al., 2012). However, the most effective instruction is one that meets the needs of the learner (Fisher et al., 2013).

Management and Safety

The final section of the edTPA lesson plan involves the educator addressing classroom management and safety issues to consider while teaching this lesson. An important part of classroom management is to make sure to have enough equipment and limit wait time for students. Since many FCS classroom topics are of a personal nature and considering the diversity of the class composition, the educator needs to ensure that no student feels ostracized, bullied, or singled out due to the topic of the lesson. It is essential that all learners feel safe, comfortable, and welcomed in the class. Creating a trauma-informed classroom can help all students feel safe and accepted, as well as prevent behavior issues (see Chapter 3 for information on how to implement a trauma-informed classroom approach). This can easily be included as a strategy to manage behaviors and ensure all students' safety.

SPOTLIGHT: LESSON PLANNING TIPS

- Always have a backup plan, especially if technology is involved.
- Lesson plans must be tied to course standards and support central focus.
- Objectives must be measurable, achievable, and tied to the course standard.
- Plan questions that can be asked throughout the lesson rather than saving all questions and feedback for the end.
- Planning gets easier the more you do it.
- For preservice teachers, make sure plans are approved by the mentoring teacher (practicum and student teacher/resident).

SUMMARY

Lesson plans are detailed outlines of the sequence of events from the beginning of the lesson to the end of the lesson. Lesson planning is essential to good teaching and learning. Although lesson planning is time-consuming, teacher preparedness increases student learning and minimizes classroom disruptions, making the time spent well worth it. The type of formal lesson plan laid out in this chapter is required for teacher education programs, edTPA, and teacher evaluations. Although the lesson plan template will differ slightly from various universities and school systems across the nation, the major components will remain consistent. Lesson preparation is key to successful teaching.

KEY TERMS

Formative assessment

Academic language

Assessment

Language function

Language demands

Supervised practice

Summative assessment

Discourse

Independent practice

Closure

Language Vocabulary

Language Syntax

Instructional strategies

Set

Concept map

Cognitive objectives

Affective objectives

Psychomotor objectives

QUESTIONS AND ACTIVITIES

1. After reading the three stages of learning in Table 6.1, provide another example to your classmates and instructor to show your comprehension of the content.
2. Choose one FCS course of interest to you. Read the course standards for your state and select one standard for focus. Practice writing three objectives using Bloom verbs.
3. Using the standard you chose in Activity 6.1, design an activity for your students that includes one of the following: language discourse, syntax, or function.
4. Using the standard you chose in Activity 6.1, design a formative assessment to assess each objective.
5. Correct the following objectives:

   a. TLW will know the best option for purchase when comparing cost/serving.
   b. Using a website, TLW analyze it.
   c. After researching mortgage interest rates, calculate the best loan.
   d. TLW know the digestive process.
   e. TLW be able to understand formal balance.
   f. TLW demonstrate knowledge of child development.

REFERENCES

Armstrong, P. (2010). *Bloom's taxonomy.* Vanderbilt University Center for Teaching. https://cft.vanderbilt. edu/guides-sub-pages/blooms-taxonomy

Broemmel, A. D., Jordan, J., & Whitsett, B. M. (2016). *Learning to be teacher leader: A framework for assessment, planning and instruction.* Routledge.

edTPA. (2020). *State participation map.* http://www.edpa.aacte.org/state/policy

Fisher, D., Fre, N., & Kroener, J. (2013). High quality support for students with disabilities. *Principal Leadership, 14*(3), 56–59.

Leland Stanford Junior College. (2019). *edTPA family and consumer scineces assessment handbook.* https:// edtpa.org/resource

Lewis, R. B., & Doorlag, D. H. (2006). *Teaching students with special needs in general education classroom* (7th ed.) Pearson Publishing.

Michael, J. (n.d.). *8 quotes to motivate you to make a plan and stick to it.* Bplans. https://articles.bplans. com/8-quotes-to-motivate-you-to-make-a-plan-and-stick-to-it/

Montgomery, B. (2019). Teaching lesson planning in family and consumer sciences. *Journal of Family and Consumer Sciences Education, 36*(1), 34–42.

Persuad, C. (2021). *Bloom's taxonomy: The ultimate guide.* Top Hat. https://tophat.com/blog/ blooms-taxonomy/

Swafford, M. D., & Dainty, H. T. (2009). Learning environments: Respecting diversity and exceptionality. *Journal of Family and Consumer Sciences Education, 27*(4), 45–59.

Swafford, M., & Giordano, K. (2017). Universal design: Ensuring success for all FCS students. *Journal of Family and Consumer Sciences, 109*(4), 47–52.

Tennessee Department of Education. (2018, January 26). *Teaching as a profession I (TAP I).* https://www. tn.gov/content/dam/tn/education/ccte/edu/cte_std_edu_tap_1.pdf

Tennessee Technological University. (2021). *edTPA lesson plan template. TK20 by Watermark. TK20– edTPA guide.* https://www.tntech.edu/education/tk20/student.php

Watts-Taffe, S., Laster, B. P., Broach, L., Marinak, B., Connor, C. M., & Walker-Dalhouse, D. (2012). Differentiated instruction: Making informed teacher decisions. *The Reading Teacher, 66*(4), 303–314. https://doi.org/10.1002/TRTR.01126.

Wiggins, G., & McTighe, J. (2005). *Understanding by design* (2nd ed.). Association for Supervision and Curriculum Development.

Youatt, J., & Hitch, J. (2001). Setting the stage. In J. Youatt & J. Hitch (Eds.), *Communicating family and consumer sciences: A guidebook for professionals* (pp. 103–113). Goodheart Willcox Publishing Co.

Figure Credits

Principles in FCS Education

Overview of Chapters 7–12

Part II provides an overview of principles used by educators in family and consumer sciences (FCS) education. The principles that are key to effective FCS education include the learning environment, instructional strategies, labs/active learning, assessments, and advocacy. Throughout the text, the authors have attempted to demonstrate the necessity of a strong link between planning instruction, delivering instruction, and assessment. Furthermore, the authors have stressed the importance of FCS being inclusive so that all individuals may gain knowledge and skills from the content that improves quality of life. It is recommended that if this text is used for both an introduction to teaching FCS and the methodology of teaching FCS in separate courses, a strong emphasis should be placed on reviewing. This will enhance the learner's ability to connect concepts of Part II with lesson planning.

Readers will note that in Chapter 7, "The Learning Environment and Classroom Management: The Impact on Learners," emphasis will be placed on how to develop a learning environment that will enhance student engagement and achievement. Emphasis will be placed on developmentally appropriate practice, theoretical approaches to classroom guidance, and a summary of Youatt and Hitch's (2002) components that support a functioning FCS classroom. Readers will be introduced to positive behavior interventions and support, as well as using a functional behavior assessment to address challenging behavior.

Chapter 8, "Instructional Strategies," provides content so the reader may distinguish between student-centered strategies and teacher-centered strategies. Research-based teaching strategies, as well as problem-based and higher order thinking strategies, will be covered. Examples of many strategies will be provided as examples for the reader. This chapter also covers two types of strategies that are required by Perkins legislation as an indication of a quality program: academic integration and differentiated instruction. Academic integration incorporates math, sciences, social studies, engineering, English, technology, art, and other disciplines with career technical education content for the purpose of improving the quality of student learning. Differentiated instruction addresses the unique education needs of diverse learners while meeting the needs of our country in preparing a quality workforce.

Chapter 9, "Planning and Implementing Labs and Other Action-Oriented Strategies," will provide the reader with content on the importance of safety during action-oriented strategies. Suggestions for classroom management are included, as the learning environment is an integral part of laboratory experiences. Labs for courses involving food/nutrition, occupational food production, clothing production and fashion merchandising, housing and interior design, and early childhood education will be covered in this chapter. Content is also included that will inform the reader about practicum and a lesson plan template. student teaching/residency in the teacher education program.

Chapter 10, "FCS Education and Technology," provides the reader with content on how to enhance student-centered learning by technology and explore the available modalities that may enhance FCS educational content. Positive as well as negative aspects of technology are included, in addition to content on developing user-friendly online courses. Being comfortable with technology promotes college and career readiness for the learner.

Chapter 11, "The Link to Effective Teaching and Student Success," provides content for preservice educators on how to assess student learning, as well as check for understanding. Through the process of assessment, decisions are made regarding curriculum, student placement/grade advancement, funding for programs, and professional development for educators. When planning assessments, one should see a link between the standard, goal/central idea, objectives/learner outcomes, and the assessment. The chapter covers how to create various types of assessments, as well as rubrics.

Chapter 12, "Advocacy," stresses the importance of FCS professionals becoming advocates in their field. Unfortunately, as with all social programs, FCS programs are often found on the proverbial chopping block of education and governmental programs. FCS professionals need to learn the art of advocating for their programs and educating people on the importance of FCS education as preventative as well as restorative. The content shared in this chapter will identify steps involved in advocacy for the profession, as well as for individuals, families, and communities.

The Learning Environment and Classroom Management

Learner Impact

Melinda Swafford, PhD, and Elizabeth Ramsey, PhD, CFLE

FIGURE 7.1 An Example of Indirect Classroom Management—Enough Supplies to Share

Chapter 7 Objectives

Upon completion of the chapter, the learner will be able to

- analyze ways to optimize the learning environment to enhance student engagement and achievement,
- analyze if a developmentally appropriate practice environment is appropriate for the FCS classroom,
- explain various techniques of direct and indirect methods of classroom management,

- contrast different theoretical approaches to classroom management,
- recognize inappropriate behavior in students and the reason for that behavior, and
- describe Youatt and Hitch's (2002) six components/functions of a positive classroom environment.

Introduction

How does one implement effective classroom management? Why are some teachers more effective with classroom management than others? What skills do these teachers possess? These are some of the questions that this chapter will address. One skill these teachers possess is the ability to positively impact the learning environment. Effective teachers who create positive learning environments develop not only a physical classroom setting but also an emotional setting that enhances student performance (Fox, 2009).

The learning environment develops over time and is defined as how an educator's expectations and the interaction with students develop a community of learners (Fox, 2009). This community of learners develops a **classroom culture** that is the atmosphere and ways educators and learners participate in common activities (Fox, 2009).

Until a quality learning environment is established, learning cannot occur. Even the most well-developed lesson plans cannot compensate for chaotic classrooms (Breaux & Whitaker, 2013). Therefore, it requires the family and consumer sciences (FCS) educator to develop classroom management techniques that keep students engaged in the learning. Additionally, preservice educators are assessed by edTPA on their ability to create a positive learning environment, and educators in the field are assessed on the quality of their learning environment. Arnett (2012) indicates that student discipline, classroom management, and facility management were major concerns of new FCS educators. Furthermore, issues with classroom management are factors that cause teachers to leave the profession. Arnett (2012) stressed that discipline and management should be covered well in all FCS teacher preparation programs.

This chapter includes content on the importance of a positive learning environment and developing a meaningful connection with all students. A wide variety of proven techniques that enhance the learning environment and student discipline will be included in this chapter. Under many current teacher evaluation models (Fox, 2009), teachers are being held accountable for student achievement, indicating the need to look at all possible avenues to improve student achievement.

We recommend that you check out the teacher evaluation rubric being used by your state. As an example, we included the current evaluation rubric from the state of Tennessee (Tennessee Team, n.d.). See Appendix B for the document. For evaluation of the learning environment and classroom management, look under "environment." The learning environment must also be addressed by the EdTPA portfolio, which must be completed during residency. The resident candidate must include written content on how the learning environment is respectful to all learners, how rapport is established with and among learners, and how the learning environment supports views to be shared within the class (Pearson, 2017).

Effective Classroom Management

Classroom management refers to all things that a teacher does to organize students, space, time, and materials so that content can be covered and student learning can occur. A well-managed classroom has a high level of student involvement, appropriate expectations, and involves using strategies of indirect and direct guidance. Wong and Wong (2009) state that effective classroom management is a major characteristic of an effective educator. The typical FCS classroom may include learners with various learning styles and classes that contain multiple grade levels (Dainty et al., 2011). Furthermore, the programs of study in the FCS curriculum include a variety of courses, each with numerous standards that include teaching materials that must be organized and managed. This can be a daunting task to keep an FCS classroom organized and well managed.

The Power of Relationships

Before investigating the learning environment and classroom management, we must address the value of a loving and nurturing teacher–student relationship. Establishing a welcoming, loving, secure relationship with each student is the first and foremost thing that any teacher should strive to accomplish in a classroom. Revisiting the trauma-informed care approach from Chapter 3, we learned that children who have experienced trauma need the stability of a loving relationship where they feel understood, validated, accepted, and emotionally secure and safe (Forbes, 2012). Learners who experience relationships where they feel emotionally secure with their educators have better academic achievement (Forbes, 2012). This is the case for not only learners who have experienced ACEs and trauma but also typically developing and emotionally secure students—positive relationships help everyone thrive!

Styles of Classroom Management

Baumrind (1971) identified styles of parenting in her pioneering research—permissive, authoritarian, and authoritative—that have later been applied to classroom teachers and classroom management. In a permissive classroom learning environment, the educator avoids imposing classroom expectations, or if expectations are set, consequences are not consistent or nonexistent (Marion, 2014). Learners regulate their own behavior. Furthermore, the educator has a tolerant attitude toward the learner's impulses, and standards for assignments are not imposed.

In an authoritarian classroom learning environment, the educator has unrealistic expectations since the educator has very little knowledge of human development. This results in the educators using force and coercion to try to maintain unquestioning obedience and classroom control. Discipline strategies are punitive and not related to the offense or to classroom expectations (Marion, 2014). Furthermore, the educator establishes the classroom expectations and confronts learners in a mean-spirited/inconsiderate way when expectations are not followed. Communication is critical and negative.

In an authoritative classroom management style, the educator is aware of human development and has reasonable classroom expectations with established limits and boundaries (Marion, 2014). Learners are supervised, yet options and choices are provided to meet learners' unique needs. Communication with learners is clear, warm, and open. Interaction with learners is consistent, firm, and kind. The authors recommend that educators adopt an authoritative style of classroom management. Discipline strategies are consequential and focus on teaching, not punishment, and learners are confronted respectfully with clear explanations of discipline encounters (Marion, 2014).

What Is a Positive Learning Environment?

How do we describe a **positive learning environment**? It is a classroom that is student-orietned—one with high expectations yet recognizes that each student has unique needs, strengths, and skill levels. Creating a positive learning environment is not new to FCS educators. Learning occurs best in student-centered environments with active engagement with content, peers, and the teacher (Marion, 2014). Positive learning environments are supported by educators who use an authoritative style of classroom management.

SPOTLIGHT: COMPONENTS OF A POSITIVE LEARNING ENVIRONMENT (SWAFFORD ET AL., 2014)

Six functions that FCS educators should consider when planning a positive learning environment are security, shelter, social contact, symbolic identification, task instrumentality, and pleasure (Youatt & Hitch, 2002).

Security and Shelter

Safety, a high priority for every school system and educator today, indicates that the environment is free from bullying and ridicule. Safety occurs when there is acceptance of diversity, assurance of confidentiality, and establishment of an atmosphere of respect. When educators establish expectations for learning and behavior, on how to succeed in the class, the learning environment is viewed as a place of comfort. Predictable routines lead to the formation of habits, therefore becoming generalized into everyday life as socially acceptable behavior. As educators, our attitudes provide the foundation of the learning climate. "Maslow before Bloom" (Berger, 2020) identifies the need for educators to first meet a student's need for safety and belonging before challenging them academically (see Figure 7.2). Bloom's Taxonomy is discussed in detail in Chapter 6.

Social Contact and Symbolic Identification

Establishing a sense of community (Magnuson, 2002) involves sharing expectations on course content, social behavior, and student achievement. Building a classroom community where students feel a sense of ownership and participate in keeping the classroom in order is part of symbolic identification. Assignments relevant to the student's personal needs lead to symbolic identification, allowing the student to gain meaning in how FCS impacts life.

To develop or enhance the social skills of the learners, plan activities such as group work and labs that involve interpersonal skills. Opportunities for choices and decision making demonstrate respect for autonomy, judgment, and values while supporting the development of freedom of expression and the development of self-esteem.

Pleasure and Task Instrumentality

Tight, cramped spaces and ill-placed items increase stress. A pleasant, well-organized classroom signifies care and control. Organized supplies/equipment should be readily accessible along with décor that changes frequently. Room arrangement should reflect specific courses. Make the classroom efficient for all types of activities by using tables for labs and group work while using desks for independent work. Consider using a U-shape configuration of desks or tables so that students are easily seen. Establishing efficient procedures for distributing work and cleaning up affects behavior while saving time and decreasing stress. Cues, such as pictures, labels, and signs, serve as reminders to help with room organization and collecting assignments.

Maslow's hierarchy of needs is visualized in a five-level pyramid (McLeod, 2020). Self-actualization cannot occur until the other four levels are met in an individual. When taking the time and effort to combine social-emotional learning in the classroom and ensuring that students feel safe and their basic needs are met, learning is accelerated (Berger, 2020).

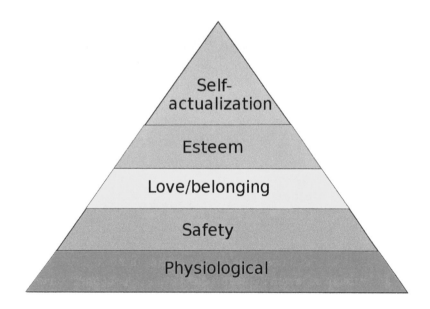

FIGURE 7.2 Maslow's Hierarchy of Needs

ACTIVITY 7.1: APPLICATION OF YOUATT AND HITCH'S CONCEPTS

Read the following examples of how several FCS educators applied Youatt and Hitch's (2002) six concepts of a positive learning environment in their classrooms. Brainstorm with fellow peers to identify two other activities that could be used to implement this in your classroom.

Application Activity

An example of symbolic identification, security, and pleasure occurred during a visit to a high school FCS classroom. The class was Life Connections; the topic and course standard included setting and attaining goals. For the assignment, each student constructed a kite to represent their personal goals for the future. The tails of the kites (five each) illustrated the action steps needed to reach the goals. Constructing a kite with tails was an effective way to make the topic of goals more concrete and appealing to ninth-grade students. Displaying each student's kite in the classroom signified the importance of each student's goals for the future and gave them a sense of pride. While visiting another school, the same course standard taught by another FCS educator used the concept behind the movie *The Bucket List*. Students made a bucket to signify a goal. Water droplets were used as action steps needed to achieve the goal.

During a visit to another high school, the FCS educator used the following strategies as a way to support symbolic identification, task instrumentally, and enhance the social skills of the learner. The students in her classroom were in charge of various routines. They distributed worksheets, laptops, and iPads, controlled classroom lighting, and collected papers. This demonstrated to the students that teamwork is necessary and provided a way to demonstrate pride in their contribution to the learning environment. Furthermore, the teacher's organization (labels, routines, baskets, etc.) enhanced the student's ability to take initiative and follow through with tasks and assignments while also providing students with important life skills.

Each of the aforementioned is an example of student-centered activities with the learners actively engaged. The benefits of these examples to the learners resulted in a sense of community in working together to keep the classroom organized and enhanced self-esteem in the daily operation of the classroom while developing skills needed for postsecondary education and job skills.

Theories of Behavior

There are multiple theories that explain behavior. Theories serve as the foundation in making decisions regarding guidance issues, as they may help educators explain behavior and understand psychological, emotional, and social needs, as theories incorporate conceptual frameworks as a way to understand and explain behavior. Some theories have a close connection to the FCS profession, such as developmental theory, social learning theory, ecological theory, and biological theory. Understanding various theories of behavior may help educators formulate a practice of managing the learning environment (Wheeler & Richey, 2005). FCS preservice educators may find how the theories summarized next influence classroom management and the learning environment. Chapter 4 includes more detailed content on the basics of learning theories.

The developmental theory was established by Jean Piaget. This theory states that learners obtain knowledge as they proceed through a sequence of development in which new knowledge and skills are obtained through active engagement with individuals and events in the environment (Wheeler & Richey, 2005). Developmental theory is the foundation for a **developmentally appropriate practice (DAP)** classroom (Wheeler & Richey, 2005). DAP is a framework that is associated with young children and is based on factors of development across all developmental domains (NAEYC, 2021). DAP is appropriate for FCS learning environments since educators accommodate the various needs of learners. Furthermore, DAP promotes authoritative guidance strategies that incorporate direct and indirect guidance strategies that are age appropriate.

In Erickson's theory of psychosocial development, most students in the FCS classroom are in the stage of identity versus isolation. Peer pressure and group conformity are more important to them than being viewed as an individual. The educator needs to realize this and avoid the isolation of individuals within the group. See Chapter 4 for information on Erickson's stage of psychosocial development.

The term **personal fable** was coined by psychologist David Elkind and usually occurs in adolescents during Piaget's formal operations stage of development. A personal fable is a belief held by many adolescents that helps explain the self-consciousness of adolescent behavior and also explains why many adolescents feel they are exempt from harm with risk-taking behaviors (Vartarian, 2000). Acknowledging the concept of a personal fable is helpful in understanding adolescent behavior.

SPOTLIGHT: AN OVERVIEW OF ADOLESCENT DEVELOPMENT

FCS educators work with middle school and high school students. Therefore, it is essential that FCS educators have an understanding of these stages of development so that they may implement DAP. An understanding of the learner will enable the educator to implement a safe and supportive learning environment, therefore enhancing retention and application of content.

Early adolescence (age 10–13) is a time when males and females begin to mature sexually, as secondary sex characteristics emerge. Many girls start their periods around age 12. Early adolescents think in terms of black or white, right or wrong, wonderful or awful. Preadolescents and early adolescents are self-conscious, egocentric, and often feel judged by those around them.

During middle adolescence (age 14–17), puberty continues, and males experience a growth spurt. Secondary sexual characteristics continue, voices in males deepen, and most girls have their periods by now. Many adolescents will begin romantic relationships, and many become sexually active. Peer pressure peaks at this age, and students are abundantly concerned with their appearance. Middle adolescents are beginning to think abstractly and can consider the bigger picture but do not always apply it. They can still be impulsive and take risks that can be potentially harmful to their health, body, and future. The frontal lobes in their brains do not fully develop well into their 20s, and this explains their limited ability to make decisions and control their impulses. Middle adolescence is marked by defining values and developing a strong sense of individuality. By the time adolescents reach 18–21 (late adolescence), they typically have improved impulse control (Healthy Children, n.d.).

In biological theory, behavior is viewed from a health and medical aspect that examines how these factors impact development and behavior. Congenital anomalies, genetic factors, and postnatal trauma may contribute to intellectual disabilities, learning disabilities, and behavior abnormalities in the learner. Furthermore, medicine and medical procedures to treat these disorders may have side effects that can impact behavior (Wheeler & Richey, 2005). In FCS education, professionals are aware of the impact of these factors on human development in human services, nutrition, dietetics, and education career clusters.

The ecological theory explains the impact of families, homes, schools, communities, economy, politics, and geography on the growth and development of the individual. The ecological theory is the foundation of our profession. This theory was developed by Urie Bronfenbrenner, and the main emphasis is on relationships and the impact of the environment on the learner. The interaction, resources, and roles played throughout the various levels in the person's environment account for the uniqueness of each individual and family.

Lev Vygotsky is also associated with ecological theory. This theory acknowledges the impact of socialization on the cognitive development of the learner and builds on the levels to promote learning, such as scaffolding and zone of proximal development (Wheeler & Richey, 2005). FCS educators incorporate strategies that involve socialization, such as cooperative learning activities and labs. FCS educators who embrace Vygotsky's theory are aware of the environmental contexts that impact the learner. See Chapter 1 for more information on ecological theory.

Social learning theory believes that learners are active in their own learning and development while being affected by their environment by exposure to modeling and imitation of behavior (Marion, 2014). This theory is associated with Alfred Bandura. FCS educators model behavior that supports building a relationship with others—behavior that illustrates respect—so that learners will see how these behaviors can be demonstrated.

Behaviorism, or behavior theory, was founded by John B. Watson and based on work by B. F. Skinner, Ivan Pavlov, and Edward Thorndike (Wheeler & Richey, 2005). Environmental responses (**consequences**) shape behaviors. When an individual's behavior is rewarded, they will likely repeat the behavior. For example, when you continuously address a learner who is creating a small distur-bance, you are rewarding the behavior with attention. A better way to address this behavior may be to distract attention away from the individual. The consequence of ignoring the behavior will not reward the individual. For more content to explain this technique, see the "Positive Behavior Intervention and Support" section later in this chapter.

Moral Development

Adolescents' moral development is impacted by the expectations of others and is heavily influenced by peer pressure (Goh, 2021). Kohlberg's theory of moral development states that moral develop-ment occurs in six stages that can be divided into three levels (see Table 7.1). Levels 1 and 2 are called *conventional.* Levels 3 and 4 are called *preconventional justice,* and Levels 5 and 6 are called *postconventional justice.* As an adolescent matures and moves to higher levels, they move from the importance of peer group identity to the development of moral thinking (Goh, 2021). As FCS content

TABLE 7.1 **Kohlberg's Moral Development (Goh, 2021)**

Stage	Focus	Moral Authority
Stage 1	Obedience and Punishment	Authority Figures
Stage 2	Individualism and Exchange	Self-Interest
Stage 3	Interpersonal Relationships	Social Approval
Stage 4	Maintaining Social Order	Obey Laws and Rules
Stage 5	Social Contract	Benefits for the Greater Good
Stage 6	Universal Principle	Human Rights and Justice

is concerned with the quality of life, this theory is relevant in helping adolescents make adult decisions in such domains as family dynamics, relationships, and careers with others.

Challenging Behavior

Learners may bring into the classroom an array of social/emotional issues that confront the teacher's expertise and resources (Moffett et al., 2008). The learners may have experienced trauma as a child, have a diagnosed learning need or physical need, speak another language other than English, or need 504 services. Furthermore, schedule changes, unsatisfactory routines, poorly designed rules, poorly designed physical environments, and adult behaviors may result in learners exhibiting challenging behaviors (Moffett et al., 2008). Keating (2002) states that 20% of any classroom population can exhibit challenging and problematic behaviors, while Owens et al. (2018) report that anywhere between 12% and 20% of students exhibit inattention, noncompliance, or impulsivity (p. 157). Also, 62% of teachers report worsening behavior that interferes with learning in the classroom over the last 5 years (Scholastic, n.d.). Yet **challenging behavior** is in the eye of the beholder. What one educator finds challenging may not be so for another educator. See Chapter 3 for a review of content on trauma-informed classrooms.

Learning is impeded in classrooms with challenging behaviors, as these behaviors may obstruct the effectiveness of an educator—in other words, obstruct learning—and they may interfere with developing relationships with peers. Yet, when faced with challenging behaviors, many teachers and adults perceive the behavior as deliberate, difficult, manipulative, and/or noncompliant. A first response may be to engage in a power struggle or attempt to "control" or "punish" the student. This strategy is not recommended, as it neglects to address the needs of the student. Various professional organizations, such as the National Association of Young Children, National Education Association, and Council for Exceptional Children, document that punitive and authoritarian guidance strategies are not appropriate or recommended for any student. These types of guidance strategies are also a violation of the organization's code of ethics (Wheeler & Richey, 2005). These professional organizations recommend using strategies of positive behavior intervention and support to address challenging behaviors.

SPOTLIGHT: MINDFULNESS IN THE CLASSROOM

Mindfulness is a popular phrase that circulates today, and is simply the practice of paying careful attention to your thoughts, body, and what is happening in your environment (Garey, 2022). Mindfulness is especially useful for students who have limited attention spans, but it is also helpful during transition times when students often struggle with shifting their focus (Garey, 2022). Mindfulness can prevent as well as disrupt meltdowns, arguments, and fights. To teach mindfulness practices, it is important to teach students to have an awareness of their emotions, as well as ways to control their emotions. FCS education is perfect for this because social-emotional learning is part of FCS content and standards.

Positive Behavior Intervention and Support

Positive behavior intervention and support (PBIS) is based on behaviorism. PBIS tracks the occurrences of challenging behaviors and delivers intervention that promotes a behavior change by teaching replacement skills to achieve the same reward or goal with a more constructive approach (Wheeler & Richey, 2005). Both authors of this chapter have doctoral degrees with an emphasis on working with exceptional learners. It would be amiss to include a chapter on classroom guidance and not include information on PBIS. This section does not include all information; websites and articles will be posted at the end of the chapter for additional information.

PBIS incorporates strategies of observation, modification of the environment, and teaching of replacement skills or behaviors, as well as a focus on prevention. In order to apply the principles of PBIS, certain principles of behavior must be understood as a basis for all behavior. **Behavior** is learned and is a form of communication (Moffett et al., 2008). Through feedback and rewards, challenging behavior can be replaced with more positive behavior. All behavior serves a function; it expresses a need, and behavior can be classified into four functions to meet that need: attention, escape, feedback, and tangible.

Since its inclusion in the 1997 reauthorization of the Individuals with Disabilities Act, PBIS is often found in most public educational settings. In fact, it is possible that your practicum placement or resident/student teaching placement may incorporate school-wide PBIS. Schools will often use slogans or logos to signify universal interventions. The major focus of PBIS is to correct skill deficits, ineffective instructional strategies, or curriculum instead of just blaming the child for the problem. This is accomplished by defining expected behaviors, teaching appropriate behaviors, and, finally and most importantly, acknowledging appropriate behaviors.

As viewed in Figure 7.3, the top portion/tier is universal interventions. All students in the school usually fall into this category. The purpose of this tier is to promote school-wide positive behavior based on a set of core values decided by a PBIS team. It involves teaching social skills and appropriate behaviors through positive reinforcement to replace undesirable behaviors that may occur in common areas of the school environment, such as hallways, lunchrooms, and auditoriums.

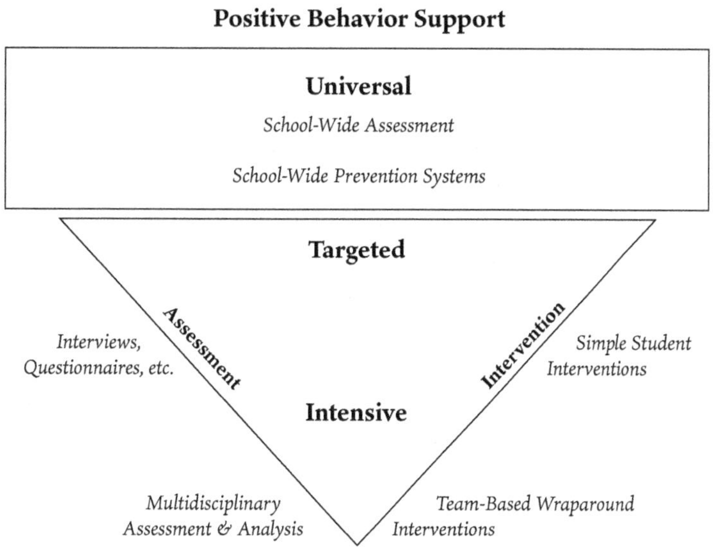

Positive Behavior Support

FIGURE 7.3 3-Tier Pyramid of PBIS

The middle portion/tier in Figure 7.3 is for at-risk/targeted students. Normally, about 20% of students need increased academic support and social skills teaching. This tier also involves an adult mentor and family training to enhance family-school collaboration. This tier is used more often in the classroom setting and may include academic support when needed. The bottom portion/tier in Figure 7.3 is intensive intervention. This includes the smallest number of students in the school and in the classroom setting. To incorporate PBIS at this level, a student may need an intensive behavior plan, intensive academic support from the school's special education department, and/or support from community agencies.

Functions of Behavior

What can we do to address challenging behaviors? Using PBIS observation and documentation, a **functional behavior assessment (FBA)** is used. With an FBA, data is collected to record the **ABCs of behavior**. "A" represents **antecedents**, events/factors that occur before the behavior; "B" stands for the actual behavior one is observing during the FBA; "C" represents consequences or what happened after the behavior as a response to the behavior (Applied Behavior Analysis, n.d.; Wheeler & Richey, 2005). Identifying the ABCs of behavior will help an educator identify the function of the behavior, or why the behavior is occurring.

Identifying the function of the behavior is essential to knowing what and when to teach appropriate replacement skills. When using the principles of the ABCs of behavior in PBIS, educators may change the environment that triggers challenging behaviors or change aspects of the environment following the behaviors. Challenging behavior is changed by either addressing what occurs before the incident or by changing the response that follows the behavior. Appropriate skills can be taught to prevent the behavior and/or can be reinforced through response by praise or consequences. Through this teaching, learners with challenging behaviors will experience enhanced learning outcomes.

Turnbull et al. (2000) recommend that teachers focus on creating a classroom environment that improves daily interactions, "making problem behavior less effective, less efficient, and less relevant therefore making the desired behavior more functional" (p. 2). For example, a learner needing attention will disrupt the class. The learner will do whatever it takes to get that attention. If we only give that learner attention when they are being disruptive, we are rewarding the learner for the disruptive behavior. Give attention when the student is on task. Reward the positive behavior.

If the function of the behavior is to escape, a learner may become disruptive when certain assignments are given. For example, a learner has difficulty with reading and math skills. From the learner's viewpoint, it is much better to be seen as disruptive than one who cannot do the assigned work. When educators send the learner elsewhere (in the hall) because of their behavior, we are teaching the learner how to escape from a task they do not want to face. Is this strategy really addressing the needs of the student? No, the consequence of sitting in the hall during the task is rewarding to the learner, as they have escaped the assignment. To incorporate PBIS, use secondary or Tier 2 strategies of academic support such as peer tutoring or collaborative groups for assignments. Also, consider using technology to help with the problem areas, or if needed, develop a behavior contract. Or an educator may refer the learner for academic tutoring.

When the function of the behavior is feedback, some learners will exhibit challenging behavior to gain a feeling of control. This behavior can be seen in the classroom with a power struggle between the educator and learner or calling another student an inappropriate name. When the function is tangible, the behavior is to gain an object or item.

As you can see from the previous examples, adult behaviors may need to be changed. Many times, our response to challenging behaviors can be reinforcing the behavior. In addition, excessive demands may contribute to the student becoming confused and possibly aggressive. For more information on PBIS, check out the website (www.pbis.org).

Classroom management is composed of both direct guidance and indirect guidance strategies. An effective educator will develop a repertoire of both strategies to promote a positive learning environment. See Figure 7.4 for visuals on classroom management strategies.

Direct Guidance

Direct guidance strategies use physical, verbal, and emotional components to guide the behavior of others. These strategies include offering choices, redirecting students, and teaching problem-solving skills (Marion, 2014). Direct strategies also include stating expectations clearly and providing visual and verbal cues as reminders. Use of specific praise and "I" messages such as "I like how ..." or "I recognize that you may be upset ..." are emotional components of direct guidance, as they provide praise and recognize emotions.

Learners with limited social skills may not be aware of options in order to change behavior. Involving the learner in conflict resolution may improve problem-solving skills and help develop empathy. Using logical consequences as a response to a mishap in behavior may also serve as a way of teaching skills.

FIGURE 7.4 Classroom Management

For physical strategies, an educator's body language can greatly impact the environment and attitude of the learners. When a learner is off task, consider using close proximity to the learner by either change of placement or standing by the off-task learner. Close proximity to a student greatly impacts behavior; an off-task student can be redirected by simply pointing to the place in their textbook or paper. Consider modeling the appropriate behavior you wish your learners to emulate. Be present in the room when students arrive. Educators are responsible for the safety of the classroom and the students (Wong & Wong, 2005).

Indirect Guidance

Indirect guidance strategies involve behind-the-scenes planning. These strategies include changing the physical setting, arranging resources that meet the learner's needs, and developing a predictable and positive learning climate with clear expectations (Marion, 2014). This will result in the learner knowing what is expected of them in order to succeed. The classroom climate should be relaxed, pleasant, but work oriented. Have assignments ready and begin the lesson quickly. Students should know assignments and tests are based on course standards and objectives, not just busywork.

A well-organized attractive room gives an "in control" image. This involves arranging floor space and keeping the traffic area clear and placing the students' desks where the teacher can see each one. The **T zone** in the classroom is a place where learners are more engaged in the lesson. These are the first two horizontal rows in the class and the center vertical row. The T zone is also a good place for students who may need a strategic location.

A welcome letter, either a hard copy or through electronic distribution, provides an opportunity to welcome students to the class and provide the families with the information covered in your class, such as course standards. This may be the only contact the educator has with families. Furthermore, if the educator has to contact a student's family for some reason over classroom management, the first contact with the family will have been the welcome letter, not to inform them the learner has been disruptive.

Since many activities in the FCS classroom involve collaborative learning, the formation of groups is essential for successful learning to occur. Again, since we are working with adolescents, choice and options are important. An effective strategy is to have students write down three people they want in their group. Students are told before this activity that the teacher would be formatting the final list, and they will have one person from the list in their group. Using this technique provides the teacher with more control and prevents the formation of groups where only one person is doing the work or groups where no one is working. When the groups are finalized, use them for food labs and cooperative learning activities, such as case studies.

ACTIVITY 7.2: TIPS ON MANAGING THE LEARNING ENVIRONMENT

The following are several tried-and-true tips that will help the new teacher become more effective with classroom management. After reading the tips, provide examples of how these tips can be incorporated into the FCS classroom. Share examples with your class.

- Your reputation as an educator will precede you (Wong & Wong, 2009). If you have a reputation for high expectations and engaging, relevant lessons that are not just busywork, students will enter your classroom with high expectations.
- Be confident but friendly. Avoid coming off as trying to be a friend to the students.
- Consider using the term *expectations* instead of *rules*. A rule is a dare to be broken (Wong & Wong, 2009). Remember, we are working with adolescents. They are searching for autonomy.
- Negative statements may be viewed by many adolescents as a challenge. Therefore, make sure all classroom expectations are stated positively and have clearly defined procedures and logical consequences. Involve students in setting expectations for the class. This can be done by class discussion or a survey.
- Classroom procedures or expectations (limit to no more than five) should be introduced on the first day and taught to the learners. Understanding the reason behind the expectation helps one adhere to the expectation.
- Interact with each student in a positive manner. Notice the positive behavior of all learners.
- When responding to a student with challenging behaviors, remain calm. Recall Erikson's stages of development and adolescent development. Testing boundaries and bending rules may be typical of this age group. If expectations and boundaries are broken, rely on logical consequences. These are consequences that fit the behavior.
- Use positive strategies that focus on teaching, not a punishment to get desired behaviors. This is accomplished by stating clear and concise expectations, modeling appropriate behaviors, using signals/cues, allowing opportunities to practice desired behaviors, and ignoring behaviors when appropriate.
- Specific praise is very important. Say what you mean and use a kind tone. Avoid sarcasm. This may be difficult to do when you are stressed and tired. An example of using sarcasm is "Amy,

what part of sit down do you not understand?" Using sarcasm will not make the educator look cool to Amy. The sarcastic response may inhibit Amy's safety, as she may feel attacked by the educator. The sarcasm may backfire, causing the educator to lose the respect of the students.

- Avoid a power struggle. No one wins in a power struggle. Instead of arguing, simply state the options. Avoid confrontation in front of the class. Speak quietly to the offender after class or in an area independently.

- Finally, treat everyone with respect; we gain respect as an educator by being respectful to others.

SUMMARY

As FCS educators, we want our learners to be successful. It is in our best interest to focus on the learning environment as a means to enhance achievement, as learners gain skills that impact success in careers, advanced education, and life. Developing a caring, nurturing relationship with the learner is the first step toward an FSC classroom with a positive learning environment. The strategies included in this chapter support a learning environment that is effective, positive, and productive while enhancing the FCS curriculum and the self-esteem of the learner. A positive learning environment supports learner achievement, and behavior will be improved. Furthermore, when these behaviors are generalized, the learner's ability to balance the demands of life and work will be enhanced (Moreno, 2008).

KEY TERMS

Developmentally appropriate practice (DAP)
Classroom culture
Positive learning environment
Indirect guidance
Direct guidance
Positive behavior intervention and support (PBIS)
Functional behavior assessment (FBA)

Challenging behavior
Antecedents
Consequences
Personal fable
Behavior
ABCs of behavior
T zone

QUESTIONS AND ACTIVITIES

1. Review the PBIS website (www.pbis.org). Summarize two additional concepts that you gained from this website regarding PBIS.
2. Describe the correlation between DAP and PBIS. In what aspects are these concepts similar?

3. Conduct a web search on classroom management. Make a list of tips that you feel are relevant to being an FCS educator.

4. After reading the Spotlight "An Overview of Adolescent Development," describe strategies that minimize self-consciousness in class.

5. You have a student in class who blurts out often and disrupts others during discussion. Through an FBA, you have determined that it is attention-seeking behavior. Discuss how you will either change the environment that triggers the behavior or how you will respond to the behavior.

REFERENCES

Applied Behavior Analysis Program guide. (n.d.). *What are the ABCs of behavior?* https://www.appliedbehavioranalysisprograms.com/faq/what-are-the-abcs-of-behavior/

Arnett, S. E. (2012). Problems encountered by beginning family and consumer sciences teachers. *Journal of Family and Consumer Sciences Education, 30*(2), 34–44. http://www.natefacs.org/JFCSE/v30no2/v30no2ArnettProb.pd

Baumrind, D. (1971). Current patterns of parental authority. *Developmental Psychology Monograph, 4*(1), 1–103.

Berger, T. (2020). *How to Maslow before Bloom, all day long.* Edutopia. https://www.edutopia.org/article/how-maslow-bloom-all-day-long

Breaux, A., & Whitaker, T. (2013). Three ways to better behavior. *Education Digest, 78*(5), 41–44.

Garey, J. (2022). *Mindfulness in the classroom.* Child Mind Institute. https://childmind.org/article/mindfulness-in-the-classroom/

Dainty, J. D., Sandford, B. A., Su, S. H., & Belcher, G. G. (2011). Factors influencing the retention of secondary family and consumer sciences teachers. *Journal of Career-Technical Education, 30*(2), 32–44.

Forbes, H. T. (2012). *Help for Billy: A beyond consequences approach to helping children in the classroom.* Beyond Consequences Institute.

Fox, C. K. (2009). Learning environment: An overview. *Journal of Family and Consumer Sciences Education, 27*(National Teacher Standards 4), 30–44. http://www.natefacs.org/JFCSE/v27Standards4/v27Standards4Fox.pdf

Goh, M. (2021). *Moral development.* LinkedIn https://www.linkedin.com/pulse/moral-development-melvin-goh/

Healthy Children. (n.d.). *Stages of adolescence.* https://www.healthychildren.org/English/ages-stages/teen/Pages/Stages-of-Adolescence.aspx

Keating, J. (2002). *Support children with challenging behaviors.* Circle of Inclusion. http://www.circle of inclusion.org

Magnuson, J. (2002). Middle school family and consumer sciences brain-based education from theory to practice. *Journal of Family and Consumer Sciences, 94*(1), 45–47.

Marion, M. (2014). *Supportive physical environments in guidance of young children* (9th ed.). Merrill Prentice Hall.

McLeod, S. (2020). *Maslow's hierarchy of needs.* Simply Psychology. https://www.simplypsychology.org/maslow.html

Moffett, K. R., Swafford, M., & Richey, L. H. (2008). Merging developmentally appropriate practice with positive behavioral support in early childhood programs. *Dimensions, 36*(2), 21–28.

Moreno, P. (2008). Incarcerated youth get a second chance with CTE. *Techniques Connecting Education and Careers, 83*(2), 18–21.

National Association of Education for Young Children. (2021). *National Association of Education for Young Children position statement.* Center on Positive Behavioral Interventions and Support.

Owens, J. S., Holdaway, A. S., Smith, J., Evans, S. W., Himawan, L. K., Coles, E. K., Girio-Herrera, E., Mixon, C. S., Egan, T. E., & Dawson, A. E. (2018). Rates of common classroom behavior management strategies and their associations with challenging student behavior in elementary school. *Journal of Emotional and Behavioral Disorders, 26*(2), 156–169. https://doi.org/10.1177/1063426617712501

Pearson. (2017). *EdTPA. Family and consumer sciences assessment handbook.*

Scholastic. (n.d.). *Classroom behavior problems increasing, teachers say.* https://www.scholastic.com/teachers/articles/teaching-content/classroom-behavior-problems-increasing-teachers-say/

Swafford, M., Bailey, S., & Beasley, K. (2014). Positive learning environment enhances student achievement. *Techniques: Connecting Education and Careers, 89*(5), 32–35.

Tennessee TEAM. (n.d.). *General educator rubric instruction.* https://team-tn.org/wp-content/uploads/2013/08/TEAM-General-Educator-Rubric.pdf

Turnbull III, H. R., Wilcox, B., Stowe, M., Raper, C., & Hedges, L. P. (2000). Public policy foundation for positive behavioral interventions, strategies, and supports. *Journal of Positive Behavioral Intervention, 2*(4), 218–235.

Vartarian, L. R. (2000). Revisiting the imaginary audience and personal fable constructs of adolescent egocentrism: A conceptual review. *Adolescence, 35*(140), 639–661.

Wheeler, J. J., & Richey, D. D. (2005). Understanding behavior in children and youth. In J. J. Wheeler & D. D. Richey (Eds.), *Behavioral management principles and practices of positive behavior support* (pp. 1–33). Prentice-Hall.

Wong H., & Wong, R. (2005). *The first days of school. How to be an effective teacher* (3rd. ed.). Harry K. Wong Publications, Inc.

Wong, H., & Wong, R. (2009). *The first days of school. How to be an effective teacher* (4th ed.). Harry K. Wong Publications, Inc.

Youatt, J., & Hitch, J. (2002). Setting the stage. In J. Youatt & J. Hitch (Eds.), *Communicating family and consumer sciences: A guidebook for professional* (pp. 103–113): Goodheart Willcox Publishing Co., Inc.

Figure Credits

Instructional Strategies

Hannah Upole, PhD; Elizabeth Ramsey, PhD; Melinda Swafford, PhD; and Caitlin Williams, MS

FIGURE 8.1 Instructional Strategies Are Often Described as Teaching

Chapter 8 Objectives

Upon completion of the chapter, the learner should be able to

- define research-based strategies, and describe how these are incorporated into a lesson plan;
- summarize methods of incorporating problem-based/higher order thinking skills in the family and consumer sciences (FCS) classroom;
- analyze pros and cons of student-directed versus teacher-directed teaching strategies;
- analyze how active homework is a teaching strategy;
- identify methods of including community in FCS instruction;

- define academic integration and how this meets Perkins requirements;
- compare and contrast a flipped classroom to a traditional classroom format; and
- summarize response to intervention and differentiated instruction.

Introduction

When developing lesson plans, instructional strategies must be considered. Instructional strategies are defined as materials and activities used by educators to engage learners in standards and objectives while meeting the needs of the learner. Strategies often vary according to grade level, class size, available resources, and the subject matter being taught. They can vary from student-centered to teacher-centered strategies.

Effective educators search for new and engaging strategies to keep the learner involved and motivated. However, for any strategy to be successful, it is vital that the educator take time to know their students, be aware of their unique history, and determine their prior knowledge. For learning to occur, the learner must first acquire new content, then have opportunities to use or to maintain the content, and finally participate in activities that allow the learner to generalize the content. Generalization of content is when true learning occurs, as learned content is applied to a new situation (Swafford & Dainty, 2009).

Family and consumer sciences (FCS) educators in the various programs of study use applied **contextual learning** strategies so that learners can see the relevance of the content in real-world situations; while these strategies incorporate critical thinking, problem-solving skills, and collaboration, the main focus on career technical education (CTE) strategies is on career development (College and Career Readiness and Success, 2013). This chapter includes descriptions and examples of various strategies used to present, maintain, and generalize FCS content to learners.

Presentation of Content

The body of the lesson includes the presentation of information; to implement this phase of the lesson, educators should have a wide variety of different strategies from which to choose. Most educators will have a few that are a favorite for a specific course and that meet the needs of the students. However, educators need to have a variety of strategies to help learners achieve desired outcomes (Rosenshine & Stevens, 1986). When selecting a strategy, keep in mind that key concepts are more likely to be applied when the learner identifies how this knowledge would be of benefit to everyday life. In other words, how does this strategy make the concepts relevant?

Miller (1990) noted that students need to be taught and assessed at various levels in the classroom. A student first needs to know the content, meaning they have a foundational knowledge of the information. Next, they need to know how to use the information in a meaningful and useful way. Subsequently, it is necessary for the student to show how they would use a particular skill or piece of information. Finally, the student should be able to independently do a task, indicating an understanding of the subject. At any point along the continuum from know to do, the instructor may formatively assess the student's knowledge to ensure they have mastered the content. Miller's theory of teaching and assessment can be incorporated into the FCS classroom in various ways, including the strategies discussed in this chapter.

Strategies may be classified as action oriented, such as simulation, role-play, debates, labs, and games. These strategies may be used in cooperative learning situations, along with case studies, jigsaw, and workstations. All of these enhance learner engagement and are student centered. Other student-centered strategies include open-ended questions, note-taking, discussions, problem-based learning, and graphic organizers. These strategies, as those previously stated, increase the likelihood of gaining knowledge and skills through application, analysis, evaluation, and creativity. See Figure 8.2 for a visual on the impact of strategies in specific areas of the brain.

Research-Based Teaching Strategies

Research indicates that evidence-based strategies have the largest impact on learners (Burns, 2010; Payne & Tucker, 2008). Killian (2015) identified strategies for educators use when teaching: provide a clear focus of the lesson, incorporate direct instruction, engage in the content numerous ways, apply knowledge from the content, use cooperative learning, pose question to assess learning, provide frequent feedback and promote learner self-efficacy.

Research-based strategies can be incorporated into a lesson plan easily. A clear focus of the lesson is accomplished during the set. The educator motivates the learner with a question or a short activity to pique the interest in the lesson. This is followed by the educator explaining the purpose of the lesson, along with an overview that provides what the learner will be doing in the lesson. During **direct instruction**, the educator shares or teaches content that the learner needs to be successful with the content. This involves having the learner take notes, identify similarities and differences, and incorporate a word wall to understand academic language, as well as using a graphic organizer to analyze connections of concepts.

Cooperative learning activities are numerous and can be easily incorporated into supervised or independent practice. These activities provide opportunities for the learner to engage in and apply the content in many ways through case studies, workstations, graphic organizers, labs/simulations, and so on. This can also be a time to summarize the main points of the lesson. During supervised practice, the FCS educator can pose questions to assess learning and provide feedback to guide the learner where improvements are needed or to provide positive affirmation when the student has demonstrated mastery.

During independent practice and closure, the learner has the opportunity to apply the concepts to demonstrate mastery of the content. This involves using critical thinking and problem-solving skills. Success at this stage enhances the learner's self-esteem.

Student-Directed Versus Teacher-Directed Strategies

Teacher-directed strategies have the following characteristics: The content flows from the teacher to the students. Teachers do most of the talking, and the teacher establishes rules and goals for the class. The major focus of instruction is on the teacher covering the curriculum (Room to Discover, n.d.). Teacher-directed strategies often include having students' desks in a row while listening to the teacher read or speak. In teacher-directed strategies, students work independently and quietly to complete worksheets or workbook pages. Teacher-directed strategies also include **rote learning,** or memorization of materials based on repetition (Merriam-Webster, 2021). As covered earlier in Chapter 6 under Bloom's Taxonomy, this type of learning is lower level. Completion of worksheets that focus on definitions and recall are examples of lower level learning.

The roots behind the student-centered approach go back to the early 20th century with John Dewey, Maria Montessori, and Carl Rogers (Richmond, 2014). **Student-directed strategies** provide opportunities for the learner to be actively engaged and interact with the content of the lesson. During planning, the educator considers the individual needs, goals, and culture of the learner. This planning provides the learner with options/choices, opportunities for collaboration with other learners, and differentiated instruction so that the lesson has relevance, interest, and meets unique learning needs. Problem-based learning, cooperative groups, case studies, and labs are examples of student-centered strategies.

Tell me and I forget, teach me and I remember, involve me and I learn.

—Chinese proverb (n.d.)

Teaching Strategies

Questioning

As mentioned previously, questioning is a research evidence-based teaching strategy. Questioning is a powerful tool in the classroom and should be used both with random individuals and class-wide—all student responses (Killian, 2014). Different question strategies can be incorporated into the classroom to randomly select students to answer a question, such as picking names from a hat or drawing popsicle sticks from a container. Making a random selection keeps students engaged and ready for involvement. When implementing a whole student response system, pose a question where the entire class responds by the use of whiteboards, five fingers (each finger represents a multiple-choice response), thumbs up/thumbs down, true/false cards, or electronic clickers (Killian, 2014). Questioning is a tried-and-true learning strategy that keeps students engaged and helps with learning and retention.

Questions should be a mixture of high-order thinking and low-order thinking. Educators should plan for questions and student responses. Questioning can also happen spontaneously as an educator picks up on cues within the classroom. A seasoned teacher recognizes when students are unclear, lost, or confused—questioning is a tool that can be used to quickly assess student comprehension and learning.

Modeling

Another evidence-based learning strategy is modeling. This strategy is valuable in any subject but can prove to be especially helpful to bring clarity to student learning when teaching FCS. Modeling is best used with a show and tell/share and model strategy (Clemson University, 2021; Killian, 2014). The educator should explain and then demonstrate the learning activity. Depending on the lesson at hand, sometimes the demonstration is a physical demonstration. For example, you might physically demonstrate how to level dry ingredients. On the other hand, modeling sometimes includes a think-aloud demonstration. For example, if students are learning how to apply child development theory in infant care, you might conduct a think aloud about Erik Erikson's first stage of development, trust versus mistrust, when working with an infant who is crying. A **think aloud** occurs when the educator literally thinks out loud: "I know Erik Erikson's theory explains the importance of infants learning how to trust their caregivers. Knowing that, the best way for me to respond to a crying infant is with tender loving care so that the baby learns he/she can trust me."

Demonstrations

Conducting demonstrations in class is another way to incorporate modeling. This strategy is used by both FCS educators in extension and in the classroom. Many FCS classroom educators use demonstration prior to a food lab in order to set a standard for a product and display a process with correct and desirable work habits. Demonstrations provide the following to learners: an understanding of why, as it brings attention to the most important points of a task and provides skill enhancement for the learner. Demonstrations are different from simulations, as they involve real action/environment (not role-play or simulation) and are appropriate for presenting information to smaller audiences (LSU AgCenter, n.d.). Effective demonstrations contain three parts: an introduction, a body, and a summary.

SPOTLIGHT: DEMONSTRATION TIPS

Prior

- Have equipment in place and checked.
- Have all necessary materials.
- Prepare measuring, chopping, and dicing before if appropriate.
- Prepare tray set up.

During

- Be sure to work in full view of the audience.
- Keep the space on the front of the worktable clear at all times—be organized.
- Be aware of time.
- Always involve your audience.
- Be able to think on your feet with flexibility and grace.

After

- A good time to summarize or have closure is when the product is being prepared for display.
- Invite questions.
- Provide samples.

(LSU AgCenter, n.d)

Graphs

Research shows the effectiveness of organizing newly learned content into graphs (Clemson University, 2021; Killian, 2014). This teaching strategy is effective when either the teacher or student organizes the information into graphs. Incorporate flow charts, Venn diagrams, mind maps, concept maps, and other graphic organizers into your classroom regularly. This strategy will build student learning both by means of summarizing content and making interrelated connections within the content.

Practice

Offer students time to practice their newly learned skills. Plan practice activities that are connected to your learning objectives. According to research, students learn better when they have time and multiple opportunities to practice over several different time periods (Killian, 2014). While students are practicing, offer feedback, both to the whole class and individualized feedback. Take time to reexplain things as needed and model again when necessary. Practice can occur both in and out of the classroom, and asking students to recall content learned from earlier in the course can help solidify content (Clemson University, 2021).

Feedback

Feedback is vital and an evidence-based teaching strategy. Giving meaningful feedback includes telling a student how they performed on a task, as well as how they can improve (Killian, 2014). Feedback is different from praise, as praise is more focused on the actual student. Feedback, on the other hand, focuses on what the student did, using tangible evidence from their work. According to research, teachers who provide meaningful feedback will see gains in their students' learning because their students understand what they did and what they can do to improve (Killian, 2014).

Lecture

Lecture is the most used teacher-directed strategy. It does have its place in FCS education, as it serves as a vehicle for the acquisition of learning new content or direct instruction. The benefits of lectures include the following: It allows delivery of large amounts of content in a short period of time; it ensures that all learners are presented the same content; it is efficient for presenting content to large groups (Youatt & Hitch, 2002). The cons of lectures include learners need to take notes and may be unengaged in the content, as learners are passive. However, educators may include a PowerPoint presentation along with notetakers and open-ended questions with lectures. This visual aid strategy with graphs and/or pictorials interspersed throughout the presentation may keep learners focused. Also, completing a graphics organizer with the content may increase learner engagement. To make the lecture more effective, the educator can vary the tone of voice for emphasis and move among the learners for observation and provide feedback.

Flipped Classroom

The Flipped Learning Network (2014) identifies four pillars to create a successful flipped learning environment. These four pillars include a flexible environment, learning culture, intentional content, and the professional educator. A flexible environment is a learning environment that can be modified to best fit the lesson, as learners may either work in groups or as individual learners. Oftentimes, a **flipped classroom** looks like small-group and/or individual attention inside the classroom and assigning lecture presentations for students to view outside of the classroom. This is often a noisy classroom environment (The Flipped Learning Network, 2014). However, students are involved in a discussion of content. The learning culture is student centered. It provides differentiated learning for the students, as well as provides various ways to show mastery of content. Intentional content provides instructional activities that are void of busywork but support understanding of the content. The opportunity for students or groups to move at their own pace while also having one-on-one interaction with the educator provides an opportunity to address any specific misconceptions for each student. The role of a professional educator in a flipped classroom is busy, as they conduct an ongoing assessment of student work, provide feedback, and incorporate reflective practice. See Figure 8.2 for a visual comparison between traditional and flipped classrooms.

SPOTLIGHT: FCS FLIPPED CLASSROOM

In an FCS classroom, imagine the FCS teacher assigning a virtual presentation on carbohydrates and a sorting activity for students to understand the foods that make up simple carbohydrates. This type of activity would be completed outside of the classroom environment, and when students return, the teacher will arrange small groups to complete the hydrolysis of the sugar in a foods/nutrition lab. The teacher provides a flexible environment for each student by presenting a variety of learning modes, including audio and text instructions. The learning culture provides rich learning opportunities, as students are working hands-on and can evaluate the process of hydrolysis together. By using teacher-created presentations, such as personal video instruction on the differences between simple and complex carbohydrates, the teacher is providing intentional content to their students. Lastly, the teacher plays the role of a professional educator when they are available to all students for efficient and effective feedback and collaborate with colleagues to enhance their teaching practices.

FIGURE 8.2 Comparing a Traditional Classroom to a Flipped Classroom

Active Homework

Active learning as a pedagogical approach is relatively well-known in classrooms, as teachers look to increase engagement with students and help with retention of knowledge through activities that emphasize thought, not just listening (Felder & Brent, 2009). Research has demonstrated the positive effects of collaborative and cooperative active learning in the classroom; however, learning does not end when the students exit your classroom (Cohn et al., 1996; Prince, 2004).

In most traditional classroom environments, homework is viewed as a means to assess students' learning, in addition to providing further experiences for interaction with course content. As demonstrated in one study, the effects of providing high- and low-achieving students with additional math homework were found to be positive, even when time spent in the classroom was not a significant contributor to test scores (Eren & Henderson, 2008). However, homework also has a history of negative engagement, as some students rank activities such as completing their chores as being more enjoyable than their homework (Corno & Mandinach, 2004).

One disconnect between student activity in the class and homework assignments could in fact be the type of homework that is being assigned. When students are presented with active learning opportunities in the classroom, their minds are engaged—they are actively thinking and doing (Auster & Wylie, 2006). With that knowledge in mind, homework assignments that promote engagement and activity allow that active learning to continue beyond the classroom.

The concept of **active homework** involves engaging students in homework activities that promote doing and thinking rather than rote learning. Active homework does not have to necessitate the development of entirely new forms of assessment but rather the way in which it is delivered to students. For instance, high engagement levels have been demonstrated in studies where students were presented with a prerecorded video or lecture discussing a chemical reaction and then asked to draw the product of that reaction before being able to move to the next module (Woodward & Reid, 2019). This technique motivates students not only by the points being offered for the activity but also by the immediate engagement of connecting content to homework. In FCS classrooms, instructors could look to a similar style of activity and modules provided by entities such as extension, in addition to other online resources, as a way to assess student learning through active homework.

SPOTLIGHT: EXAMPLE OF ACTIVE HOMEWORK

An example of this can be demonstrated through the Rethink Your Drink campaign, presented by the Centers for Disease Control and Prevention (CDC, 2021), which aims to teach consumers about ways to reduce added sugars in their beverages. The CDC offers literature on their web page that could be presented to students in the form of a lecture in class or a quick online module, regarding the definition of sugary drinks, why they should be concerned about this, and how to read nutrition labels to locate additional sugars in their drinks. Following the review of this module, students would then be presented with an active homework assignment: Trick-and-Treat—Rethink

Your Drink! In this homework assignment, provide each student with a nutrition label for a popular sugary drink (make sure to provide the name of the drink for clarity purposes) and an image of an empty glass of water. Instruct students that their job is to add low- or no-sugar alternatives, such as slices of fruit or adding a splash of juice to the water, to try to mimic the taste of the sugary drink they were provided with a nutrition label for. On the image of the empty glass of water, they should draw the ingredients they plan to add to mimic the taste without adding new sugars to the drink, in addition to explaining how their solutions would decrease the added sugars found on the nutrition label for their beverage. In this homework assignment, students are still having to do something (make the new drink) in addition to thinking about the correlations between the lesson they learned in class and this task they have been assigned. Rather than teaching the lesson and asking students to answer questions about added sugars, this active homework technique requires them to be engaged with the content in a more hands-on manner, thinking about what they have learned and demonstrating an understanding through a physical activity rather than passively writing about it.

Jigsaw

Another approach for higher level activities is offered by Buijs and Admiraal (2013), who suggest using a **jigsaw-style assignment** to increase student engagement through an active homework approach. This technique, adapted from Aronson's (1978) jigsaw classroom technique, requires that students assess their learning both individually and as a combined unit. This homework begins by dividing students into groups of three to four and selecting a generalized research topic for each group, such as sustainability in the design industry or the importance of play in child development. Then divide the research into four equal parts. For example, if students are assigned to read articles about the topic, assign a number to each article and have students in each team randomly select a number from a box to learn which article they will need to read.

Once students have their unique articles within their groups, assign each student to read that article at home and answer a series of questions to demonstrate understanding. When the class meets again, collect the students' answers and ask the groups to join back together. Instruct each group to take turns leading the discussion, to compare their unique articles and responses to the questions they answered. Ask students to try to come to a consensus on the most important points and to check among group members for understanding before moving to the next point.

Then, assign the next part of the homework: to work as a group to develop a 5- to 10-minute lesson about their topic, which they will teach to the class. The students will then have to work together outside of class to develop their lesson, including how to present and deciding on the most important information to address from their unique articles. Students may then be assessed on their individual work in reading and responding to their article, in addition to their work as a combined member of the team in presenting their lesson to the class, using defined rubrics for flipped classroom experiences.

EXAMPLE OF ACTIVE HOMEWORK USING JIGSAW

This homework activity uses the jigsaw approach of having students analyze content individually to gain knowledge, for then being brought together to discuss, to then learn they must work together to complete the full puzzle of the required safety issues involving early childhood education. In Tennessee the course Early Childhood Education I, Standard 1 states the following:

> Compile and critique procedures for maintaining a safe and healthy learning environment for children present in a childcare facility. Cite information for the Occupational Safety and Health Administration (OSHA), including but not limited to CPR, First-Aid, and Bloodborne Pathogens, to identify precautionary guidelines to prevent illness, communicable diseases, and injuries. Incorporate safety procedures and complete a safety test with 100 percent accuracy. (Tennessee Department of Education, 2019)

To prepare students for success with the safety test, students have to pull from the knowledge they gained through reading their unique articles to complete their first homework assignment, then use that knowledge to teach the peers in their group, thus recalling content and creating action around the activity. However, students then have to continue to actively work on the assignment to develop a lesson that is appropriate and interesting to their peers while still remembering they are an "expert" in just one area of this topic and will need to rely on their peers for additional knowledge.

While somewhat complex, the jigsaw approach introduces active homework as a meaningful technique, showing students that even more passive homework (such as memory recall from a reading) will still be used in active learning settings, in addition to homework that requires students to work together to generate meaning through the active learning technique (Aronson, 1978; Buijs & Admiraal, 2013). Regardless of depth, active homework can provide a unique way to assess students through active learning outside of the classroom, increasing overall student engagement with their homework assignments.

Discussion-Based Learning

Research has demonstrated the importance of discussion in the classroom, specifically in regard to how discussion can be used to build meaning and gain new perspectives (Flynn & Klein, 2001; Griffith & Laframboise, 1997; Levin; 1995). For many educators, the concept of discussion in the classroom may seem obvious; however, there is a clear distinction between recitation and a true discussion-based classroom (Gall & Gillett, 1980). By definition, a discussion-based method for instruction is "a strategy for achieving instructional objectives that involves a group of persons, usually in the roles of moderator and participant, who communicate with each other using speaking, nonverbal, and listening processes" (Gall & Gillett, 1980, p. 99).

The key to a discussion-based method of learning is that students are working collectively with their peers, both in the roles of listening and speaking, while also encouraging collaboration between students (Gall & Gillett, 1980). In contrast, recitation is predominantly focused around a recall pattern, with students merely repeating the statements they are taught, which does not focus on actively developing meaning or gaining new perspectives regarding the content. While there is certainly a time and place for recitation in the classroom, discussion-based learning focuses on encouraging students to explore ideas and engage in meaningful conversation, two techniques that benefit students far beyond the classroom (Larson, 2000).

While discussion-based learning has its fans, it also has its critics, with educators often wondering how to implement discussion-based learning into classrooms with students who do not want to participate or in classes where time is a concern. As most educators would likely agree, time is at a premium in the classroom—there is only so much time in a class to instruct, assess, and move on to the next stage of learning. There may just be moments where discussion seems impossible because of a lack of time. However, in these contexts, the discussion does not have to extend for hours at a time. Rowe (1987) found that by training teachers to extend their wait times for responding to students' points of discussion to 3–5 seconds, mere seconds from the average of just 1 second between student discussion and teacher response, the quality and quantity of student responses increased.

In the classroom, educators may often quickly respond to student discussion with follow-up questions or additional instruction without addressing the need for student reflection (Wilen, 2004). When allowing a brief time delay for reflection, the class shifts from a focus on recitation to true discussion. By asking students to stop and think about what they just heard from their peers, you are no longer reciting information but rather building meaning around a topic. During this time delay, students have the opportunity to think about the response they just heard before adding to the conversation or reflect to build meaning about this point of discussion. These mere seconds can make a major impact in the discussion, as students take a moment to think, without having to quickly move on to the next topic. In the instances where time is a concern, discussion-based learning may look as simple as posing a higher cognitive-level question to students or calling on volunteers to share responses. This is followed by allowing all students in the class to reflect on this discussion.

Another critique of the discussion-based learning approach is that students do not want to participate in the discussion, which may actually stem from teacher involvement in the discussion (Wilen, 2004). One study found that educators have a tendency to try to control discussion in the class by assuming the role of moderator too often (Klinzing & Klinzing-Eurich, 1988, as cited in Wilen, 2004). In most instances, this is often unintentional, as educators are looking to reinforce students' points with their own responses or additional questions. However, in some cases, this can actually deter students from wanting to participate in the discussion, as it moves control of the conversation from peer to peer back to teacher to student, which reverts back to a more recitation-based method of learning (Wilen, 2004). Instead, try to focus on using your role as the educator in a manner of facilitation by encouraging more student-to-student interaction through only intervening with comments or questions at key points in the discussion (Wilen, 2004).

SPOTLIGHT: THINK-PAIR-SHARE

One technique to help with increasing student participation and to encourage discussion is to develop **think-pair-share** activities. The think-pair-share strategy implements three steps: (1) asking students to think critically about a question or discussion topic on their own, (2) pairing up with a classmate or a group of peers to discuss their individual thoughts, and (3) sharing their collective thoughts with the class, another group, or the instructor (Kaddoura, 2013). This technique also helps to increase participation by engaging students in discussion that has lower barriers to entry, as all students enter the pairing stage with their own unique thoughts and ideas (Wilen, 2004).

The think-pair-share strategy begins by posing a question to students on an individual level (Kaddoura, 2013). For instance, in an upper division housing and design course, educators could pose a question regarding how to maximize space in cityscapes where land is at a premium (i.e., no more space exists for new buildings). Be sure to structure the question in a way that promotes critical thinking while still addressing any necessary parameters of the course content or standards. Once students have been presented with this question or topic of discussion, ask them to think about what their solution would be and make a quick sketch of their ideas or write down a few sentences that explain their thought processes. Make sure each student has time to think about the problem they were presented with and reflect on their thoughts.

After allowing students the opportunity to think on their own for a few minutes, ask students to pair up, or join into small groups in larger classes, and to share their ideas with their partner(s). If working in groups, keep the group sizes small so that each student has the opportunity to fully share their ideas within the group setting. In the pairing process, encourage students to find the similarities and differences between their ideas; however, only interject when you feel it is necessary to move the discussion forward. Allow the groups time to work through their ideas together, toward developing shared meaning.

The final step is to ask groups to share their ideas with the class as a whole. In this step, cooperation is a vital concept, as groups must work together to share their thoughts cooperatively (Kaddoura, 2013). Research suggests that during this share phase, cooperation is one element that helps students to be more willing to listen to others' views, clarify similarities and differences, and build new understanding, through the sharing of new ideas (Gilles, 2008). In essence, it is the structure of this activity—the promotion of individual accountability in the think phase and the peer interaction during the pair phase—that helps students to build this cooperative environment necessary to share freely with the class (Kaddoura, 2013). Through think-pair-share, students are encouraged to generate new ideas with peers, from their own ideas and thought processes, leading to more robust discussions of course content.

While the impact of discussion-based learning is widespread, one final element to consider is that discussion is only effective when students learn how to discuss. As preservice and in-service educators, the first step in leading enriching classroom discussion is knowing how to guide the discussion. Teacher educators may need to spend time modeling the principles of good discussion with their students, such as thinking out loud and showing the difference between moderating and participating in a discussion (Larson, 2000). Educators should be careful, however, not to dominate the discussion, as this can actually lead to a decrease in student engagement, and should instead switch their lens to a facilitative perspective, helping to guide the discussion in a meaningful way (Wilen, 2004). With practice, discussion-based learning can provide a wealth of knowledge to a classroom by teaching students how to communicate and generate meaning through both speaking and actively listening to other perspectives.

Suggested Discussion Strategies

Several different discussion strategies can be implemented in the classroom to build rich discussion among students. Using observation, the educator may also use these strategies as formative assessment. Strong academic questions are central to supporting rich discussions and can be teacher created or student created. If the class discussion is over a reading assignment, it is important that everyone reads the text prior to the discussion. To ensure that students read the text, we suggest that some sort of evidence of reading is presented as an entrance ticket to class, such as a chapter outline, brief summary, or notetaker. This will help with building a rich discussion. Additionally, ground rules regarding discussions should be included. Because of the personal nature of content in FCS classrooms, ground rules are an important part of the discussion, as students may end up sharing personal information about their families of origin or personal experiences relating to class content. A sample of ground rules used in class is provided in the following Spotlight.

SPOTLIGHT: CLASS GROUND RULES FOR DISCUSSION

- The discussion stays in the room. You may speak for yourself outside the room, but you will not presume to speak for others or about others.
- Listen respectfully. This is a dialogue, not a debate.
- Speak from your own perspective. Use lots of "I" statements: "I think," "I feel," "I believe," and so on.
- Use textual evidence. Statements such as, "In the text, it states...," "According to the text—," "The author said...," "On page ___, the author says..."
- Agree to disagree.
- Try not to interrupt classmates.
- Practice active listening. Use conversation stems when needed to clarify, paraphrase, agree, disagree, elaborate, or summarize.
- Be aware of your nonverbal behavior. Body language sends subtle messages.
- Be sensitive to others—they have experiences that you may never know about or begin to understand.

(adapted from Richey, 2013)

Fish Bowl

The fishbowl is a discussion strategy that is useful with any size group and is easy to implement because no additional supplies are needed. Prior to class discussion, arrange the chairs so that you have an inner circle and an outer circle. The inner circle is the fishbowl; the outer circle, which circles around the inner circle, is known as the gallery. Ask students to take a seat, half of them being in the fishbowl and half in the gallery. The students in the fishbowl will be responsible for discussing the questions. Leave one empty seat in the fishbowl so that students from the gallery can come and go as they have things to add. If a student in the gallery would like to participate in the discussion, they join in the fishbowl with an extra seat. Usually, about halfway through the discussion, ask the students in the gallery and fishbowl to switch spots so that every student has an opportunity to contribute to the discussion. As the facilitator of the discussion, you will need to create meaningful questions prior to the discussion.

Gallery Walks

In order to properly implement gallery walks, you will need poster-size sticky notes or posters with tape, markers, and small sticky notes. Depending on class size, you will divide students into small groups. In a class of 30, you might have six small groups of five each. However, if you have a small class of only eight, students could work in pairs to form four groups. Either way, determine your groups as it works best for your class size. Give each group a different section of the text as a focus. Instruct students in their small groups to determine the major points of the text or their major take-aways. Ask them to record this information on their large sticky note or poster. Once complete, they will hang their poster/sticky note on the wall. Once everyone has finished, the students begin the gallery walk with their small group. Instruct students to travel in their small groups and view each group's poster/sticky note. As they read over the information, ask each student to leave a comment on the poster/sticky note with a small sticky note note. This note can be a personal application, additional comment from the text, or another takeaway. After all posters/sticky notes are viewed, finish class by asking the groups to view the comments left for them on their original poster/sticky note and to share outcomes and findings with the class.

Thoughts, Questions, and Epiphanies

Rich discussions occur when implementing the thoughts, questions, and epiphanies (TQEs) discussion strategy. Start by asking the students to read the text prior to class discussion. Divide the students into small groups and ask them to discuss the text by including their thoughts—this can be subjective. Ask them to discuss any questions they might have regarding the text. These can be questions that need clarification or questions for deeper study. Ask the students to include epiphanies—any "aha" moments that they might have had while reading the text. Suggest the following stems to guide students' small group discussion:

What is your favorite quote?

Why would the author _____?

What questions do you have?

What notes did you take on the chapters?

How can this be applied to families and/or children?

List some favorite statements, insights, or questions.

Give the students about 15 minutes for discussion, asking the group to pick two of their most meaningful group TQEs. After the students have discussed in small groups, have a representative from each group write their two favorite TQEs on the board. After every group has recorded two TQEs, begin a whole-group discussion regarding the TQEs. Experience tells us that this method really ignites deep discussion and thinking.

Conver-stations

Conver-stations are a nice way to get students moving while conducting meaningful conversations. With conver-stations, students are divided up into small groups and each group is given a discussion question. After enough time has passed for students to develop a nice conversation about their discussion question, the group will appoint one to two students (depending on group size) to rotate to the next group. The new group members will begin discussing at their new station, sometimes bringing points from previous groups. After ample time has passed, the one to two more students move to the next station, typically group members who have not traveled yet. This way, the groups at each station are continually evolving and changing.

ACTIVITY 8.1: DISCUSSION STRATEGIES ASSESSMENTS

Identify various ways to assess each of the aforementioned discussion strategies.

Higher Order Thinking/Problem-Based Learning

Higher order thinking goes beyond rote learning and memorization, as it incorporates the advanced levels of Bloom's Taxonomy (Anderson & Krathwohl, 2001) and involves the neocortex (see Figure 8.3). Higher order thinking and problem-based strategies allow the learner to dig deeper and go beyond the surface to understand cause and effect, implications of an action, and create possible solutions.

Various teaching strategies that relate to Bloom's Taxonomy can be traced to various parts of the brain, as documented by research in neuroscience (Kaufer, 2011). For example, lower levels of learning use the hippocampus. Teaching strategies that involve the hippocampus focus on understanding and remembering.

Higher level learning involves the neocortex of the brain. These strategies can be classified as active and student centered and involve decision making, comparison, analysis, and creativity (Kaufer, 2011). **Problem-based learning** is also included under higher order thinking. It is a student-centered

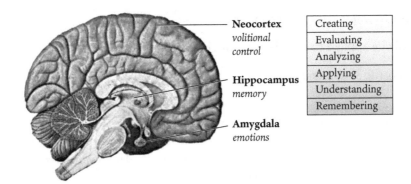

FIGURE 8.3 Bloom's Taxonomy, Teaching Strategies, and the Brain

strategy that involves the learners working in groups to solve an open-ended problem. Steps to problem-based learning involve (1) defining the problem, (2) identifying what content is needed to solve the problem, (3) identifying various ways to solve the problem, (4) finding solutions to the problem, and (5) reporting findings to the class (Nilson, 2010). The varied and repeated use of instructional strategies that encourage problem solving and higher order thinking skills will help provide a creative and dynamic classroom (Smith, 2012).

FCS has included higher order thinking skills, discussion, and problem-based learning in the profession since its beginning. Ellen Swallow Richards founded the discipline in 1899 on the premise of improving quality of life for individuals, families, and communities by using in-depth reasoning and understanding of concepts that enabled the learner to solve real-world problems, including those related to health and wellness, family relationships, child guidance, interpersonal communication, consumer economics, and career goals (Swafford & Rafferty, 2016).

ACTIVITY 8.2: APPLICATION OF STRATEGIES THAT STIMULATE AREAS OF THE BRAIN

Review Figure 8.3. Select a course standard from a program of study in FCS content in your state. Identify strategies that involve specific portions of the brain. Analyze how these support the hippocampus or the neocortex. Be prepared to share with your peers.

Case Studies

Using **case studies** encourages problem-based learning, as students are given a situation that provides the opportunity for them to explore how the content they have covered in class applies to the situation. Case studies can be used in group work or with an individual and provide the learner with opportunities to use analytical skills and discuss outcomes with active engagement.

SPOTLIGHT: EXAMPLE OF HIGHER ORDER THINKING USING PROBLEM-BASED LEARNING

An FCS educator plans a lecture addressing obesity that includes a PowerPoint on portion control, along with an activity on USDA MyPlate. To incorporate higher order thinking and problem-based learning, the educator expands upon this lesson to include a project. The learners, placed in heterogeneous groups, are required to research and discuss the correlation of factors impacting obesity, such as socioeconomic levels, racial and ethnicity factors, age and gender factors, and activity levels across the life span. The learners research how public policy addresses obesity causes and prevention. These activities require the learners to read, evaluate, listen to viewpoints, and analyze the complex underlying principles impacting obesity in modern society. Learners apply the knowledge and skills learned through this lesson by addressing nutritional needs in life. Critical thinking, synthesis, and evaluation are required for the learners to accurately and successfully help change an individual's dietary and exercise habits (Swafford & Rafferty, 2016).

Academic Integration

Academic integration incorporates math, sciences, social studies, engineering, English, technology, art, and other disciplines with CTE content for the purpose of improving the quality of student learning. Why integrate other academics into FCS lesson plans? The Perkins Acts requires academic integration in CTE programs as an indicator of quality programs; therefore, funding is increased when a program demonstrates academic integration in reports. Furthermore, The brain is a pattern seeker; therefore, experiencing new concepts in relation to more than one area allows neurons and synapsis to generalize the content. Students learn more quickly and easily in situations of contextual learning. In other words, academic integration highlights the sciences, technology, engineering, arts, and math in FCS content.

Academic integration may be accomplished by either team teaching with other educators or by integrating another discipline within the lesson. During team teaching, two or more educators representing different academic disciplines align course standards and/or curricula to teach concepts. When integrating another discipline, an educator incorporates an authentic problem from a career field that requires an understanding of an academic concept to solve. Projects usually work well with both types of approaches, as learners are required to conduct research, use reason to solve problems, and plan, organize, and present information (Bottoms & Sharpe, 1996). It can also serve as recruitment for FCS courses in various programs of study when working with other educators. It is easy to incorporate English, language arts, math, biology, and chemistry into the FCS curriculum.

SPOTLIGHT: FCS EXPERIENCE OF ACADEMIC INTEGRATION

By Melinda Swafford, PhD

My experience with academic integration with other educators usually involved projects. My students and I collaborated with the humanities teacher with a Greek Feast that was planned. I was covering foreign foods in a nutrition and foods course. During this project, my students converted recipes to feed large groups; they gained knowledge and skills when they were exposed to Greek food customs and preparation techniques, and they demonstrated and explained scientific principles of food safety and sanitation to others when a goat was roasted with a spit. Social and emotional skills were also addressed as students collaborated with students from another class. My students were exposed to Greek culture, which included Greek drama, and apparel. The quinceañera event was also an opportunity to include academic integration, as it exposed the learners to the Hispanic culture of food, dance, and celebrations. See Chapter 2 for details on quinceañeras.

In another example, my students collaborated with the drama program for several years on a dinner theater production. The drama teacher and I split the profits from the plays to use as funding for our classes. During this activity, my students planned a menu that supported the play, converted recipes to feed larger numbers, prepared the food for the event, served the patrons who attended the play, and cleaned up after the meal. The following day both classes met together to reflect on the activity.

While teaching social health to eighth-grade students, I planned an activity during a consumer education learning segment that had students determine which brand of popcorn had the lowest percentage of kernels that did not pop. The result would let them know which brand of popcorn was the better value. Students were divided into groups. Each group had a particular brand of popcorn. Popcorn popped according to directions. Total kernels that popped were counted, and total kernels that did not pop were counted—a percentage was determined. Each group presented the data. Better value in popcorn was determined.

During a residency observation, I evaluated an FCS resident student (student teacher) who planned and presented a lesson for the interior design class entitled International Design. The course standard was that students will assess current housing trends and issues. The lesson she presented was an excellent example of integrating concepts of geography into an FCS lesson, as well as providing various research-based strategies in the lesson.

For direct instruction, the FCS resident presented an outline of each area being discussed with students. Students were also provided a list of popular trends from each area/country. Students were required to take notes. Tactile samples were provided of some fabrics, wall coverings, and flooring. Pictures were also projected for visual learners. For supervised practice, the students, using laptops, participated in an online shopping trip. The groups shared the various furnishings, accessories, and backgrounds that are available for purchase in the United States from particular countries with classmates during class. The FCS resident student monitored cooperative groups and provided assistance and feedback when needed. For independent practice and for closure, the students were provided a map of the world. Students were to locate the following countries: China, France, Madagascar, Cuba, Chile, India, and Afghanistan. They were to label each country and identify each country's design trend and/or product.

Differentiated Instruction

One requirement to receive Perkins funding mandates that FCS educators provide instruction that meets the needs of students with exceptionalities and those for whom English is a second language. This requirement meets the needs of our country in preparing a quality workforce, but ultimately, it is an ethical action to provide for the educational needs of all students. An academically responsive classroom incorporates differentiated instruction. Please see Chapter 2 for content on serving students with diverse needs.

Differentiated instruction provides a means of creating a learning environment that is accessible for all individuals (Swafford & Giordano, 2017), as it challenges the notion that all students learn the same content the same way (Tomlinson, 1999). Although the practice dates back to earlier times, owing to the Education for Handicapped Children Act (P.L.94-142), the term has become more commonly used since the reauthorization of the Individuals with Disabilities Act 2004 and response to intervention (Fisher et al., 2013; RTI, n.d.). Differentiated instruction uses the same curriculum for all students but modifies the learning tasks and/or outcomes while providing a variety of strategies, as well as accommodation and modifications in the areas of content, process, assessment, and environment.

Content

Curriculum content and materials are often easy to accommodate (Broemmel et al., 2016). To differentiate instruction in the content, it is important that educators know their students. This can be accomplished by having learners complete a learning style and/or interest inventory. It is also important to view student records and attend individualized education program meetings. All this information will allow you to identify learners' strengths, preferred styles of learning, and recommended adaptations and modifications. "Indeed, unsuccessful, unmotivated students have experienced academic growth when exposed to multifaceted intervention and techniques" (Stanford, 2003, p. 81). Next, review course standards to identify content learners should master. Once content is identified, incorporate pretests to assess prior knowledge and skills. Class time is precious and should not be used for content that is already known (Swafford & Giordano, 2017).

Process

To differentiate instruction during the process, use a variety of cooperative group activities with heterogeneous members that will encourage learners to use their strengths. Use visual and verbal cues to enhance recall. **Task analysis,** or breaking down the content and/or outcomes into small steps, may help with comprehension, application, and analysis (Wheeler & Richey, 2005). Frequently posed higher order thinking questions encourage thinking at various levels and keep learners challenged. Make sure to have content in a learner's native language for an English language learner student or pair a student with one who speaks the specific language (Beecher et al., 2015). If one learner needs a larger print, make all the handouts in larger print. It will save you time, and no one will be identified as being different.

Assessment

Differentiated instruction applies to assessment, as learners may demonstrate mastery in various ways, some of which are less conventional when accommodations are needed (Swafford & Giordano, 2017).

For example, a student with a learning disability in written expression or a physical disability that prevents them from writing or using a word processor may demonstrate mastery of content orally. A student who has a learning disability in reading comprehension or visual acuity may have difficulty with a long assessment of 20 matching or true-false statements. Instead, formulate the assessment in groups of five true-false or five matching. This will make the assessment less overwhelming for the learner. See Chapter 11 for more information on assessments.

Learning Environment

To differentiate instruction in the learning environment, plan for time, space, and storage of materials. During labs, projects, and workstations, not all learners will be working on the same activity at the same time. Have planned routines so learners may access needed materials without disruption to others (Swafford & Giordano, 2017). Plan time for one-on-one help or opportunities to redo work if needed.

Providing accommodations and modifications through differentiated instruction in planning, implementing, assessment, and the learning environment is essential in teaching. Differentiated instruction strategies ensure that all students, regardless of learning style, ability, disability, and/or language barriers, can be successful in the FCS classroom. These practices should be embraced by all educators.

Involving Community in the Classroom

Individuals throughout the community can provide another strategy for the classroom. Community and family involvement is a sign of a successful school (O'Brien, 2012). Involving the community in the classroom is a vehicle for implementing the FCS body of knowledge (BOK; Swafford et al., 2015). Bronfreenbrenner's ecological theory, a component of the FCS BOK, stresses the importance of understanding the impact of multiple environmental layers on the individual, as well as the reciprocal relationships among individuals and their various environments (Swafford et al., 2015). For a review of the FCS BOK and Bronfreenbrenner's ecological theory, see Chapter 1.

According to Bronfreenbrenner's ecological theory, the stronger the linkage, the more influence the layer may have on the microsystem. A strong relationship between schools and local communities works to meet the needs that often are beyond what the school can provide for the students. Community collaborations may come from businesses, religious organizations, senior's groups, cultural groups, government agencies, and universities (Ramsey, 2014). These collaborations may provide support to educators in curriculum, training (Ramsey, 2014), guest speakers, field trips, school adoption programs, practicum/internship placements, and membership on various councils (Ramsey, 2014). Furthermore, involving the FCS classroom with local communities addresses a quality indicator of Perkins's requirements for CTE programs.

Ramsey's (2014) study demonstrated the importance of school-community collaboration. Ramsey found in her qualitative case study of a rural school district in the southeast that schools benefited from various types of school-community partnerships. In the school district examined, community partners would "adopt" a school. In doing so, they contributed to the schools in various ways. Ramsey found that the types of agencies that adopted schools and their interactions varied.

For example, a successful fast-food chain adopted three schools in one community and provided food, gift cards to students and faculty, and donated various items. Another school was adopted by a church. The congregation volunteered time with students—tutoring, eating lunch with at-risk students, and their building skills—and built a pavilion that could be used as an outdoor classroom. An elementary school was adopted by a nursing home. This was an especially enduring school/community relationship, as the children would often visit for various activities, such as parades, chorus singing, and special group readings. The interactions between the residents and students were beneficial to each, as they were emotionally and socially valuable interactions. The nursing home made donations to the school as well.

SUMMARY

This chapter contains content on a variety of strategies used to teach concepts in FCS courses and enhance student engagement. In teacher-directed strategies, the learner takes on a more passive role in learning as the content comes directly from the educator. Student-directed strategies promote student engagement, as they enhance the relevance of the content to the real world. The use of research-based instructional strategies, academic integration, and differentiated instruction is mandated by legislation to make education equitable for all learners. To further student engagement, FCS educators should incorporate a variety of strategies into their repertoire when presenting content.

KEY TERMS

Rote learning	Student-directed strategies
Contextual learning	Flipped classrooms
Direct instruction	Teacher-directed strategies
Academic integration	Differentiated instruction
Problem-based learning	Task analysis
Jigsaw-style assignment	Think-pair-share
Response to intervention	Think aloud
Active homework	Case studies

QUESTIONS AND ACTIVITIES

1. Research the strategies in each group. Summarize each strategy and indicate how to use each strategy in an FCS classroom to teach a course standard.

   a. Games, case studies, journals
   b. Sole play, simulations, debate
   c. DVD, charts, graphic organizers

2. Select a course standard and summarize how to incorporate problem-based/higher order thinking skills in the supervised and independent practice of the lesson.

3. Write a paragraph on the benefits of and how you plan to include the community in your classroom.

4. Read the pdf about the Learning Network by visiting the link https://flippedlearning.org/wp-content/uploads/2016/07/FLIP_handout_FNL_Web.pdf Explain the benefits of flipped learning. Identify problems with flipped learning. Brainstorm with peers on how to address the problems.

5. How is a think aloud a form of modeling? Explain when it is best to physically model something versus a think aloud.

6. Research some educational websites such as Edutopia or the IRIS center by Vanderbilt and make a diagram of how feedback and praise are different.

7. Conduct a search to locate a case study to support a course standard in FCS content.

REFERENCES

Anderson, L. W., & Krathwohl, D. R. (2001). *A taxonomy for learning, teaching, and assessing: A revision of Bloom's taxonomy of educational objectives.* Longman.

Aronson, E. (1978). *The jigsaw classroom.* SAGE Publications.

Auster, E. R., & Wylie, K. K. (2006). Creating active learning in the classroom: A systematic approach. *Journal of Management Education, 30*(2), 333–353.

Beecher, L., Artigliere, M., Patterson, D. K., & Spatzer, A. (2015). Differentiated instruction for English language learners as "variation on a theme." *Middle School Journal, 43*(3), 14–21. https://doi.org/10.1080/00940771.2012.11461807

Bottoms, G., & Sharpe, D. (1996). *Teaching for understanding through integration of academic and technical education.* Southern Regional Education Board.

Broemmel, A. D., Jordan, J., & Whitsett, B. M. (2016). *Learning to be teacher leaders: A framework for assessment, planning, and instruction.* Routledge.

Buijs, M., & Admiraal, W. (2013). Homework assignments to enhance student engagement in secondary education. *European Journal of Psychology of Education, 28*(3), 767–779.

Burns, M. (2010). Response-to-intervention research: Is the sum of the parts as great as the whole? *Perspective on Language and Literacy, 36*(2). http://www.rtinetwork.org/component/content/article/10/293-response-to-intervention-research-is-the-sum-of-the-parts-as-great-as-the-whole

Centers for Disease Control and Prevention. (2021). *Rethink your drink.* https://www.cdc.gov/healthy-weight/healthy_eating/drinks.html

Clemson University. (2021). *Evidence based teaching strategies.* Office of Teaching Effectiveness and Innovation. https://www.clemson.edu/otei/evidence-based.html

Cohn, D. A., Ghahramani, Z., & Jordan, M. I. (1996). Active learning with statistical models. *Journal of Artificial Intelligence Research, 4*, 129–145.

College and Career Readiness and Success. (2013). *How career and technical education can help students be college and career ready: A primer.* American Institutes for Research.

Corno, L., & Mandinach, E. B. (2004). What we have learned about student engagement in the past twenty years. *Big Theories Revisited, 4,* 299–328.

Eren, O., & Henderson, D. J. (2008). The impact of homework on student achievement. *The Econometrics Journal, 11*(2), 326–348.

Felder, R. M., & Brent, R. (2009). Active learning: An introduction. *ASQ Higher Education Brief, 2*(4), 1–5.

Fisher, D., Frey, N., & Kroener, J. (2013). High quality supports for students with disabilities. *Principal Leadership, 14*(3), 56–59.

Flipped Learning Network Hub. (2014, March 12). *Definition of flipped learning.* https://flippedlearning. org/definition-of-flipped-learning/

Flynn, A. E., & Klein, J. D. (2001). The influence of discussion groups in a case-based learning environment. *Educational Technology Research and Development, 49*(3), 71–86.

Franklin, B. (n.d.). *Benjamin Franklin autobiography famous quotes and life sayings.* Quotes Charger. https:// quotescharger.blogspot.com/2016/03/benjamin-franklin-autobiography-famous.html

Gall, M. D., & Gillett, M. (1980). The discussion method in classroom teaching. *Theory into Practice, 19*(2), 98–103.

Gilles, R. M. (2008). The effects of cooperative learning on junior high school students' behaviors, discourse and learning during a science-based learning activity. *School Psychology International, 29*(3), 328–347.

Griffith, P. L., & Laframboise, K. (1997). The structures and patterns of case method talk: What our students taught us. *Action in Teacher Education, 18*(4), 10–22.

Kaddoura, M. (2013). Think pair share: A teaching learning strategy to enhance students' critical thinking. *Educational Research Quarterly, 36*(4), 3–24.

Kaufer, D. (2011). *Neuroscience and how students learn.* Berkley Graduate Division. http://gsi.berkeley.edu/ gsi-guide-contents/learning-theory-research/neuroscience/

Killian, S. (2014). *10 evidence-based teaching strategies—the core list.* Evidence-Based Teaching. https:// www.evidencebasedteaching.org.au/evidence-based-teaching-strategies/

Killian, S. (2015). *8 strategies Robert Marzano & John Hattie agree on evidence based teaching.* Evidence-Based Teaching. http://www.evidencebasedteaching.org.au/robert-marzano-vs-john-hattie/

Larson, B. E. (2000). Classroom discussion: A method of instruction and a curriculum outcome. *Teaching and Teacher Education, 16*(5–6), 661–677.

Levin, B. B. (1995). Using the case method in teacher education: The role of discussion and experience in teachers thinking about cases. *Teaching and Teacher Education, 11*(1), 63–79.

LSU AgCenter. (n.d.) *4-H How to give method demonstration.* https://www.lsuagcenter.com/MCMS/ RelatedFiles/%7BD4E91CD0-EA91-4041-9326-C2BBF3694450%7D/How-to-Give-a-Method-Demonstration.pdf

Merriam Webster. (2021). Rote. In *Merriam-Webster.com dictionary.* Retrieved August 31, 2021 from https://lsuagcenter.com/portals/4h

Miller, G. (1990).The assessment of clinical skills/competence/performance. *Academic Medicine, 65*(9), 63–67.

Nilson, L. B. (2010). *Teaching at its best: A research-based resource for college instructors* (2nd ed.). Jossey-Bass.

O'Brien, A. (2012, March 21). *The importance of community involvement in schools: It is all about making connections.* Eutopia. https://www.edutopia.org/blog/community-parent-involvement-essential-anne-obrien

Payne, R., & Tucker, B. (2008). *Research-based strategies: Narrowing the achievement gap for under-resourced students.* ha! Process, Inc.

Prince, M. (2004). Does active learning work? A review of the research. *Journal of Engineering Education, 93*(3), 223–231.

Ramsey, E. (2014). *Perceptions of school partnerships: Connections uniting schools and community agencies* [Unpublished manuscript]. Department of Curriculum and Instruction, Tennessee Technological University.

Richey, L. (2013). *Class ground rules for discussion* [Unpublished work].

Richmond, E. (2014, April 2). *Student centered learning.* Stanford Center for Opportunity Policy in Education. https://edpolicy.stanford.edu/news/articles/1193

Room to Discover. (n.d.). *The 6 signs of a student-centered classroom.* https://roomtodiscover.com/student-centered-classroom/

Rosenshine, B., & Stevens, R. (1986). Teaching functions. In M. Wittrock (Ed.), *Handbook of research on teaching* (3rd ed., pp. 376–391). MacMillan.

Rowe, M. B. (1987). Using wait time to stimulate inquiry. In W. Wilen (Ed.), *Questions, questioning techniques, and effective teaching* (pp. 95–106). NEA Professional Library, National Education Association.

RTI Action Network. (n.d.) *What is RTI? A program of the National Center of Learning Disabilities.* http://www.rtinetwork.org/learn/what#:~:text=Response%20to%20Intervention%20(RTI)%20is,in%20special%20education%2C%20or%20both

Smith, B. P. (2012). Curriculum development standard for family and consumer sciences teachers. *Journal of Family and Consumer Sciences Education, 30*(1), 1–16. http://www.natefacs.org/JFCSE/v30no1/v30no1Smith.pd

Stanford, P. (2003). Multiple intelligence for every classroom. *Intervention in School and Clinic, 39*(2), 80–86. https://doi.org/10.1177/10534512030390020301

Swafford, M. D., & Dainty, H. T. (2009). Learning environment: Respecting diversity and exceptionality. *Journal of Family and Consumer Sciences Education, 27*(National Teacher Standards 4), 45–59. http://www.natefacs.org/JFCSE/v27Standards4/v27Standards4Swafford.pdf

Swafford M., & Giordano, K. (2017). Universal design: Ensuring success for all FCS students. *Journal of Family and Consumer Sciences, 109*(4), 47–52.

Swafford, M., & Rafferty, E. (2016). Universal design: Ensuring success for all FCS students. *Journal of Family and Consumer Sciences, 109*(4), 47–52.

Swafford, M., Ramsey, E., & Mullens, L. (2015). Family and consumer sciences body of knowledge promoting strong community alliances with public schools. *Journal of Family and Consumer Sciences, 107*(2), 18–22.

Tennessee Department of Education. (2019, February 8). *Early childhood education careers I (ECEC I).* https://www.bartlettschools.org/Curriculum/CTE/EarlyCEI.pdf

Tomlinson, C. A. (1999). Mapping a route toward differentiated instruction. *Educational Leadership, 57*(1), 12–16.

Wheeler, J. J,. & Richey, D. D. (2005). Understanding behavior in children and youth. In J. J. Wheeler & D. D. Richey (Eds.), *Behavior management: Principles and practices of positive behavior supports* (pp. 1–33). Person/Merrill/Prentice Hall.

Wilen, W. W. (2004). Refuting misconceptions about classroom discussion. *The Social Studies, 95*(1), 33–39.

Woodward, R. L., & Reid, C. S. (2019). You've got mail (and homework): Simple strategies for promoting student engagement with prelecture videos. *Journal of Chemical Education, 96*(9), 2055–2058.

Youatt, E. J., & Hitch, J. P. (2002). *Communicating family and consumer sciences: A guidebook for professionals.* Goodheart-Willcox Company, Inc.

Figure Credits

Planning and Implementing Labs and Other Action-Oriented Strategies

Hannah Upole, PhD; Elizabeth Ramsey, PhD, CFLE; Melinda Swafford, PhD; Samantha Hutson, PhD; and Caitlin Williams, MS

FIGURE 9.1 Culinary Arts in Action

Chapter 9 Objectives

Upon completion of the chapter, the learner should be able to

- identify the benefits of labs in Family and Consumer Science (FCS) education,
- discuss the importance of safety in relation to FCS labs,
- analyze effective strategies to keep students engaged during labs, and
- develop an activity to support specific course standards involving the following:
  - o nutrition/food labs or culinary arts
  - o housing and design

o   fashion and clothing production

o   early childhood education and careers

Introduction

Labs are an important aspect in the family and consumer science (FCS) classroom, as labs provide an opportunity for learners to be actively engaged in the concepts through synthesis and application. FCS career clusters of hospitality/tourism; architecture and construction; arts, audio/visual technology, and communication; and education and training rely heavily on the implementation of labs for learners to grasp needed concepts involved in appropriate career preparation. This active engagement allows learners to implement concepts that are difficult to grasp by only reading and through lecture. Providing a follow-up activity with labs provides an opportunity for additional higher order thinking and problem-based learning, as learners are able to reflect on the activity through synthesis and evaluation. This chapter includes content on how to plan strategies in various career cluster genres of FCS that promote student engagement. Preplanning that includes occupational safety concepts, correct use of equipment, planning sheets, and follow-up activities to enhance student learning will also be included.

Food Preparation Labs

Food preparation is directly related to the core concepts of the FCS body of knowledge (Nickols et al., 2009). Food fulfills a basic need, promotes wellness, and can build unity within a family. However, eating and tasting prepared food is more effective at engaging students than just studying it (Cheng et al., 2020). Education regarding food preparation is innately active. Programs of study in culinary arts, as well as nutrition and dietetics, include labs involving food preparation and service. While students need a foundational knowledge of nutrition, food safety, and sanitation, as well as basic food preparation skills, to safely navigate a laboratory setting, they benefit greatly from hands-on experiences that cement their knowledge and skills.

Furthermore, in our current world, it is also important to address and teach concepts of food sustainability and global interdependence as they relate to food preparation and management. Food preparation labs allow students to not only learn basic food preparation skills and the science behind food preparation but also to explore various cultures, learn teamwork skills, and explore controversial topics such as genetically modified foods and food insecurity (Ellis & Gruber Garvey, 2013). FCS educators have a unique opportunity to greatly impact the daily lives and routines of children and families through effectively teaching food preparation.

Safety and Sanitation

Before planning any food labs, it is important to begin with a unit on food safety and handling. Safety might include safe food handling, proper cooking temperatures, food thermometer usage, knife skills, dishwashing protocols, handwashing skills, and foodborne illness. To meet the requirements of career technical education (CTE), students must be tested on their safety knowledge. This exam is to be kept on file for 4 years and should indicate that the student passed the exam with a score of 100. There are many websites available that provide free resources on food safety and handling, such as the Food and Drug Administration (FDA), National Restaurant Association and ServSafe, and U.S. Department of Agriculture Food and Nutrition Service (2017).

Culinary Arts

FCS educators who add the additional endorsement of food production and management to their FCS licensure may teach Culinary Arts I–IV in the career cluster of hospitality and tourism. *Culinary arts* refers to preparing, presenting, and serving food (Hospitality Net, 2020). This is a growing field, as many individuals and families consume meals from various genres in the foodservice industry. Careers in culinary arts may range from catering and restaurants to food service establishments in cafeterias, hospitals, and/or food trucks.

According to the Tennessee Department of Education (2021a), culinary arts is an applied-knowledge program of study that prepares learners for careers as fast-food employees or in the culinary field as entry catering assistants or other entry-level food preparation/service employees and for post-secondary training by providing work experience in commercial food production and service. Upon completion of this program of study, proficient students will have knowledge of proper use and care of commercial equipment and food preparation tools, safety and sanitation, history and careers in food service and hospitality, food preparation skills, nutrition, dining room service, and food presentation. Learners will prepare a portfolio to document training. Learners will create a portfolio that documents training provided throughout the entire sequence of courses.

Culinary arts programs in high schools vary according to the needs, as some programs provide a restaurant that serves lunch for students, teachers, and administrators. Other culinary programs provide catering for the community and other special events. In addition to the focus on safety/sanitation and quality food, educators must also stress teamwork, time management, and service/food presentation.

Lab planning sheets and lab evaluation sheets are dependent on the type of facility of the culinary program and the type of food service provided by the program. Some school districts teach culinary arts in a traditional FCS classroom with individual food labs that are set up like individual kitchens in a home setting. Other school districts operate culinary arts programs in a commercial kitchen area with commercial equipment. Still other school districts do a combination of both.

Safety and Sanitation

As in all areas of food preparation, safety and sanitation are of high priority. In the occupational culinary art program, ServSafe is a food handlers' certification from the National Restaurant Association that signifies an individual has received comprehensive training in the prevention of foodborne illness and food allergies (Boston Food Safety, n.d.). Students who receive this certification must pass a comprehensive examination in best practices for preparing and serving food. Each FCS educator in culinary arts will have standards that must be followed in the lab. See the following Spotlight for a sample lab procedure document used in a culinary program.

SPOTLIGHT: EXAMPLE OF A HEALTH POLICY AND LAB PROCEDURES FOR CULINARY ARTS LAB

By Melinda Anderson, PhD, RD, LDN

Employee Health Policy Statement:

Beginning July 1, 2015, all food service establishments in the state of Tennessee are required to have an employee health policy. Ill food workers are a leading cause of foodborne illness outbreaks. An effective employee illness policy reduces the risk of food contamination by ill food workers.

Responsibility of Food Handlers

1. Report the following symptoms to the person in charge (PIC):
    *   Vomiting*, diarrhea*, jaundice, sore throat with fever, infected cuts or burns on hands or wrists
2. Report the following diagnosed illnesses to the PIC:
    *   Salmonella typhi (typhoid-like fever)
    *   Nontyphoidal salmonella
    *   Shigella spp. (causes shigellosis)
    *   E-coli 0157:H7
    *   Hepatitis A virus
    *   Norovirus

Note: Employees may not return to work until they have been asymptomatic for at least <u>24 hours</u>.

Responsibility of the PIC

1. Exclude all ill employees from the establishment while they have diarrhea and/or vomiting.
2. Appropriately exclude or restrict employees diagnosed with E.coli 0157:H7, salmonella, shigella, and/or hepatitis A.
3. Notify the local health department of any employee diagnosed with any of the illnesses listed above or exhibiting jaundice (yellowing of the eyes or skin).

COVID-19 Policy

All students entering the lab for the first time each week will answer the following questions and have their temperature taken with a no-touch thermometer.
*   Have you been in close contact with a confirmed case of COVID-19 in the past 14 days? (Note: This does not apply to medical personnel, first responders, or other individuals who encounter COVID-19 as part of their professional or caregiving duties while wearing appropriate personal protective equipment.)
*   Are you experiencing a cough, shortness of breath, or sore throat?

- Have you had a fever in the last 48 hours?
- Have you had a new loss of taste or smell?
- Have you had vomiting or diarrhea in the last 24 hours?

Any student who answers "yes" to any question should leave the lab immediately, call Health Services at 931-372-3320, and self-quarantine for the appropriate number of days. Students who exhibit any of these symptoms or answer "yes" to any of the questions must present evidence of a negative COVID-19 test before returning to the lab.

Face Coverings: All students participating in labs are required to wear an appropriate face covering or mask. There is no exception to this policy. State of Tennessee Health Department Restaurant guidelines require food service workers to wear a face covering (https://www.tn.gov/governor/covid-19/economic-recovery/restaurant-guidelines.html).

Uniform

The correct uniform for students in the lab is a clean shirt and pants with rubber-soled nonskid shoes. Male and Female students must have hair contained in a hair restraint and/or an approved hair covering. Male students with beards must wear a beard net. Approved hair coverings include hair net or bonnet, kerchief, or clean cap.

All students must wear a head covering and a clean apron or lab coat when working in the lab.

NOT PERMITTED: Sandals, flip-flops, or other shoes with straps are not permitted. Halter tops and shorts are not permitted. Dirty clothes, uncovered hair, excessive jewelry, excessive makeup, or perfume/cologne are not allowed.

Servers: The correct uniform for servers is a shirt with appropriate pants and closed-toe, rubber-soled shoes. A black apron is provided in the lab. Servers should also have their hair neatly styled, and long hair should be in a hair restraint. Managers should wear closed-toe, low-heeled shoes, no jewelry, and keep hair restrained.

All Students: Clean fingernails are essential, and nail polish/artificial nails are not permitted to be worn during any lab assignment. NO NAIL POLISH AT ANY TIME IS ALLOWED IN THE LAB. Servers should maintain clean, neatly groomed nails (male and female). Jewelry should be left at home: A plain wedding band is the only kind of ring permitted to be worn during lab assignments. DO NOT WEAR EARRINGS, NECKLACES, WATCHES, BRACELETS, OR RINGS OF ANY KIND in the lab.

Handwashing

It is essential that students follow correct handwashing procedures when working in the food lab. The instructor reserves the right to give a lab grade of 0 if a student willingly fails to observe the handwashing procedures.

Upon entering the lab for the first time, students should have hair coverings already in place and put on a clean apron or lab coat. Then wash hands thoroughly using hot water and soap. Always dry hands with paper towels, never dishcloths.

(Continued)

Hands should be washed again when

1. a student leaves the lab and returns;
2. a student coughs, or sneezes, or touches face or hair;
3. a student handles raw meat or eggs;
4. after every food preparation procedure is completed;
5. when going from dirty dishes to putting up clean dishes; or
6. any other time as instructed by manager or instructor.

Safety Procedures

- Never sit on tables or counters.
- Dish towels never go on the shoulder.
- Clean up spills immediately, and alert other students if the floor is wet.
- Always use dry potholders when handling hot pots or pans. Damp potholders will cause burns. Never use a dish towel to handle hot pots or pans.
- Always use a cutting board; never prepare food directly on the countertop or any other work surface.
- Use knives with extreme caution.
- No Bare Hand Contact With Ready-to-Eat Foods.

Miscellaneous

Backpacks and personal items should be stored in lockers in the restrooms or on hooks in the kitchen; do not leave on the floor.

Always use a separate, clean spoon for tasting. After tasting, do not stir or return the tasting utensil to the common pot or plate of food; put it in the dishwasher to be cleaned.

Handle glasses at their base; never put fingers inside glass to carry it. Do not carry clean glasses by putting hand inside the rim.

Handle clean silverware by its handle; do not put hands on the end of the silverware that will be used for eating.

Handle clean plates on the edges to minimize contact with hands.

Consequences for Noncompliance

Students should realize that the foods lab is a professional kitchen, and food safety and sanitation guidelines will be enforced. The 2017 FDA Food Code and the ServSafe course will be the source of food sanitation regulations (http://www.fda.gov/Food/GuidanceRegulation/RetailFoodProtection/FoodCode/).

The instructor reserves the right to give a grade of "0" or "F" for the lab or for the course to any student who knowingly fails to comply with these guidelines

I have read and understood the above foods lab guidelines. I agree to comply with these guidelines, as well as adhere to the highest food safety and sanitation techniques while working in the Quantity Foods/Friday Cafe Lab. I understand the consequence for noncompliance is a grade of "o" for the Lab or "F" for the course following Tennessee Technological University (TTU) academic misconduct procedures.

Students will sign the Food Lab Safety form as documentation of their understanding of these guidelines and consequences.

The Lab Experience

FCS educators in both culinary arts and nutrition and foods labs are responsible for planning a safe, applicable, and informative lab experience. This includes creating labs that align with the course standards while considering the ability of the students, class size, available equipment, and food budget. Oftentimes, students will work in groups during food labs. This can serve several purposes. First, it can help the teacher control food cost if a group of students prepares a recipe, as opposed to individual students. Second, in addition to being cost-effective, it is time efficient. For example, each group may be provided with a recipe or task or may choose to prepare a specific, teacher-approved item. After preparing the item or completing the task, one student is responsible for teaching the class about their group's work. Taste-testing stations can be set up to allow each student in the class to gain knowledge of and taste multiple recipes. In addition, this provides the student who is the spokesperson for their group with an added learning opportunity.

Students learn in various modalities from various lab-based experiences. Jones and Rathman (2020) suggest providing students with content-specific videos that directly relate to lab experiences. This not only re-teaches the content but also may help those students who are visual learners feel more confident in the lab setting. In addition, Ebert-May et al. (2005) suggest employing **active homework** for classroom or lab preparation. Researching and providing a recipe that will align with the week's content is an example of engaging in active homework. The instructional method helps students apply and analyze the subject matter to increase understanding (Ebert-May et al., 2005). In addition, it serves as a method of formative assessment for the instructor. For example, if the recipe submitted by the student contains gluten during a gluten-free lab, the instructor can then re-teach this concept. In addition, this technique requires little commitment relative to the benefit for the student while increasing student engagement and accountability (Ebert-May et al., 2005). If a student is responsible for locating a recipe that their group will prepare and eat, they are likely to be more motivated to find a suitable option.

Forming Lab Partners

Prior to labs, educators need to group the learners into heterogeneous groups. This process takes time and much thought, as it may influence the success of the lab. Heterogeneous groups simulate real-world experiences, as the learners who make up the groups are different in abilities and strengths.

Students of all abilities generally benefit from heterogeneous grouping, as lower level students are able to follow leaders at level, and above level students are able to gain another perspective in the learning process and become leaders (Mugabi, 2019). Furthermore, heterogeneous groups provide an opportunity for the Vygotsky zone of proximal development and scaffolding to occur naturally (Lynch, 2021).

As an FCS educator, on the first day of class as I was providing an overview of the course, I distributed each student a note card. I instructed my learners to identify three classmates they would like to work with in a group setting. I promised them only one student. During the next few weeks, I carefully observed the interactions between students and became familiar with the strengths of each student.

Since my food labs had three home-style kitchens, I would put learners in two groups of three or four depending on class size. In the state of Tennessee, CTE courses are not to go above an average of 25. For food preparation labs, I would have a 2-day lab with one group working on supporting group activities while the other group did lab work. The next day, the groups would switch roles.

An educator may also use the same grouping of learners for other collaborative activities used in the class. For case studies and other group activities, a group of three students works well. In the case of groups that are four or more, one could divide the groups in half.

The Lab Planning Process

A key component in conducting a successful lab, no matter the content being taught, is planning. Commonly, the content of the course is taught, students are prepared for the lab experience, students complete the lab, then they are given the opportunity to reflect on the lab experience in some way. One method of ensuring these criteria are met is by using **lab planning sheets**. Allowing students to actively participate in the planning process increases their engagement in the lab (Ebert-May et al., 2005). For example, when preparing a food for lab, the planning sheets should contain, at a minimum, teaching objectives, pre-lab work, a list of recipes and tasks to be completed in the lab and who is responsible for each, a list of equipment, a list of necessary ingredients (a market order), cost of ingredients, and post-lab work, which includes evaluation of procedures and food items, as well as cost/serving. FCS educators may allow students to select a recipe that coordinates with the topic of the lab (e.g., muffins) or offer the learners a choice. The educator may provide options of recipes that coordinate with the topic of the lab (e.g., different types of muffins—apple cinnamon, banana, oatmeal raisin, or jelly muffin). Each lab group could select a choice.

Monitoring Food Labs

When planning food labs, it is crucial to structure the lab so that students succeed and unruly behavior is minimized. As stated before, the educator needs to consider the ability of the learner, available time, available equipment, a grouping of the students, and the budget. Careful planning results in lab success. We highly recommend that educators have learners complete in detail lab planning sheets and use them for all labs. Prior to the lab, learners complete the lab handout as a group by assigning each student a role and specifying the team members, recipe, kitchen number, yield of the recipe, ingredients needed, cost of ingredients, equipment needed from the supply table, equipment needed from the kitchen, and task assignment. The educator will evaluate the plan sheet, provide feedback, and make the shopping list from each lab planning sheet submitted. This will help control food costs, as well as ensure that each student has an active role in the lab. Please see Figure 9.2 for an example of a lab planning sheet for a nutrition and foods lab.

Kitchen Manager: _____

- Supervise all work
- Retrieve and return extra equipment
- Set table
- Clean counter
- Inspect kitchen at end of period

Cook: _____

- Get out all equipment
- Prepare main recipe
- Measure and mix
- Put away all equipment

Assistant Cook: _____

- Get ingredients from the supply table
- Help cook or make second recipe
- Dry dishes

Dishwasher: _____

- Get out towels, washcloths, potholders
- Fill dishpan and get out drainer
- Wash dishes as they are used
- Clear table, scrape dishes

Assistant Kitchen Manager: _____

- Dry Dishes
- Fold towels, etc. from dryer and put away in kitchen
- Clean tables and floors
- Put away folders
- Check off roles (this sheet)
- Empty soiled laundry into washer
- Fill in for absences

FIGURE 9.2 Kitchen Roles Plan Sheet

The time available for labs is dependent upon the number of students in the class, the number of food labs in the department, and the school schedule. In larger classes, educators may divide the class and have 2 days of the lab for one topic. For example, Group 1 (one half of the class) participates in the lab while Group 2 (the other half of the class) participates in a group project that supports the topic of the lab. The next day, repeat the process with Group 1 working on the project and Group 2 participating in the lab. This is how food labs are typically conducted in public schools on 90-minute block schedules. Other FCS programs have enough food labs that allow each student to participate, and the entire lab can be completed in 1 day. Still other FCS programs have 45-minute class periods, which may result in food labs being 3 or more days.

Lab Evaluation

Evaluation is another key component of successful food labs. Be clear with students about how they will be evaluated. As students work in their groups, use the example in Figure 9.3 as a checklist, or one like it, and monitor student effort. Actively monitoring students by perusing the room will keep student behaviors on task and encourage engagement with the instructor as you move throughout the room. Some labs may require product evaluation for quality food preparation techniques for items such as muffins, pie crust, biscuits, or yeast breads.

Food evaluation sheets and product evaluation sheets can be found in ancillaries from various publishers' textbooks used to teach the course Nutrition and Foods or from websites like UEN.org or the Family and Consumer Sciences Facebook page.

Kitchen: (insert kitchen label here, Example Kitchen 1)					
Followed lab demonstrations	5	4	3	2	1
Listened to verbal directions	5	4	3	2	1
Read directions/recipes	5	4	3	2	1
Performed assigned lab plan duties	5	4	3	2	1
Adhered to lab safety rules and procedures	5	4	3	2	1
Effectively worked together to finish in a timely manner	5	4	3	2	1
Product meets expectations	5	4	3	2	1
Proper etiquette and manners	5	4	3	2	1
Comments:					
Total points:					

FIGURE 9.3 Lab Evaluation Sheet

Each lab is worth 25 points.

Criteria	6	4-5	2-3	0-1
Written lab completed	All (100%): • Pre-lab assignments, • <u>All</u> handouts provided in class, whether informational or to be completed, • Lab time assignments (including questions/tables/charts not completed by your Kitchen), and • Post-lab questions are included.	Most (80-99%): • Pre-lab assignments, • handouts provided in class, whether informational or to be completed, • Lab time assignments (including questions/tables/charts not completed by your Kitchen), and • Post-lab questions are included.	Some (40-80%): • Pre-lab assignments, • handouts provided in class, whether informational or to be completed, • Lab time assignments (including questions/tables/charts not completed by your Kitchen), and • Post-lab questions are included.	Very Little (<40%): • Pre-lab assignments, • handouts provided in class, whether informational or to be completed, • Lab time assignments (including questions/tables/charts not completed by your Kitchen), and • Post-lab questions are included.
	13	**10-12**	**5-9**	**0-4**
Team work & performance	Students completed tasks as needed. Actively engaged with team members. Volunteered to help where needed.	Students completed tasks as needed. Engaged with team members. Did not volunteer to help complete tasks outside of those assigned to him/her.	Students completed some tasks as needed. Did not engage with team members. Did not volunteer to help complete tasks outside of those assigned to him/her.	Students did not complete tasks as needed. Did not engage with team members. Did not volunteer to help complete tasks outside of those assigned to him/her.
	Final product was as intended.	Final product was mostly as intended; students recognized where errors occurred.	Final product was mostly as intended; students were unable to recognize where errors occurred.	Final product was not as intended; students were unable to recognize where errors occurred.
	Participated in teaching classmates about tasks completed in their kitchen.	Somewhat participated in teaching classmates about tasks completed in their kitchen.	Had to be encouraged by the teacher to participate in teaching classmates about tasks completed in their kitchen.	Did not participate in teaching classmates about tasks completed in their kitchen.
	6	**4-5**	**2-3**	**0-1**
Safety, sanitation	Student was dressed according to lab procedure guidelines.	Students did not adhere to, or forgot, one aspect of appropriate lab attire.	Students did not adhere to, or forgot, two aspects of appropriate lab attire.	Students did not adhere to, or forgot, more than two aspects of appropriate lab attire.
	Students demonstrated correct and safe use of kitchen equipment.	Students demonstrated correct and safe use of kitchen equipment. Only one correction was needed.	Students demonstrated correct and safe use of kitchen equipment. Multiple corrections needed.	Did not use equipment in the correct manner.
	Students adhered to all sanitation guidelines.	Students adhered to most sanitation guidelines; only one correction needed.	Students adhered to most sanitation guidelines; more than one correction needed.	Students did not adhere to most sanitation guidelines.

FIGURE 9.4 Culinary Lab Evaluation Rubric

Housing and Design

The field of housing and design contributes significantly to basic human interactions, as the housing unit provides many benefits to the individual, from the economic impact of homeownership to the memories that are formed beneath that roof (Femenías & Hagbert, 2013). Beyond the symbolism of the housing unit, many homeowners also find satisfaction in maintaining and improving their homes by creating living environments that support their lifestyles and increase their happiness with the look, and function, of their homes (Rohe et al., 2001). Then there is the movement to establish more environmentally friendly building practices and toward developing more sustainable home design, such as the green building movement (Reynolds, 2021). FCS educators have the opportunity to help impact the lives of individuals, families, and communities by instructing students on the effective development and use of the built environment.

Students in housing and design courses need the opportunity to develop foundational knowledge and thorough instruction using the lowest levels of Bloom's up to the highest level of taxonomy—creation (Armstrong, 2016). As housing and design is a constantly evolving field, it is imperative that students understand the foundational aspects of the field while also being encouraged to explore their personal creativity through analysis and evaluation. One valuable way to achieve this style of learning is through the use of laboratory activities, as lab-based activities combine theoretical content with hands-on experiential learning (Abdulwahed & Nagy, 2009).

As housing and design typically encompass an interest in architecture and interior design, students should begin with lessons that illustrate the concepts of visual art, specifically those that teach the elements of design—color, line, shape, form, space, and texture—in addition to the principles of design—balance, emphasis, scale/proportion, rhythm, and harmony (Evans & Thomas, 2012; Lovett, 1998; McClurg-Genevese, 2005). At their core, the elements and principles of design are rooted in understanding and recall, as they have defined parameters that must be identified properly to then be used in analysis or evaluation.

Anchor Charts

Educators can also implement elements of analysis and creativity in this foundational learning through the use of a helpful teaching tool: the anchor chart. **Anchor charts** support instruction by "anchoring" learning through situating thinking as a visual process (Mulvahill, 2020). In their most traditional sense, anchor charts are created at the classroom level, where teachers and students work together to create a visual representation of the most important content and relevant learning strategies for remembering that content. These charts do not have to be complex. In fact, they should focus on the most important content and convey it in new, visual ways that promote classroom engagement and recall of the most important course content, such as the example of an anchor chart for teaching secondary color formation in Figure 9.5. The charts may then be displayed around the lab for the duration of a lesson or throughout the semester, whichever is deemed most appropriate to learning (Murray, 2014).

Anchor charts can also be constructed on the individual level, through a series of handouts, where students are provided with basic prompts on a topic and then asked to express their learning in a visual format. When teaching the elements and principles of design, individual and classroom anchor charts on topics such as the color wheel, types of shape and form, and the importance of emphasis in a design allow for students to recall important facts about each topic while also encouraging creativity through the development of unique charts by each student or class.

SPOTLIGHT: EXAMPLE USING AN ANCHOR CHART

An anchor chart that can be used for teaching the basic elements of design is a simple color wheel. In this lab, students are presented with a worksheet that displays the basic 12-hue wheel, which is used to demonstrate the primary, secondary, and tertiary colors, in addition to color schemes, such as analogous or complementary colorways. Underneath the color wheel, students could be presented with a series of furniture pieces or interior design items, such as a sofa or a vase, then prompted to use their knowledge to add color to these pieces. One task may be to use a primary and secondary color to create a complementary color scheme on a pillow. The students may then select any primary-secondary complementary color relationship to complete this task, in addition to drawing their own patterns on the pillow. Another task may be to assign one color, such as the primary hue red, and ask students to create a monochromatic mural that could be featured as an accent wall in a bedroom. Students can then label their creations with the appropriate color schemes and names to provide a secondary level of information recall. The sheets can then be kept in the lab space for further practice with the color wheel and can even be re-created in future activities once further knowledge has been obtained.

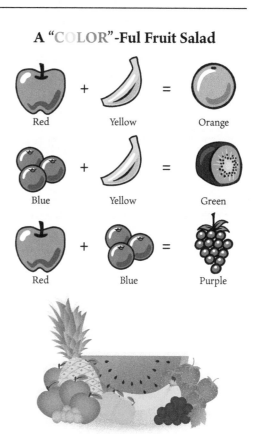

A "COLOR"-Ful Fruit Salad

FIGURE 9.5 Anchor Chart Used to Teach the Formation of Secondary Colors Using Primary Colors

The use of anchor charts for foundational knowledge allows students to cocreate their learning environment in a format that makes sense for their individual schemas. By implementing a higher level Bloom's activity—individual creativity—educators are also able to help students begin to think about the ways to take this foundational knowledge and integrate it into their own ideas.

Application and Analysis of Content

Once students have gained a solid foundational knowledge of design elements and principles, they are then able to move into applying and analyzing that content. In the housing and design lab environment, this can be achieved in a variety of ways. In lessons focused on architectural structure and form, students can be challenged to use their knowledge of design elements other than color to construct architectural features made of spaghetti noodles and marshmallows. See the Spotlight titled "Spaghetti and Marshmallow Buildings." This simple activity asks students to apply their understanding of the other design elements, such as line and shape, to build a space that uses unique geometric features or textural aspects to create visual interest without relying on color to add emphasis. This hands-on design experiment allows students to interact with a unique medium, noodles and marshmallows, in an unconventional format, challenging their problem-solving and design thinking capacity while still being focused on application of material.

SPOTLIGHT: SPAGHETTI AND MARSHMALLOW BUILDINGS

Did you know that uncooked spaghetti noodles and marshmallows could be turned into building materials?! When teaching students about architectural form, especially in regard to how design elements work to add visual interest, it can often be a challenge to have students think beyond simply adding color to a structure. This easy-to-complete activity shows students that a simple line may be all they need to add unique features to their structures. Divide students into groups of three to four. Provide each group with their "building materials"—a handful of uncooked spaghetti and 10 marshmallows. Then have each group randomly select famous pieces of architecture to re-create using just these two materials. Allow each group 5–10 minutes to construct their masterpiece, encouraging them to be creative while still maintaining the form of the piece of architecture they selected. Once teams have finished their structures, walk around the room and try to match the famous piece of architecture to the correct spaghetti and marshmallow recreation. This activity provides a great opportunity to challenge students' creativity, pushing them to think about using the simplest element—a line—to create complex pieces of architecture!

Hand Drafting

Learners may also benefit from learning basic hand drafting techniques in the lab environment. While many college curricula focus on the use of digital technology to create architectural renderings, there is still a tremendous benefit to learning the skills of sketching and hand drafting, including teaching how to communicate ideas quickly and efficiently, in addition to improving design quality through creative thinking (Fakhry et al., 2021). Students may be instructed on the skills of sketching and basic hand drafting through a series of unit work in the lab, focused on the ideas of creating technical illustrations, techniques for sketching, the types of architectural sketches, and using proper proportion and scale when sketching.

Students can be encouraged to practice their sketching in the lab by keeping a sketchbook, where they start and end each lab by producing one quick sketch (5 minutes or less), with a set of parameters from the day's lesson. This formative type of assessment could then be used to ensure proper knowledge of content, through a review of the sketchbook, with the teacher being able to provide ongoing feedback and revisit concepts that may have been missed in the initial sketches. This knowledge could then be evaluated through summative assessment at the end of the unit through an activity aimed at producing a specific type of sketch for a sample client, using only grid paper and a pencil. Rubrics for the evaluation would be provided to each student upfront to provide guidance for assessment purposes, with flexibility for unique student applications of the content in their sketch.

Community of Practice

Upon successful application and analysis of the course content, students can then use the lab environment to reach the highest level of Bloom's Taxonomy: creation. In housing and design labs, educators should encourage students to explore their creativity through individual and group design projects while still emphasizing the importance of learned skills and foundational knowledge. One way this can be achieved is through creating a **community of practice (CoP)** within the lab environment (Kavousi & Miller, 2014).

Using this approach, design thinking is fostered through creating a shared lab space where students learn while also socializing and interacting with each other (Kavousi & Miller, 2014). The first step is creating a space where students feel comfortable to gather and share ideas as a group. In schools with dedicated lab spaces, this may include allowing students to decorate workstations or placing large sheets of paper on the wall for free thinking. In schools where labs are taught in the classroom, this could be as simple as pushing desks together to create large workstations rather than singular, defined desk units or having the class come up with a unique name for their lab, which is displayed on the board each day when they enter the room. The goal is to have the space feel, and function, like a community, where the social engagement of students and teachers is enhanced by the physical space (Kavousi & Miller, 2014).

Once the lab space has been established as the CoP, students can then be presented with realistic design challenges, with the point being to encourage sharing of ideas among peers and exploring new ways to solve problems by learning from the experience of others (Kavousi & Miller, 2014). One interesting method to foster this creativity and shared learning environment is to present groups of students with a design problem. *Design problems* (Table 9.1), which are addressed through design thinking, are issues that have no singular solution, as they are constantly evolving with the population or changes in society (Razzouk & Shute, 2012; Rowe, 1987). These problems encourage students to think beyond traditional means, as they have to find a solution that works best for the parameters they are provided, not necessarily a solution that will "solve" the problem.

Addressing Design Problems

Once presented with their design problem, students are encouraged to use the lab space like a think tank or creative sandbox—as a place to explore the problem in detail and begin constructing solutions in any capacity, from the smallest detail to big picture solutions. Students may be provided

TABLE 9.1   **Sample of Design Problems for Activities in Housing & Design Labs**

Create an office building that will house twice the number of tenants as the old building; however, it will not take up any more space than the old building did.	Design a kitchen with the option to bring the outdoors to the indoors, emphasizing the importance of the lived environment to healthy eating habits.
Design a playroom for a 5-year-old child that can also be used as a guest bedroom, taking into consideration the safety needs of small children.	Create a home design for a young couple who wants to incorporate modern elements into the barn-style home they just purchased in a rural community.
Create a patio space that includes an area for outdoor cooking, in addition to a seating area, taking into consideration any safety measures associated with an open flame.	Design a bed for an assisted-living home that allows for easy entry and exit while still taking into account current design trends and color palettes.

with some parameters to further challenge creativity, such as total cost for the project or a timeline for completion. Students should also be provided with tools for creation, from pens and pencils to more tactile objects such as sculpting clay, to begin prototyping their initial solutions. Once these solutions are drafted, students can then rotate around the lab space to view other groups' proposed solutions. The shared, collaborative nature of the lab environment should be encouraged, with groups modifying each other's solutions to address potential concerns or areas of improvement. Through this revision process, groups learn the importance of sharing ideas and building from others' experiences, as there is no singular solution to the problem presented. Groups may be assessed using rubrics to determine adherence to specific parameters or feasibility of the solution, in addition to a reflection by each student on how they utilized new ideas or experiences from their peers to reach their solution, as a means of demonstrating higher level Bloom's thinking.

Safety Issues in Housing and Design

There are many safety hazards and safety issues in housing and design, from construction hazards and various chemicals to knowledge of building codes. These hazards and building codes have resulted in interior design courses in the career cluster in architecture and construction to have a standard on safety. Students must document the passage of safety exams in a portfolio. These tests should include safe handling of tools, equipment, and materials, as well as knowledge of local, state, and national regulations. Since cooperative learning is a part of housing and design, safety should include acceptance and respectful acknowledgment of diverse opinions, as well as cultural diversity.

Lab experiences in housing and design should focus on the progression of learning from understanding to creativity, through the use of both theoretical and conceptual activities. The emphasis should be placed on creating a CoP in the lab environment that is focused on shared learning between students and their teachers. Housing and design is a constantly evolving field with a sincere impact on the lives of individuals, families, and communities. Teachers should focus on using lab time in housing and design courses to move from teaching basic understanding of core concepts, such as design elements and principles, to application through hands-on experimentation, ultimately culminating in the creation of unique products through creating a CoP focused on compassionate design thinking. It is through this approach that students in housing and design learn the ways in which their field significantly impacts the lives of those around them and beyond!

Fashion and Clothing Production

Fashion and clothing production, in addition to textiles, also contributes significantly to the advancement of the individual, family, and community. First and foremost, clothing contributes to one of human's most basic needs—survival—as it provides a protective layer from the elements (Shirley & Kohler, 2012). However, clothing and textiles go much deeper than basic survival. Clothing has been shown to serve as an important element of identity development and growth, in addition to societal impacts of dress, such as group identification (Davis, 2013; Entwistle, 2014). And there are countless ways that dress impacts culture, from traditional dress of cultural significance to the rise and fall of trends, and brands, in modern media (Hansen, 2004; Siggelkow, 2001).

The current course standards in the fashion design program of study have changed from a major focus on constructing clothing from patterns to a focus on creating, testing, merchandising, and marketing textile goods. In the state of Tennessee, one standard in the course Fashion Design is dedicated to clothing construction. However, three courses in the program of study include a standard on occupational safety (Tennessee Department of Education, 2021i). Therefore, safety should be a priority. Just as in food preparation labs, the educator must document the learners passing a safety test with a grade of 100. Content of the test should include safe use of materials, tools, and equipment; knowledge of safe storage of tools, materials, and chemicals used in the production of textiles and fashion; as well as knowledge of Occupational Safety and Health Administration regulations. When incorporating collaborative strategies in labs, it is wise to include content on safety that demonstrates respectful interaction with peers and acceptance of diversity and culture. These are skills needed by all individuals in the workforce.

When an educator begins teaching clothing production, it is imperative that learners demonstrate safe operation of sewing equipment, as well as pressing and cutting tools. To become familiar with the safe operation of a sewing machine, having the learner sew paper with various designs is helping in learning how to pivot, stop, and, sew curved seams. These paper designs include straight lines, squares, triangles, large zigzags, and large circles.

Design Thinking Framework

Current course standards provide a unique opportunity for FCS educators to implement new teaching strategies in their classrooms and to cover a broad range of topics through experiential learning. One meaningful way to integrate these broad-based topics in fashion and clothing production is to utilize a design thinking framework. At the core, design thinking is an innovation-based method of solving complex problems (Rowe, 1987). It encourages individual thought while also addressing the concept that no problem has a single, "correct" solution. While several variations of the **design thinking process** (Linke, 2017) exist, they all are centered on five fundamental core elements, as proposed by the Hasso-Plattner Institute of Design at Stanford, known as d.school (Brown &

Wyatt, 2010; Dam & Siang, 2020; Interaction Design Foundation, n.d.). The five elements of design thinking are empathize, define, ideate, prototype, and test (Brown & Wyatt, 2010; Carlgren et al., 2016; Dam & Siang, 2020; Interaction Design Foundation, n.d.). As illustrated in Figure 9.6, the five elements of design thinking do not function in a simple linear pattern. Instead, they function simultaneously, with reflection playing a major role in determining the practicality of a solution.

At its basic unit of function, design thinking refers to both seeing and thinking your way through a problem (Liu, 1996). As humans, we are often quick to see problem solving as an either/or process. We don't always take the time to see what is truly in front of us, just like we may not always stop and think about ways our "solutions" could truly impact a problem. Design thinking addresses these concerns by asking individuals to (1) see what exists in terms of problem solving and conceptualization; (2) draw relationships between ideas to think about the most beneficial, not the easiest or most straightforward, way to solve a problem; and (3) view the "solutions" as further informing future design efforts (Carlgren et al., 2016). Indeed, design thinking never stops: It is a process of reflection, communication, and critique, toward continual innovation, not just finding one solution. This works extremely well in the laboratory environment for all design concentrations, as modern design necessitates careful reflection and continuous innovation to serve complex needs; however, it works particularly well in fashion and clothing production laboratories. In fashion and clothing production labs, students are often engaged in a variety of independent projects and focused on acquiring necessary skills while also exploring individual creativity and thought.

One way to achieve this is by structuring labs to include defined variables or parameters while also allowing for individualized approaches to solutions. Begin by introducing the class to a problem that exists in our world that cannot have a single solution. As you work through Bloom's Taxonomy, begin with a topic that can demonstrate basic understanding while still encouraging creativity.

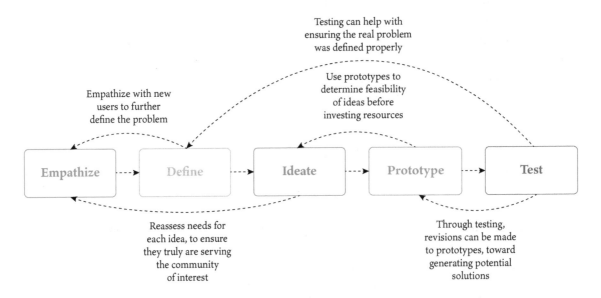

FIGURE 9.6 Five Stages of the Design Thinking Process (Linke, 2017)

SPOTLIGHT: FASHION LAB EXAMPLE

In fashion and clothing production labs, a great option is to have students work to design a sock! But why a sock specifically? A sock is a relatively simple product, consisting of basic stitches and often natural textile components, in addition to being offered in neutral colorways, providing a blank canvas for creativity. Socks also carry a functional component, as they must be comfortable for the wearer and provide protection, which requires the student to understand the basic principles of usability and focus on what clothing does, not just how it looks (Watkins & Dunne, 2015). Additionally, if labs do not contain sewing machines for physical construction or modification of a product, a two-dimensional image of a sock can be just as effective in design thinking, through the medium of crayons, markers, or even paints.

With most design thinking labs, the first step will involve presenting students with a problem. For this sock experiment, provide students with a prompt that encourages creativity while still providing specifics that must be addressed. An example of this could be the following:

> Your team has recently been hired by a world-famous designer to create a new design for their collection. This design needs to be innovative while still being marketable to a specific audience, in addition to cost-effective. The designer encourages you to be creative, to use any mediums that you feel are best for creation of your design, but to always remember who the consumer is who will purchase this item. And what product type is this designer currently working on? A sock!

At this stage, the team now has a design problem with no singular solution. The next step is to begin demonstrating the reflective nature of the design thinking process. Instead of moving into empathizing or even defining the true problem, allow students to move straight into the ideation phase, which is likely where most students will initially want to begin. Provide each team with a way to begin collecting their thoughts and ideas. A fun, and effective, way to do this is by providing each team with a pack of sticky notes. Encourage the team to write down one idea on each sticky note and then begin placing them around their work station. This way, the team can see all their ideas in one place and can then begin to physically piece them together, by moving the sticky notes into groupings. Allow each team ample time to work through their thoughts, which includes having each team decide on an initial design, before beginning to illustrate the importance of the iterative nature of the design thinking process.

Once each team has their idea, introduce a new element to the project: the importance of empathizing before defining or ideating. Using a random draw process, have teams select one target consumer for their sock. When determining target consumers, encourage thoughtfulness by selecting consumers who are not within their own markets and price points that will challenge innovation. A sample of target consumers can be found in Table 9.2 as a reference guide; however, focus on higher level Bloom's thinking by integrating new demographics or psychographics into target consumer profiles based on the environment.

(Continued)

TABLE 9.2   Sample of Target Consumers for Sock Design Experiment

Engineering student with a part-time job at a grocery store and doesn't have time between school and work to change socks	Seventy-two-year-old magazine editor, only wears socks that are "interesting," walks 3 miles a day to and from work in New York City
Woman, 40-years-old, full-time job at real estate agency that has a business-casual dress code, predominantly wears sneakers to work	Kindergarten student, doesn't like wearing socks (in fact, they will actually throw them away some days!), likes the color red
Retired male, 58-years-old, married, no children, enjoys hiking and bird watching	Resident of assisted-living home, enjoys fashion tv shows, requires no-slip socks

One element to focus on when selecting consumers is creating profiles that have broad and specific elements. Allow some groups to decide on the age of their consumers or to determine if gender identity exists; however, also create parameters that require empathizing with specific life-style needs. This creates new layers of depth for students to begin assessing needs of a consumer who may not share similarities with their own lives.

After each team has selected their target consumer, have them assess what the needs of that individual would be. This could be using more sticky notes or even having students fill out a profile sheet for their consumer. Encourage students to return to the original problem—creating a sock that is innovative and creative while still being marketable to a specific audience, in addition to cost-effective—while also examining what that means to their target consumer. In the empathize stage, allow students to conduct independent research on their consumer, as this encourages them to explore how individuals with unique traits can be segmented into their target market groups, which are the primary audiences products are sold to (Beane & Ennis, 1987). To determine if teams are empathizing with their unique consumer, implement the three-question approach. When walking around the lab space, ask each group three questions about their consumer that encourages new schools of thought, such as "What is the most challenging part of designing a sock for this specific consumer?" or "In what ways would you have to advertise your sock to encourage this consumer to purchase it?" When presented with the challenge of modifying their original design to meet the needs of this new consumer, groups may initially overlook all of the aspects of this consumer's demographics, psychographics, personality, or generalized needs. Encourage deeper, more empathetic thinking by pushing groups to address the unknowns of their target consumer, such as what would deter them from purchasing or questions of function versus design.

After thoroughly addressing the needs of their target consumer, through empathizing with them, then have each group define the true problem that exists for their consumer. This will be different from the overall design problem, as it will focus specifically on the individual they are now designing for. For instance, the defined problem for a kindergarten student may be creating a product that makes them actually want to wear socks, potentially through creating a design with their favorite cartoon characters, while also ensuring the product is easy to care for, as parents may need to wash these socks more frequently. Another example could be that the true defined problem for someone who prefers function over fashion is creating a sock that has specific performance features while still being interesting enough for a designer to want to feature in their new collection. Remind each team that while they are defining the true problem for their target consumer, they also need to keep the larger design problem in mind, which may require using the design thinking process to return to empathizing with consumer needs and the needs of the designer that hired them!

Now that teams have their defined problem, ask them to return to their original sock design and answer a simple question: Would their original design work for their target consumer and the problem they have just defined? In most instances, the answer will likely be that the design needs some modification to meet new needs or better address the specific problems they have identified. This allows teams to move on to the ideation and prototyping phase. Ask teams to go back through the ideation process, now focusing on exploring ideas based on the new parameters of their design. This may also be blended with the prototyping phase as they work to determine what ideas are the most realistic to move onto the testing phase. Encourage creative ideation through prototyping by providing students with basic supplies to explore their ideas, such as paper, pencils, markers, stickers, and even clay to sculpt potential additions from. If sewing machines are provided in the lab or hand sewing is an option, students could be presented with sewing tools and notions to create a three-dimensional prototype of their sock. Throughout the ideation and prototyping phases, meet with each team and ask them to explain their design, asking questions from the empathize and definition stages to ensure understanding of their problem while also encouraging creativity.

While teams can develop several prototypes to test feasibility, functionality, or aesthetics of design, ask teams to decide upon one prototype to move on to the testing phase. This should be the prototype they feel best solves the larger design problem and the more specific defined issue for their target consumer. Upon selecting their prototype, teams will then need to move into testing their product to determine if it truly was the best solution given the problem. To illustrate the iterative nature of the design problem, one option is to test prototypes outside of the lab setting. Select a different class, either a new section of the same course or an entirely different class depending on course offerings, to introduce the products created for a new population. The goal here is to gather feedback from a new group of students, who may empathize with the target consumer in a new way or see new ideas that may help further refine a product. Present the new class with each sock and a brief description of the target consumer, along with the larger design problem. Then ask the new class to provide at least three pieces of constructive feedback about the design—from aesthetic choices to the function of the product for the specific target consumer, or even new questions for groups to assess based on a second appraisal of the target consumer's needs. Along with teacher feedback, present this to the original class with an explanation of how reflection and feedback help to create the best possible version of a product by assessing elements that may otherwise be overlooked or forgotten. Then encourage students to revise their prototype based on feedback, which may, in turn, require moving back to developing new ideas or even re-defining the specific problem of their target consumer. This is the iterative nature of the design thinking process!

(Continued)

Assessment

In terms of assessment, groups can be graded based on adherence to specific variables, which should be predetermined before the lab. Provide each group with a rubric that shows elements that must be addressed, such as making significant changes to the original design or the creation of at least three working prototypes; however, be sure to leave room for creative elements. An example of a scoring rubric for this activity is provided next for reference. A final layer of design thinking can also be achieved by having students assess their own work through a reflective activity. Students should be provided with a scoring rubric of their own that addresses elements of the design thinking process, such as their work toward defining the design problem or the changes made during the revision process, in addition to asking students to reflect on the experience as a whole.

Before presenting their final designs, have each group go back to their original sock creation—the first image they created without knowing their target consumer or hearing feedback from others. Encourage students to reflect on the changes in their designs and how each of those changes came about. Use this time to show a model of the design thinking process; explain each step and how the process moves fluidly, which is essential for good design. Discuss with students how the final product they created is in fact not finalized at all. Ask them to imagine what changes might be made to their sock design a year from now, then 10 years from now, based on how their target consumer may change or how technology advances. The goal with this lab is not to have students create a singular sock design but rather to understand how to create the best possible solution to a design problem at this moment in time, realizing this solution will likely need to be revisited with time or new variables. And that is good design thinking in labs for fashion and clothing production!

Safety Issues with Fashion and Clothing Production

There are many safety hazards and potential safety issues in fashion and clothing production, from the proper use of a sewing machine, to the careful handling of sharp sewing tools, and even the use of chemicals in textile-testing labs. A standard for safety in the fashion and clothing production lab should be established within the first days of the course, ensuring that students are aware of proper safety protocols in the lab environment. Students should be provided with appropriate tutorials when handling sewing tools or operating a sewing machine, in addition to having access to a lab manual that highlights all lab rules. Students must document the passage of safety exams in a portfolio and should document their agreement to follow all rules in a lab safety contract. Lab safety tests should include safe handling of tools, equipment, and materials, as well as knowledge of appropriate behavior in the lab environment. Since cooperative learning is a part of fashion and clothing production, safety lessons should also address acceptance and respectful acknowledgment of diverse opinions during class discussion and activities, as well as the acknowledgment of cultural diversity.

Early Childhood Education and Careers

FCS educators who have the additional endorsement in occupational care and guidance of young children may teach courses in the early childhood education program of study in a high school setting. In many cases, this involves having a childcare program in a high school setting. This type of setting can vary according to the school system and the needs of the community. Some occupational programs serve as half-day childcare programs for 3- to 5-year-olds in the community. Others serve as inclusive childcare programs for children with various disabilities, with a few children without disabilities to provide an inclusive setting. Still others may use local childcare settings as placements for students to gain practical experience. In each type of setting, an adult other than the occupational FCS educator is the lead teacher in the childcare program. The occupational FCS educator is in charge of preparing students for careers in early childhood education, modeling appropriate child-adult interaction, and evaluating the early childhood education learner.

The four courses in the program of study focused on early childhood education. The content from these four courses include curriculum planning, student learning, safe and healthy learning environments and relationships with young children, knowledge of and the ability to perform screening and assessment instruments on young children, and techniques on developing an optimal family-school partnership. A major topic in the early childhood education program is developmentally appropriate practice (DAP). See Chapter 4 under "Piaget" for more content on DAP.

During the courses in the program of study, learners will have the opportunity to observe and/or work with educators; they will collect artifacts that document their experience and become prepared for postsecondary education for careers with children (Tennessee Department of Education, 2021e). The FCS educator may have students use lesson planning templates to help them with lesson planning. See Figure 9.7 for an example. Educators may also have evaluation sheets that are used during microteaching in the early childhood education child care lab. Make sure your learners are familiar with all planning and evaluation sheets.

Safety

As in all other FCS courses that involve lab work, educators must prepare learners to pass a safety test with 100% accuracy (Tennessee Department of Education, 2021e). This would include content involved in providing a safe and healthy learning environment for children. Developmentally appropriate child guidance strategies that promote social and emotional well-being in children are also included. The safety test that must be passed with 100% accuracy includes content on CPR, first aid, prevention of communicable diseases, and regulations from the Occupational Safety and Health Administration (Tennessee Department of Education, 2021e).

Microteaching

Microteaching, an effective technique for practicing teaching, is an integral part of teacher preparation programs. Microteaching was developed at Stanford University of California in 1963 (Sa'ad et al., 2015). Through classroom simulations, preservice teachers practice their skill sets before

ECED III Lesson Plan Template

Lesson Title: Grade/Subject:

State Standards	Topic
List 3 TDOE or TN-ELDS Standards. Two should be from your subject area.	What is the overall topic you are teaching?

Lesson Objective(s)

List three specific skills or outcomes you want the child to accomplish. Objectives are measurable.

Vocabulary

What vocabulary words could be used for this lesson? List three. Include definitions.

Assessment

How will you ensure the student understands the concept(s)?

Instruction

What are the steps you will use to introduce the lesson and activity? Be specific; another teacher should be able to use these plans.

Materials Needed

Include all necessary materials and a book that could be used in the lesson.

Adaptations to Meet Individual Needs:

How will you adapt the instruction to meet the needs of individual students?

Safety Concerns

FIGURE 9.7 Lesson Plan Template for Occupational Early Childhood
Tennessee Technological University, 2021

entering the field or student teaching/residency. This lower risk classroom experience of micro-teaching provides opportunities to teach among peers for shorter time periods, which may range from 5 minutes for a set or closure to a 20-minute instructional strategy (Allen et al., 1972; Allen & Eve, 1968; Reddy, 2019).

Microteaching simulation typically involves three steps: a planning phase, a teaching phase, and a reflection phase (Karlström & Hamza, 2019). In most traditional microteaching settings, there are three groups of participants: the preservice teacher, the class instructors or supervisor, and a small group of peers. The skills acquired through microteaching include preparing a lesson plan that the student will actually teach, speaking in front of a group, managing time, observing the learning environment during instruction, posing questions to students, and assessing student performance. Through these sessions, preservice teachers are able to practice and refine their teaching techniques, even beyond the reflection stage, in a controlled environment with the assistance of their instructors or mentors before putting them into practice with actual students. This allows preservice teachers the opportunity to explore new teaching techniques, assessment types, methods of explanation, demonstrations, and even effective communication in a lower risk environment. Moreover, a microteaching preservice teacher is evaluated by the instructor and peers in the class, providing the peers with experience in providing feedback and constructive criticism. Sa'ad (2015) stated that preservice educators that participate in microteaching learn the benefits of good planning and gain confidence as a teacher.

The three steps of microteaching help to guide preservice teachers through the process of knowledge acquisition, application, and reflection. First, preservice teachers will need to be instructed on a specific educational technique or theory, through lecture, text, demonstration, or other forms of knowledge dissemination. The preservice teacher will then need to take the content they have learned and begin the planning phase, where attention should be placed on developing appropriate objectives and planned sequences for the content (Reddy, 2019). In most traditional microteaching simulations, each student teacher has just 5–10 minutes to instruct on their topic to the small peer group, meaning they must plan effectively to present content that is concise and relevant yet still aimed at active learning.

Once the student teacher has developed the content, they then move into the teaching phase, where their lesson plans can be instructed within the simulated environment to their instructor and small peer group. Additionally, research suggests that videotaping this teaching experience can also serve as a tool of reflection, so the student teacher can review their own teaching techniques outside of the simulation (Allen et al., 1972; Ostrosky et al., 2013). This allows for both an active and reflective component to the teaching simulation, gathering feedback in real time and after instruction, which is mirrored in the traditional classroom experience.

FCS educators who teach in the career cluster of education and training will be involved in microteaching with their students. The programs of study teaching as a profession and occupational early childhood courses have practicum/field experience and internships. Therefore, presenting preservice educators with knowledge of teacher evaluation and constructive criticism is helpful in the preparation of FCS education.

Field Experiences, Practicums, Internships, and Student Teaching/Residency

During the teacher education program, preservice teachers will be placed in classroom settings for **field experience**, **practicum**, and student teaching/residency. For students not seeking licensure, field experiences and internships with community cooperative extension or state/government agencies will be used. Both of these situations require FCS educators to collaborate with employers in the community to provide opportunities for preservice teachers to practice skills and learn to address problems and challenges faced by those in real-world experiences. Furthermore, these experiences provide an opportunity to gain additional skills essential for employment (College Career Readiness and Success, 2013).

These experiences are usually different from microteaching, as they occur in the actual workplace setting with guidance and evaluation on a daily basis by the mentor. Most teacher preparation programs require that each preservice FCS educator be formally evaluated by a university supervisor one to five times during the period of the experience, depending on the course requirements. This is also a wonderful time to gain one-on-one mentoring from an FCS licensed educator, as many placements are for the entire semester.

Consequently, since all of the career clusters include a course that is an internship or a practicum, it is vital that content be provided on how to manage the preservice teachers during practicum and internships. It is also important to communicate the role of mentor, communicate how and when to evaluate the students, and consider transportation of students to and from the site.

SUMMARY

Labs are hand-on experiences for both the educator and learners. Career clusters of human services, education and training, nutrition and dietetics, housing and interiors, fashion and clothing production, and early childhood education all provide opportunities for labs and action-oriented experiences. The educator is responsible for facilitating learning, answering student questions, and ensuring learners are safe. Furthermore, educators should also use teaching strategies to promote learners' use of critical thinking skills such as synthesis/creativity and evaluation throughout the lab experience. Benefits of labs and action-oriented learning may include opportunities to understand why they are doing a task, opportunities for practice of skills, opportunities to gain experience in a real-world setting, opportunities to practice time management, opportunities to gain collaboration skills that promote teamwork, and opportunities to gain confidence and self-esteem.

KEY TERMS

Active homework

Design thinking process

Anchor charts

Community of practice (CoP)

Lab planning sheet

Microteaching

QUESTIONS AND ACTIVITIES

1. Prepare a food lab planning sheet for a lab in which students are learning to make muffins. The planning sheet should include teaching objectives, a list of pre-lab tasks the student should complete, at least one recipe or task, and post-lab questions. In addition, include food items and equipment needed and the cost of each food item.

2. Develop handwashing and dishwashing procedure posters that could be posted above sinks in your future classroom. The procedures should follow the FDA Safe Food handling guidelines (2017).

3. Develop a safety quiz that is appropriate for a nutrition and dietetics food lab.

4. Develop a safety quiz that is appropriate for either housing and design or fashion and design.

5. Develop a lesson plan for occupational early childhood education using the lesson planning template included in the chapter.

REFERENCES

Abdulwahed, M., & Nagy, Z. K. (2009). Applying Kolb's experiential learning cycle for laboratory education. *Journal of Engineering Education, 98*(3), 283–294.

Allen, D. W., Cooper, J. M., & Poliakoff, L. (1972). *Microteaching* [No. 17]. U.S. Department of Health, Education, and Welfare, Office of Education, National Center for Educational Communication.

Allen, D. W., & Eve, A. W. (1968). Microteaching. *Theory into Practice, 7*(5), 181–185.

Armstrong, P. (2016). *Bloom's taxonomy.* Vanderbilt University Center for Teaching.

Beane, T. P., & Ennis, D. M. (1987). Market segmentation: A review. *European Journal of Marketing, 21*(5), 20–42.

Boston Food Safety. (n.d.). *What is ServeSafe?* https://bostonfoodsafety.com/what-is-servsafe

Brown, T., & Wyatt, J. (2010). Design thinking for social innovation. *Development Outreach, 12*(1), 29–43.

Carlgren, L., Rauth, I., & Elmquist, M. (2016). Framing design thinking: The concept in idea and enactment. *Creativity and Innovation Management, 25*(1), 38–57.

Cheng, S. C., Ziffle, V. E., & King, R. C. (2020). Innovative food laboratory for a chemistry of food and cooking course. *Journal of Chemistry Education, 97,* 659–667. https://dx.doi.org/10.1021/acs.jchemed.9b00465

Dam, R. F., & Siang, T. Y. (2020). *What is design thinking and why is it so popular?* https://www.interaction-design.org/literature/article/what-is-design-thinking-and-why-is-it-so-popular

Davis, F. (2013). *Fashion, culture, and identity.* University of Chicago Press.

Ebert-May, D., Linton, D. L., Hodder, J., & Long, T. (2005). Active homework: Preparation for active classes. *Frontiers in Ecology and the Environment, 3*(5), 283–284. https://www.jstor.org/stable/3868491

Ellis, J., & Gruber-Garvey, E. (2013). Introduction: Teaching food. *The Journal of Inclusive Scholarship and Pedagogy, 23*(2), 13–16. http://web.njcu.edu/sites/transformations

Entwistle, J. (2015). *The fashioned body: Fashion, dress and social theory.* John Wiley & Sons.

Evans, P., & Thomas, M. A. (2012). *Exploring the elements of design*. Cengage Learning.

Fakhry, M., Kamel, I., & Abdelaal, A. (2021). CAD using preference compared to hand drafting in architectural working drawings coursework. *Ain Shams Engineering Journal, 12*(3), 3331–3338.

Femenías, P., & Hagbert, P. (2013). The habitation lab: Using a design approach to foster innovation for sustainable living. *Technology Innovation Management Review, 3*(11), 15–21. https://timreview.ca/article/741

Food and Drug Administration. (2017). *Safe food handling*. https://www.fda.gov/food/buy-store-serve-safe-food/safe-food-handling

Hansen, K. T. (2004). The world in dress: Anthropological perspectives on clothing, fashion, and culture. *Annual Review Anthropology, 33*(2004), 369–392.

Hospitality Net. (2020). *What is culinary arts?* https://www.hospitalitynet.org/news/4101329.html

Interaction Design Foundation. (n.d.). *Design thinking*. https://www.interaction-design.org/literature/topics/design-thinking

Jones, G., & Rathman, L. (2020). Blended learning: Use of instructional videos in undergraduate food preparation lab. *Journal of Nutrition Education and Behavior, 52*(7), S20. https://doi.org/10.1016/j.jneb.2020.04.055

Karlström, M., & Hamza, K. (2019). Preservice science teachers' opportunities for learning through reflection when planning a microteaching unit. *Journal of Science Teacher Education, 30*(1), 44–62.

Kavousi, S., & Miller, P. A. (2014). The community of practice: Teaching pedagogy in the architecture foundation design lab. *EDULEARN14 Proceedings*, 2548–2557.

Linke, J. (2017). *Design thinking explained*. Ideas Made to Matter. http://mitsloan.edu/ideas-made to matter/design-thinking-explained

Liu, Y. T., & Group, A. (1996). Is designing one search or two? A model of design thinking involving symbolism and connectionism. *Design Studies, 17*(4), 435–449.

Lovett, J. (1998). *Original design overview: Design features*. https://www.johnlovett.com/design-overview

Lynch, M. (2021). *What is heterogeneous grouping all about*. The Edvocate. https://www.verywellfamily.com/heterogeneous-grouping-1449185

McClurg-Genevese, J. D. (2005). The principles of design. *Digital Web Magazine*, 13. https://www.digital-web.com/articles/principles_of_design/

Mugabi, T. (2019). *Heterogeneous vs. homogeneous grouping: What's the best way to group students?* Classcraft. https://www.classcraft.com/resources/blog/heterogeneous-vs-homogeneous-grouping-whats-the-best-way-to-group-students/

Mulvahill, E. (2020, July 14). *Anchor charts 101: Why and how to use them*. We Are Teachers. https://www.weareteachers.com/anchor-charts-101/

Murray, T. (2014, December 17). *Using anchor charts as an effective teaching/learning tool*. Northwest Area Education Agency. https://www.nwaea.org/connections-blogs/reading-blog/2014/12/17/using-anchor-charts-as-an-effective-teaching-learning-tool

Nickols, S. Y., Ralston, P. A., Anderson, C. L., Browne, L., Schroeder, G. A., Thomas, S. L., & Wild, P. (2009). The family and consumer sciences body of knowledge and the cultural kaleidoscope: Research opportunities and challenges. *Family and Consumer Sciences Research Journal, 37*(3), 266–283.

Ostrosky, M. M., Mouzourou, C., Danner, N., & Zaghlawan, H. Y. (2013). Improving teacher practices using microteaching: Planful video recording and constructive feedback. *Young Exceptional Children, 16*(1), 16–29.

Reddy, K. R. (2019). Teaching how to teach: Microteaching (A way to build up teaching skills). *Journal of Gandaki Medical College-Nepal, 12*(1), 65–71.

Razzouk, R., & Shute, V. (2012). What is design thinking and why is it important? *Review of Educational Research, 82*(3), 330–348.

Reynolds, M. (2021, May 20). *Efficient home design, or how to design a home to use less energy.* EcoHome. https://www.ecohome.net/guides/2406/efficient-home-design/

Rohe, W. M., Van Zandt, S., & McCarthy, G. (2001). The social benefits and costs of homeownership: A critical assessment of the research. *The Affordable Housing Reader, 40,* 00–01.

Rowe, P. G. (1987). *Design thinking.* MIT press.

Sa'ad, T. U., Sabo, S., & Abdullahi, A.D. (2015). The impact of micro-teaching on the teaching practice performance of undergraduate agricultural education students in college of education. *Azare, Journal of Education and Practice, 6*(26), 109–115.

Shirley, L. M., & Kohler, J. (2012). Clothing and textiles: Reinforcing STEM education through family and consumer sciences curriculum. *Journal of Family & Consumer Sciences Education, 30*(2), 46–56.

Siggelkow, N. (2001). Change in the presence of fit: The rise, the fall, and the renaissance of Liz Claiborne. *Academy of Management Journal, 44*(4), 838–857.

Tennessee Department of Education. (2021a, May). *Culinary arts 1.* https://tinyurl.com/28f2dwdp

Tennessee Department of Education. (2021b, May). *Culinary arts II.* https://tinyurl.com/mry5r5tn

Tennessee Department of Education. (2021c, May). *Culinary arts III.* https://tinyurl.com/bdeskce2

Tennessee Department of Education. (2021d, May). *Culinary arts IV.* https://tinyurl.com/42tkh8vd

Tennessee Department of Education. (2021e, May). Early childhood education and careers I (ECEC I). https://www.tn.gov/content/dam/tn/education/ccte/hlth/cte_std_early_childhood_1.pdf

Tennessee Department of Education. (2021f, May). Early childhood education and careers II (ECEC II). https://www.tn.gov/content/dam/tn/education/ccte/hlth/cte_std_early_childhood_2.pdf

Tennessee Department of Education. (2021g, May). Early childhood education and careers III (ECEC III). https://www.tn.gov/content/dam/tn/education/ccte/hlth/cte_std_early_childhood_3.pdf

Tennessee Department of Education. (2021h, May). Early childhood education and careers IV (ECEC IV) https://www.tn.gov/content/dam/tn/education/ccte/hlth/cte_std_early_childhood_4.pdf

Tennessee Department of Education. (2021i, May) *Fashion design.* https://www.tn.gov/content/dam/tn/education/ccte/art/cte_std_foundations_fashion_design.pdf

Tennessee Technological University. (2021). *edTPA lesson plan template. TK20 by Watermark. TK20–edTPA guide.* https://www.tntech.edu/education/tk20/student.php

Watkins, S. M., & Dunne, L. (2015). *Functional clothing design: From sportswear to spacesuits.* Bloomsbury Publishing USA.

Figure Credits

FCS Education and Technology

Elizabeth Ramsey, PhD; Melinda Swafford, PhD; and Caitlin Williams, MS

FIGURE 10.1 Technology Impacting Education

Chapter 10 Objectives

Upon completion of the chapter, the learner should be able to

- describe the benefits of the appropriate use of technology in family and consumer sciences (FCS) education;
- identify problems associated with the use of technology in education;
- analyze appropriate websites, apps, and free teaching resources for use in FCS education;
- identify components of a user-friendly learning module and required components of an online course; and
- create an online module that includes a variety of teaching strategies, including higher order thinking, as well as resources and assessments.

Introduction

Technology is a part of everyday life and has become an integral part of education. Family and consumer sciences (FCS) educators use technology in a variety of ways: planning instruction and assessments, administrative tasks such as attendance and recording grades, and searching the web for reliable resources (Hirose, 2011). The frequent use of technology in FCS classrooms is commonly observed by the use of web searches and visual displays (PowerPoints) during lectures. Students who have been exposed to various types of technology may be more comfortable with it's use. This exposure has both positive and negative effects (Schmitt, 2021). This chapter focuses on how to enhance student-centered learning with technology and explore the available modalities. At the end of the chapter, students will describe three types of online learning environments of FCS content, as well as create a user-friendly learning module.

Technology in the FCS Education

It is expected that preservice FCS education and new FCS educators be proficient in incorporating technology with higher order thinking strategies (Hirose, 2011). This fact is supported by the National Standards for Teachers of Family and Consumer Sciences that state preservice FCS educators and current FCS educators should engage learners in higher order thinking and problem solving in FCS content by use of varied instructional strategies and use of technology (Borr et al., 2013). In addition, the Council for the Accreditation of Educator Preparation includes standards that require learners to gather information, evaluate data, and be creative with digital formats (Hirose, 2011). This requires educators to go beyond using audio/visuals in the classroom. Technology is always changing, and FCS educators have a responsibility to implement various technologies in FCS content programs of study in all content areas. Consequently, being familiar with technology prepares the learner to be college and career ready.

Online FCS Education

During the COVID-19 pandemic, many school systems and institutions of higher education were forced to move all coursework to online platforms (Hess, 2021). As a result of this, many individuals are more comfortable with this platform and technology, resulting in increased use of the format (Hess, 2021). Online FCS education can be designed and presented in a variety of ways. Instructors may design their online courses by allowing students to follow a curriculum calendar on their own or providing a pace to the content for a more controlled learning environment. **Student-centered learning** and **teacher-centered learning** are educational terms that also apply to online education. Student-centered online learning allows learners to be actively involved in the content, as well as with peers and instructors while providing opportunities for reflection (Riggs, 2020). Whereas in teacher-centered online learning, students read or listen to lectures and do not collaborate with peers or the instructor.

Blended/hybrid learning occurs when students learn partially through online instruction and partially in a brick-and-mortar (in-person) setting. The student's role in this type of instruction would be considered synchronous or asynchronous. **Synchronous learning** allows learners to view the material anytime on their own schedule during a specific time frame, whereas **asynchronous learning** requires learners to log in at a particular time and participate in class (Scheiderer, 2021). **Web-based learning** occurs when all learning materials are available to students through the online learning platform (see Figure 10.2). Studies show that learners prefer synchronous learning over asynchronous learning because of the perception of increased opportunities for discussion with the instructor (Betz-Hamilton, 2021). A mixed-method study to compare university students' experiences with the FCS consumer affairs course delivered hybrid/blended as compared to 100% web based and 100% in-person courses in consumer affairs, and the results of the study indicate that hybrid courses are the preferred mode of delivery (Betz-Hamilton, 2021).

Regardless of the delivery of an online course, Picciano (2017) shares the following components that could be used coherently to provide a framework for online education: content, social and emotional, dialectic/questioning, reflection, collaborative learning, and evaluation. Students should be aware of the organization of the course and the expectations set by the instructor. Instructors can state the course expectations through a written syllabus, as well as an introductory video, such as a screen recording introducing themselves, the platform being used, and any other vital information.

FIGURE 10.2 Online Education

SPOTLIGHT: ONLINE COURSE DEVELOPMENT

When developing a course that will be implemented through a web-based platform, one strategy for course development is to create the course around the standards. When creating a course in a web-based learning platform, it is best to take each standard and create a module/unit that focuses solely on each standard. For clarity, the terms *module* and *unit* are used interchangeably. For example, in the course Introduction to Human Studies in Tennessee, there are 18 standards. With that said, the educator should create 18 modules/units. The first standard states, "Describe the different levels of human growth (using research such as Maslow's hierarchy of needs) and articulate the different characteristics of each level. Make a graphic that illustrates the pattern of metamotivation as humans fulfill each type of need." According to this standard, students will be exploring Maslow's hierarchy of needs. The following are suggestions for a module/ unit for Standard 1:

- Title: Unit/Module 1, Maslow's Hierarchy of Needs

   This section should be simple and clear. Be sure to include a well-rounded title, including the unit/module number.

- Standard with Objectives:

   This section should include the standard with the objectives clearly identified.

- Media Checklist:

   This section should include a checklist of everything the student needs to view, explore, or watch. For example, compile web resources for students to view, short video clips, and websites to explore.

- Reading Checklist:

   This section should include chapters or articles that the student should read. If there are copyright concerns, consider listing the chapters only and not embedding them in the course.

- Assignments:

   This section should include all assignments. The authors suggest including a formative assignment that checks for reading, like a quick 10-item quiz, discussion post over the readings, or a brief summary of the readings. Most students will bypass reading assignments unless there is some type of assignment connected to it.

   This section should also include the summative assignment that is required in the standard, in this case, a graphic. Each assignment should have a rubric attached (unless it is a test or quiz) with clear instructions and due dates.

User-Friendly Online Courses

Inequities do exist within internet technology. For example, 1 in 4 U.S. learners do not have what they need for success with online education, as not all areas in the United States have access to broadband services (NEA Today, 2021). When planning online education, it is important that the program be user-friendly. User-friendly is a subjective term; however, common features are identified for an online program to be user-friendly. These features include flexibility, student support, and cost savings (Scheiderer, 2021). Flexibility allows the learner to schedule a class that supports the individual needs of the learner, such as working from home or during the weekend. Cost savings provide the learner the benefit of taking courses while being employed full time during the day or evening. Student support includes access to the instructor, timely feedback on assignments, and opportunities to collaborate with peers.

Student-Centered Approach with Online Courses

In a student-centered learning environment, the instructor may supply the learning activities for students, but the learning responsibility is that of the student. Discussion postings provide opportunities for the learner to connect with peers in the online course. These postings as well as higher order thinking/problem-based assignments provide an opportunity for students to reflect and apply the content. In this approach, students find a connection between the learning activities and real-world experiences, a benefit for any career technical education course (Richmond, 2014). Furthermore, online formats provide educators with avenues for feedback and encouragement in one-on-one situations or within groups.

Benefits of Technology

There are numerous benefits to incorporating technology into the classroom. Research documents that technology may improve communication, as many educators post assignments, class notes, and information for families on school websites (Hirose, 2011). This may improve partnership building between families, schools, and educators. Through technology, learners are exposed to new visual experiences beyond the classroom and their social environment, which provides opportunities for learners to grow emotionally and understand cultures beyond their microsystems (Schmitt, 2021). Technology also promotes critical thinking skills and demonstrates real-world application of FCS content to learners (Hirose, 2011).

In the spring of 2020, the COVID-19 pandemic resulted in government officials requiring public and private education to go online for spring and summer terms. In the school year of 2020/2021, educational programs had the option to go 100% online or provide an option of hybrid courses for learners. Current research documents university students perceived that online learning provided more opportunities for participation than face-to-face learning. However, students also reported problems with technology and the heavy workload to be barriers to online learning, and students reported retaining less content and missing fellow students (Betz-Hamilton, 2021).

SPOTLIGHT: MY COVID-19 EXPERIENCE AS AN FCS EDUCATOR
By Cailtin Williams

In the spring of 2020, my school district closed schools and encouraged students to continue learning from home. As a secondary instructor, lesson planning and implementation of learning activities were put at a standstill as our school district created content-specific activities and made those accessible for all students and parents through printed packets or online activities. The sole learning responsibility quickly shifted to students. In my FCS classroom, students were already familiar with a student-centered learning environment, as they were often presented with learning opportunities that promoted the development of their critical thinking skills, as well as self-reflection skills. During the pandemic, many students developed new technological skills, including web conferencing and email communication.

In my postsecondary environment, students were already familiar with a student-centered learning environment, as my course was solely online when the pandemic occurred. Students understood the course environment and expectations in the very beginning, which is very important for online learning. However, all university courses were impacted by the pandemic so not only did students have to shift their technological skills in their face-to-face environments but they also had to build organization, time management, and problem-solving skills.

Challenges of Technology

Research by Smith (2015) indicates several challenges school systems face with technology, which range from limited budgets, to untrained educators, unreliable software, inadequate infrastructures, and educators who are resistant to change. Access to technology varies among the states and regions of the United States, requiring FCS educators to rely on textbooks and other hard-copy resources rather than digital resources for learning. Consequently, research by Borr et al. (2013) indicate that most FCS educators use technology only for word processing and software presentations. Implications of the study urge FCS educators to be fully competent with technology. All these identified barriers make it difficult for school systems to address technology needs for learners as education moves to a digital age.

The effects of technology on adolescents, both positive and negative, are constantly monitored in today's society. FCS educators and professionals are oftentimes instructed on, or use in their practice, Maslow's hierarchy of needs. If technology disrupts a student's physical needs, they may perform lower in the classroom, as their additional needs cannot be met. Research also states that the use of the internet may present distractions and steal time from other activities, which may lead to isolation (Rehm & Keller, 2020). Dienlen and Johannes (2020) state, "Positive relations between excessive screen time and insufficient sleep, physiological stress, mind wandering, attention deficit-hyperactivity disorder (ADHD)-related behavior, nonadaptive/negative thinking styles, decreased life satisfaction, and potential health risks in adulthood" (pp. 137–138).

Social media also presents a problem with adolescents, as their developmental stage of ego-centrism and brain synapses makes this age group vulnerable to foster addiction and risk-taking behaviors that may expose them to cyberbullying, sexting, breaches of confidentiality, and online predators, as well as extensive time with inappropriate gaming platforms (Schmitt, 2021). As technology decreases the need for face-to-face interactions, students are acquiring fewer social and emotional development opportunities.

FCS professionals can use programs of study standards to incorporate safe use of technology and social media platforms into **modules**, which is a unit of instruction that covers a topic (Merriam-Webster, n.d.; Schmitt, 2021). Furthermore, it is important for teachers to acknowledge their purpose behind integrating technology in the FCS classroom. A tech-rich instructional environment provides students with technological resources to support traditional instruction. However, to successfully integrate technology into a blended learning environment, educators must promote student-centered learning outcomes for classroom content and instruction (Maxwell, 2016). While educators are not only tasked with how to use practice, it is also necessary for educators to have extensive knowledge of teaching students within varying contexts (Kim et al., 2019).

Although years of experience and training sources were not significantly correlated to technology adoption, some teacher-level barriers were to blame, such as technology anxiety, age, and technology training and availability (Redmann & Kotrlik, 2009). Technology in the FCS classroom has been around for many years; however, there has been a recent shift from computer software to cloud-based applications. Lokken et al. (2003) conducted a 3-year study that showed after technology training, there was no anxiety reported by the participating FCS teachers. In addition to basic technological skills, teachers should also have training geared toward integrating instructional technology in order to minimize stress and anxiety.

SPOTLIGHT: FCS WEBSITE

In December of 2013, FCS educator Sarah Puddy, along with 15–20 FCS educators from Wisconsin, created a private Facebook page for FCS teachers to share ideas and resources. At the time of this publication, the site has over 184,000 members worldwide. Members are able to post assignments, tips, and resources, as well as ask questions. However, one can only be a member if you have FCS in your profile. The website contains five Google resource sites that are free, easy to download, listed in a table of contents alphabetically, and located under the announcement icon on the home page. Resource topics range from bulletin board ideas, to cell phone policies, classroom setup, extra credit, rubrics for general presentations, bell ringers, and exit slips. Lesson plans and information on 504 and individualized education plans are also included. The site also has a place for the job posting of available teaching positions in FCS across the United States. In addition to all these resources, members may also participate in an FCS blog on current issues. For example, #distantonlinevirtuallearning was a recent topic at the beginning of the 2021/2022 school year.

ACTIVITY 10.1: WEBSITE ANALYSIS

Use the rubric in Table 10.1 to analyze the following website for a user-friendly environment. Instructional Practices :: iCEV | Online CTE Curriculum & Certification Testing (icevonline.com).

TABLE 10.1 Activity Rubric

	Below Standard	Approaching Standard	At Standard
Lesson Objectives	• are not provided to educators	• are provided to educators • are clear and cohesive to only a select group of educators • some, but not all, are obtained through lesson	• are provided to educators in an easy-to-read format • are clear and cohesive for all educators • all are obtained through lesson activities
Lesson Activities	• do not offer a variety of modalities • do not provide opportunities for accommodations/ or modifications • provides an incomplete lesson plan	• are provided for one to two various modalities • provide opportunities for some accommodations and modifications • provides a lesson plan	• are presented for a variety of modalities • provide opportunities for accommodations and modifications • provides a clear lesson plan for educators to follow effectively
User-Friendly and Student Centered	• 100% Teacher centered • No flexibility • No choices or options	• some student choice available • provide opportunities for some flexibility	• opportunities for reflection • provides much flexibility • provides opportunity for support with peer and instructor

SUMMARY

Teacher education preparation programs require that preservice educators be proficient in technology. Technology provides exposure to new visual experiences beyond the classroom and the learner's social environment. During the COVID-19 pandemic, we have all witnessed the impact of technology on education. Currently, problems exist with school systems and technology, which range from limited budgets, to untrained educators, unreliable software, inadequate infrastructures, and educators who are resistant to change. However, student-centered learning with higher order thinking activities and feedback from educators is still possible with online education.

KEY TERMS

Synchronous Learning

Teacher-centered learning

Web-based learning

Asynchronous dearning

Module

Blended/hybrid learning

Student-centered learning

Social media

QUESTIONS AND ACTIVITIES

1. Analyze the benefits of technology in FCS education.
2. Describe a user-friendly online environment.
3. Conduct a web search for two Facebook pages devoted to FCS education. Compare and contrast resources and content.
4. Create a student-centered online module that includes a variety of teaching strategies including higher order thinking, resources, and assessments.
5. Locate five teaching strategies from the FCS educator website that support two different course standards. Share with your peers why you selected these strategies. Are these strategies student centered? Support your response.

REFERENCES

Betz-Hamilton, A. (2021, Spring). Student perceptions of learning experiences during the COVID-19 pandemic: An examination of post-secondary hybrid, in-person, and online consumer affairs courses. *Journal of Family and Consumer Sciences Education, 38*(1), 13–23.

Borr, M., Napoleon, L., & Welch, A. (2013). Technology access and use in North Dakota family and consumer sciences classrooms. *Journal of Family and Consumer Sciences Education, 31*(2), 11–24. http://www.natefacs.org/Pages/v31no2/v31no2Borr.pdf

Dienlin, T., & Johannes, N. (2020). The impact of digital technology use on adolescent well-being. *Dialogues in Clinical Neuroscience, 22*(2), 135–142. https://doi.org/10.31887/DCNS.2020.22.2/tdienlin

Hess, A. J. (2021). *Online learning boomed during the pandemic—but what happens when students return to classrooms?* CNBC. https://www.cnbc.com/2021/03/26/online-learning-boomed-during-the-pandemic-but-soon-students-return-to-school.html

Hirose, B. (2011). Family and consumer sciences teacher use of technology to teach higher order thinking skills. *Journal of Family and Consumer Sciences Education, 29*(1), 36–45. http://www.natefacs.org/JFCSE/v29no1/v29no2Hirose.pdf.

Kim, S., Raza, M., & Seidman, E. (2019). Improving 21st-century teaching skills: The key to effective 21st-century learners. *Research in Comparative and International Education, 14*(1), 99–117. https://doi.org/10.1177/1745499919829214

Lokken, S. L., Cheek, W. K., & Hastings, S. W. (2003). The impact of technology training on family and consumer sciences teacher attitudes toward using computers as an instructional medium. *Journal of Family and Consumer Sciences Education, 21*(1), 18–32.

Maxwell, C. (2016). *What blended learning is—and isn't.* Blended Learning Universe. https://www.blendedlearning.org/what-blended-learning-is-and-isnt/

Merriam-Webster. (n.d.). Module. In *Merriam-Webster.com dictionary.* Retrieved July 26, 2021, from https://www.merriam-webster.com/dictionary/module

NEA Today. (2021, January). First and foremost. *National Education Association, 39*(3), 13.

Picciano, A. G. (2017). Theories and frameworks for online education: Seeking an integrated model. *Online Learning, 21*(3), 166–190.

Redmann, D. H., & Kotrlik, J. W. (2009). Family and consumer sciences teachers' adoption of technology for use in secondary classrooms. *Journal of Family and Consumer Sciences Education, 27*(1), 29–45. http://www.natefacs.org/JFCSE/v27no1/v27no1Redmann.pdf

Rehm, M., & Keller, M. K. (2020, Fall). Family and consumer sciences college students and the perceived role of the internet in developing a spiritual blueprint. *Journal of Family and Consumer Sciences Education, 37*(1), 14–27.

Richmond, E. (2014). *Student centered learning.* Stanford Center for Opportunity Policy in Education. https://edpolicy.stanford.edu/news/articles/1193

Riggs, S. (2020). *Student-centered remote teaching: Lessons learned from online education.* Teaching & Learning. https://er.educause.edu/blogs/2020/4/student-centered-remote-teaching-lessons-learned-from-online-educationer.

Schmitt, M. (2021, Spring). Effects of social media and technology on adolescents: What the evidence is showing and what we can do about it. *Journal of Family and Consumer Sciences Education, 38*(1), 51–59.

Scheiderer, J. (2021). *What's the difference between asynchronous and synchronous learning?* Ohio State Online. https://online.osu.edu/people/juliana-scheiderer

Smith, D. F. (2015). The 7 greatest challenges facing education technology. *EdTech Magazine.* https://edtechmagazine.com/k12/article/2015/11/7-greatest-challenges-facing-education-technology

Figure Credits

Assessments

The Link to Effective Teaching and Student Success

Elizabeth Ramsey, PhD, and Melinda Swafford, PhD

FIGURE 11.1 Planning Assessments

Chapter 11 Objectives

Upon completion of this chapter, the learner should be able to

- summarize the purpose of assessments,
- compare and contrast assessment to evaluation,
- relate validity and reliability to assessments,

- describe the correlation between planning and assessment,
- define preassessments and their purpose in lesson planning,
- distinguish between subjective and objective assessments,
- summarize various methods of student assessment,
- categorize various ways to assess patterns of student learning into formative/summative assessments,
- create a rubric to assess a specific task,
- summarize the various measures that evaluate students in public schools, and
- identify the teacher evaluation instruments in a specific school district.

Introduction

An effective family and consumer sciences (FCS) educator needs to understand the relationship between assessment and instruction. When planning instruction, one should see a link between the standard, goal/central idea, objectives/learner outcomes, and assessment. The focus of this chapter is on assessments informing instruction, how assessment improves an educator, and how assessments measure student achievement. A wide variety of measures exists that document student achievement. These vary from measures that rely on empirical data to teacher observation. Assessment is an essential part of education, as it is an indicator of individual and whole group patterns of student learning and successful attainment of a goal/central idea and objectives/learner outcomes (Edutopia, 2008). At the end of the chapter, the learner will demonstrate various ways to assess student learning.

Assessment and Evaluation

Assessment is a complex process involving data collection. The purpose is to evaluate student content, measure student performance, evaluate programs, and make decisions regarding teaching. Through the process of assessment, decisions are made regarding curriculum, student placement/grade advancement, funding for programs, and professional development for educators.

Course standards and objectives determine the content that should be taught and at what level. Objectives have a direct relationship to what will be assessed and how it will be assessed; therefore, assessments should support the objective. See Table 11.1 for examples.

TABLE 11.1 Relationship of the Objective to How It Will Be Assessed

Objective	Assessment
TLW demonstrate	Application activity
TLW analyze	Evaluation activity
TLW identify	Recall activity
TLW summarize	Comprehension activity

When planning assessments, an educator must ensure that the assessment selected to measure the objective is valid. **Validity** refers to the soundness of the assessment. If an assessment is valid, it measures what it was intended to assess, and to what extent.

Content validity ensures that the assessment items measure what they were intended to measure. For example, the objective is the learner will (TLW) identify the components of a budget. A test question asks, "Why should families use a budget?" Although this question at first glance might seem like a good question, an educator must evaluate this question regarding the learner's objective. Does this sample test question evaluate the components of a budget? The resounding answer is no.

ACTIVITY 11.1: CONTENT VALIDITY

Discuss a way to assess the previous objective (TLW identify the components of a budget) that demonstrates content validity. Share with the class and support your choice.

To achieve **construct validity**, the performance on the assessment must relate to the objective or standard. In other words, the student must perform or do what is stated in the objective. For example, if the objective states TLW analyze the principles of interpersonal communication, the student must actually analyze interpersonal communication. This could be accomplished through analyzing a case study about interpersonal communication and answering discussion questions. When considering this objective, true/false quiz items would not demonstrate the learner's ability to analyze principles of interpersonal communication. Because analyzing requires high-order thinking, it is difficult to assess the analysis of interpersonal communication with true/false quiz items. Typically, true/false items assess lower level recall concepts. That being said, a case study with a discussion question would be a much better way to assess the higher order thinking response required for the analysis of the principles of interpersonal communication.

Reliability refers to the consistency of the assessment. When a test is reliable, the results are consistent over time with similar populations. In other words, if a test were given again, to similar students, under the same circumstances and the results were similar, the test would be reliable. When an assessment is reliable, it is an indication that the data produced by the assessment were accurate. Assessments need to be reliable in order to be valid (Silverstein, 2019). Therefore, it is important that assessments are both reliable and valid.

Program Evaluations

Assessment and evaluation do not have the same meaning, although the two terms can be mistakenly used for one another. Assessment is a data collection process. **Evaluation** is placing judgment on the data that is collected through analysis of the data. Evaluation quantifies the assessment data of the student toward the progress of reaching the course standard, goal, and objective. Having learners complete formative assessments provides the educator with data toward the learner's progress of the lesson of the day. Through observation or a checklist, the educator makes the decision to either move forward or reteach. However, during a summative assessment, the educator evaluates the progress by categorizing the data to show how well the learner has made progress in gaining knowledge of the concepts. Terms commonly used in evaluations are mean, median, and mode. Mean is the average score, the median is the midrange score between the highest and lowest score, and mode is the most common score. Numerical quantities may also be used to quantify assessment data.

Standardized tests involve all participants answering the same questions and using consistent scoring scoring to evaluate students. Districts use standardized tests to determine how their students are doing in comparison to students in similar situations around the state or nation. These tests can be used for program evaluation and for funding, as these tests provide data on how well students, teachers, school districts, and states are performing and show patterns of strengths and weaknesses. Types of assessments for program evaluation include your state's standardized testing, such as the Tennessee Comprehensive Assessment Program (TCAP) and Terra Nova, which is a complete battery of diagnostic tests for grade level kindergarten-12 (Terra Nova, n.d.). Data collected from these tests measure student-level proficiency. Districts and states use the data to make decisions on programs. Other types of standardized tests for individuals include aptitude tests such as IQ, or tests like ACT or SAT. Terms associated with standardized tests include **norm reference**, which compares students to others that are the same age, and **criterion reference**, which assesses a child's performance on a specific task. Standardized tests are also used to qualify students for special education services.

Standardized tests provide a variety of scores. The term *raw score* means the number the student got correct on a standardized test. It is helpful to have a basic understanding of these scores. A standard score is a statistical average based on the performance of students tested in the norming process of the development of the test (Logsdon, 2020). Standard scores on tests estimate if a student's scores are above average, average, or below average as compared to their peers. A standard score on a norm-referenced assessment compares one student's performance on a test to the performance of other students their age.

Age/grade equivalent scores are formed from a mental age standard that was obtained by identifying the age at which most children pass a particular test. These scores should not be used in the high-level analysis of student achievement. For example, if a second-grade student has a reading equivalent to a fourth grader, it doesn't mean the student reads on a fourth-grade level. This means the student reads second-grade material like you would expect a fourth grader to read.

The bell-shaped curve is a graph that represents a normal distribution of scores. The highest point of the curve represents normal or the majority. The left of the curve represents below normal, and the right of the curve represents above normal. The bell curve represents student scores on evaluations. Consequently, an educator may observe the bell curve in many situations. For example, consider the timing when students complete an exam. A smaller number will complete the exam early, the majority of students will complete the exam close to the same time, while fewer of the students will complete the exam later. Even though a bell curve can be observed in situations

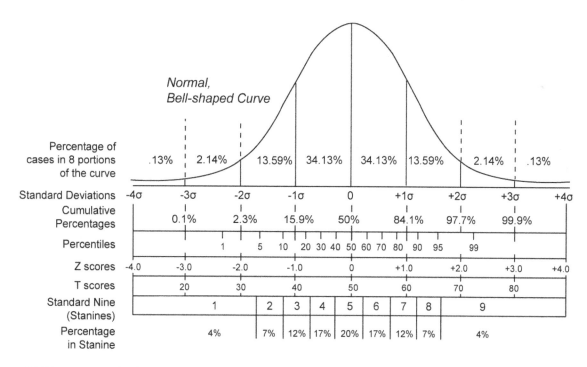

FIGURE 11.2 Normal Bell-Shaped Curve

like the aforementioned, we know that there is no correlation between the time it takes a student completes a test and the score.

A **stanine** is a way to scale test scores. Stanines are integers and can be used to convert a test score into a single digit. Stanine indicates nine statistical units on a scale of 1 to 9, which are used to indicate a performance level on a psychological or educational test. Stanines provide the same information as other standard scores; however, they are less accurate. The mean is always 5 with a standard deviation of two. Low-level scores are 1–3, average scores are 4–6 average, and high scores are 7–9. An alternative to stanines is percentile scores.

A **standard deviation** is a measure of the variation in the distribution of a data set and is used to determine what scores are average, above average, or below average (see Figure 11.2). These scores can be useful in understanding a relative range of a performance such as TCAP or TerraNova. Standard deviation scores are different for each test.

Percentile scores are more accurate and easier to explain to others. The percentage of subjects in a normative sample that is scored at or below the particular score you're interpreting. So if you score at 90 percentile, your score is the same or higher than 90% of others in the same grade taking the same test. See Figure 11.2 for a visual depiction of normal standard deviations and percentile scores.

Formative and Summative Assessments

Formative assessments are used to monitor learner progress on a daily basis during instruction and provide feedback to the student. This type of assessment is part of the instructional process and is key to providing effective learning experiences for the learner. Formative assessments can be as informal as teacher observation or as formal as a pen and paper assessment; this type of assessment may also be conducted with an individual, small group, a partner, or the entire class. When educators pay attention to the data from formative assessments, they monitor the progress of the learner and adjust instruction accordingly—either reteach or move forward.

By varying the types of formative assessments during the lesson or learning segment, the educator will get a true picture of how much learning has occurred. During the body of the lesson, formative assessments can occur during the set, presentation of content, supervised practice, and independent practice and closure. Examples of formative assessments are paper-and-pencil activities, anecdotal notes, oral questioning, checklists, completion of graphic organizer, closure, homework, and other activities that are ungraded.

Summative assessments are evaluations that are intended for the purpose of assigning a grade, as they are used to determine how much learning has taken place at the end of a lesson or learning segment/unit. As with formative assessments, the educator reviews the data to determine the next step for instruction. Summative assessments usually carry more weight in the course average. Examples of summative assessments include end-of-unit or chapter tests, semester or final exams, ACT and SAT, benchmark assessments, and state exams. New or preservice educators may be confused by the differences between formative and summative assessments.

The common features of both formative and summative assessments are necessary for the education of learners. From both, educators can use data to plan future learning. Each form of assessment can be used to provide feedback to learners (see Figure 11.3).

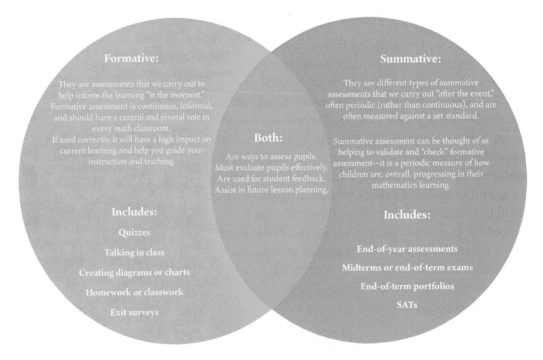

FIGURE 11.3 Venn Diagram of Formative and Summative Assessment

Methods of Assessment

Assessment instruments serve the following purposes. They provide the educators some indication of the actual achievement of learners to make educational decisions of reteaching or moving on to the next learnings segment. Assessments also identify trends among groups. Effective educators incorporate a variety of formative assessments in each lesson. Several distinctive categories of assessment are included in the following sections.

Questioning

Questioning is a method that provides feedback to the educator regarding how the learners are grasping the content. Effective educators formulate and pose questions to learners throughout the entire lesson. This may be difficult for the preservice and first-year educator, but with practice, formulating and posing questions will get easier. There are several types of questions: open-ended, closed-ended, knowledge questions, skills questions, and reflection questions (Wiggins & McTighe, 2005). Knowledge questions ask students to recall facts and ideas, skill questions require them to apply knowledge, and reflection questions require the learner to give meaning and connect facts to overall themes or concepts (Wiggins & McTighe, 2005). Knowledge questions are appropriate to use in the set and in the closure as educators are asking learners to recall facts. Skill questions are appropriate for independent practice during the lesson, as well as during closure. Reflection questions are also appropriate for independent practice and during closure.

Observation

Observation of learners is a reliable form of assessment. Observation is classified as formative assessment, and much can be learned by noting the body language and facial expressions of learners in the classroom. Puzzled looks, a turned head, or lack of eye contact may mean that the concept covered needs more explanation or there is a lack of understanding from the learner. Furthermore, the educator can require the learner to use thumbs up or head nods to illustrate agreement or disagreement with a statement. Educators may also use observation as a way to assess behavior, as observation is a part of positive behavior intervention and support. Scatterplots, checklists, and anecdotal records are involved in the collection of data. Please see Chapter 7 for more information on positive behavior intervention and support.

Feedback

An important part of the assessment process is feedback for both formative and summative assessments. Serving as a form of self-evaluation, feedback can be the vehicle for self-improvement. Feedback that is timely, constructive, and meaningful to the learner helps them to gain an understanding of what they know and how to make improvements. Feedback can be provided orally, visually (with the type of body language, like smiles, nods, thumbs up, fist bumps, or high five), and through written comments on student work. Effective written feedback begins with a positive comment and then includes a comment on how to improve or gain additional knowledge.

Closure

As previously stated in Chapter 6, closure is a way to conclude a lesson. It also serves as a formative assessment, providing the educator with the knowledge to determine if content needs to be retaught. Several methods of assessment may be used with the closure of a lesson. A common method is an exit ticket. This may be in the form of a response to a written or oral question posed by the educator. Also, having students summarize their notes in a written paragraph can serve as a formative assessment. Orally, students individually or in a group can share a question they have about the content or one thing learned about the content. Other forms of activities in a closure that assess student knowledge include key ideas, thumbs up, KWL (what the learner **k**nows, what the learner **w**ants to know, what the learner **l**earned) charts, the Five Ws of a lesson, and think-pair-share, where partners respond to a question posed by the educator or share with your partner some content covered in the lesson, while having someone from the pair share with the class (Mulvahill, 2021).

Writing Measurement Items for Assessments

Writing items for assessments is an important step in evaluation and is often used when creating tests and quizzes. Creating assessment items is a time-consuming process but well worth the time for educators and students to have excellent products to measure student performance. The goal of any assessment

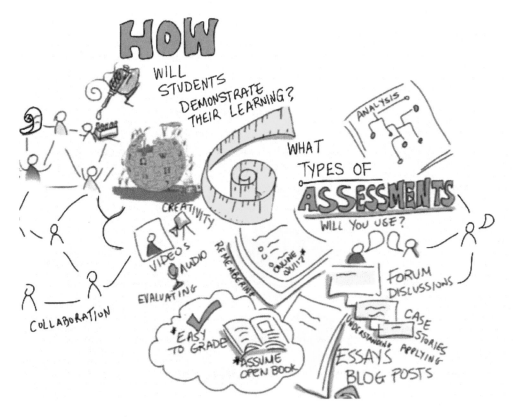

FIGURE 11.4 Types of Assessments

tool should be to determine student mastery but also determine adequate instruction. Considering the time educators invest in creating assessment tools, educators may want to consider textbooks and curricula that supply test banks. Test banks can be useful resources for educators, as they are typically screened for reliability and validity. However, test banks are not always included in textbooks and curricula; therefore, we will examine various types of assessment items and how to successfully write those items. As always, with any assessment, there should be clear instructions. See Table 11.2 for a comprehensive list of assessment items and when each is appropriate and inappropriate to use.

When constructing true/false items, focus on one concept for the item, as items that contain more than one concept can be confusing or misleading. When an item has more than one concept included, it is considered a **double-barrel** item and will lack validity. It is best to include statements that are entirely factual and not opinion based (Hitch & Youatt, 2002). It is best to keep true/false statements short and concise; in other words, avoid long and complicated sentences. Also, avoid superlative statements, like always, never, best, and generally (Weber State University, n.d.). When creating true/false assessments, use an equal number of true/false answers and randomize the items.

Multiple-choice items include the following structure: the item **stem**, which is the introductory question or statement to be answered or solved, and the **alternatives**, which are the list of possible solutions or responses (Brame, 2013; Hitch & Youatt, 2002). When writing multiple-choice items, there are some guiding concepts. First, the stem should address a single problem, should be more complex in nature than the alternatives, should avoid irrelevant material, should be a question or incomplete statement, and should not be negative unless necessary (Hitch & Youatt, 2002; Brame, 2013). In turn, the alternatives should be plausible, homogenous, grammatically correct with stem, and have four to five options. The alternative items should also be vertically listed, somewhat equal in length, and should be free from clues (Hitch & Youatt, 2002; Brame, 2013). Additionally, alternatives should avoid the responses "all of the above" or "none of the above" (Brame, 2013). Multiple-choice items on an assessment should have an equal number of alternatives. In other words, one item should not have five responses while another item has four alternatives—be consistent. Additionally, avoid any pattern in responses and avoid clues to other items.

TABLE 11.2   **Various Test Items and Appropriate Use**

Assessment Item	When to use
True/False	Use when testing factual content. Do not use it when the content is not entirely true or false.
Multiple Choice	Use with a variety of content and learner outcomes.
Matching	Use when learners need to construct relationships between concepts.
Short Answer	Use to demonstrate student knowledge by responding with a word, phrase, or few sentences without any choices.
Essay	Useful when students need to express ideas, generalize content, or organize and integrate ideas rather than simple rote memorization. Requires the student to synthesize ideas, express ideas, and write coherently.

Informed by Hitch & Youatt (2002).

Constructing matching items on assessments typically consists of creating two columns. The left column contains the premise, and the column on the right contains the response, and each column should be homogenous (Hitch & Youatt, 2002; University of Wisconsin, n.d.). There should be at least a few more responses than premises (Hitch & Youatt, 2002; University of Wisconsin, n.d.). When columns are homogeneous, that means they are the same, so for example, the right-hand column might contain all definitions, and the left-hand column would contain all vocabulary words. Hitch and Youatt (2002) suggest writing the premise, the longer item, in the left column and shorter items in the right-hand column. For clarity, the matching items should fit neatly onto one page, and there should not be more than 10–12 items.

Constructive response items include both short-answer and essay items. Short-answer items are best written when they are clear and concise, and there should be only one plausible answer. Short answers should be written to specific units of measurement (e.g., pounds, ounces, inches, etc.). For example:

At birth, the average neonate weighs _____ (pounds).

Short-answer responses are best written with the missing word or phrase at the end of the item (Hitch & Youatt, 2002). Short-answer responses should all contain the same blank length for each item. When students are required to label an illustration or diagram, make it big enough to be seen well along with clear lines and arrows.

Essay items give an educator the opportunity to test higher order thinking skills. Essay items also take less time to construct, yet take more time to grade. When creating essay items, create a scoring key or rubric prior to grading responses (Hitch & Youatt, 2002; Kelly, 2019). Be clear in the instructions about how spelling, punctuation, and grammar will be addressed. Include a suggested completion time on each essay question, along with arranging essay questions in order of complexity. Be sure to provide sufficient space to respond to each essay question within the exam. Essay items should be constructed from learner lesson objectives, should be positioned at the end of the exam, and should contain a point value (Kelly, 2019).

Creating Rubrics

Rubrics are commonly used to help students understand expectations while adding to the ease of grading. Rubrics are useful when assigning individual or collaborative work projects. When teachers provide students with a rubric, students know how they will be assessed while teachers can easily check off the criterion in a neat, organized way. Rubrics can be time-consuming to create, but once they are created, they will cut back on the time spent grading. There are three components to a rubric: the evaluation criteria, scoring strategy, and quality definitions for each criterion (Hitch and Youatt, 2002). When creating a rubric, begin with the criteria. For example, if you have students creating an infographic of indicators that affect healthy brain development, begin with each criterion. After selecting the criteria, develop quality definitions, starting with a strong definition of exactly what you require. Use a graded scale and work your way down to what you would consider unsatisfactory. In the example, you will see four levels for each criterion. Notice how each level is labeled with a point value included.

SPOTLIGHT: EXAMPLE OF RUBRIC: HEALTHY BRAIN DEVELOPMENT INFOGRAPHIC

Instructions: Create an infographic differentiating between healthy and unhealthy brain development. Please include at least 10 items that can impact healthy development and 10 items that can impact unhealthy development. Document at least three quality sources used in APA format in a reference section at the bottom of the infographic. Please be as creative as possible. Free infographic templates can be accessed through Canva, PicMonkey, Venngage, or Piktochart. You may use other templates as desired. See the following Spotlight for a rubric example on the assignment Healthy Brain Development.

TABLE 11.3   Healthy Brain Development Rubric

Example: Healthy Brain Development
Total Value: 100 points

Criteria	Excellent 25 points	Good 20 points	Fair 15 points	Poor 10 points
Content	Content is accurate and included required 10 examples of each healthy and unhealthy development.	Content is accurate and required 10 examples of each healthy and unhealthy development component are present, with one or two minor mistakes.	Some of the content is inaccurate and some of the required components are missing or have mistakes.	Content is inaccurate and components are missing.
Organization	Content is organized exceptionally well and easy to follow. Components are clearly labeled and easily identifiable.	Content is organized well and easy to follow. Components are labeled and identifiable.	Content is somewhat organized and can somewhat be followed. Components are somewhat labeled.	Content is difficult to follow and not well organized. Components are not labeled.
Spelling and punctuation	Correct grammatical construction, free of typos; clear, correct technical vocabulary, correct punctuation.	A few mistakes with the following: Correct grammatical construction, free of typos; clear, correct technical, vocabulary; and correct punctuation.	Five or more mistakes with the following: Correct grammatical construction, free of typos; clear, correct technical, vocabulary; and correct punctuation.	Infographic contains numerous grammatical, punctuation, typos, and/or spelling errors.
APA sources	Three or more quality sources were correctly cited in APA format.	Three or more quality sources were cited in APA format with a few minor mistakes.	Two quality sources were cited in APA format with mistakes.	Quality sources were lacking or missing from infographic or APA format was disregarded.

Differentiated Assessments

A requirement for career technical education educators is to make sure the classroom is respectful and accommodating of diversity. Differentiated assessment is one way to meet the needs of individuals with diverse learning needs. By incorporating differentiation assessments, students may demonstrate mastery in a variety of ways (Broemmel et al., 2016) as educators reflect back on students' strengths and interests for ways to differentiate assessments (Swafford & Giordano, 2017). Everyone gains when educators incorporate modifications and accommodations into the lesson. The teacher avoids developing a separate lesson plan for each student with diverse needs. The learner with diverse needs is included in the activities to the appropriate extent possible and becomes an active part of the community of learners. Our society gains, as the student will learn needed content that will impact quality of life and improve capacity building of the individual (Swafford & Giordano, 2017).

An example of accommodations is when educators adapt tools or other equipment in the food lab to accommodate learners with physical disabilities involving eye-hand coordination (such as a pizza cutter to cut green onions or other vegetables). Furthermore, someone with a learning disability in written expression may demonstrate mastery of content orally instead of writing a summary or a reflection (Swafford & Giordano, 2017). Using these examples illustrates that the learners are held to the same standards as other students. However, remember that a modification is when the standard has been changed and the learner is held accountable for the revised standards.

edTPA and Assessments

The edTPA, Teacher Performance Assessment, is a national assessment tool used to assess preservice teachers' readiness to teach specified content and is designed to incorporate theory and research (Pearson, 2019). The edTPA has three major tasks that are assessed through a total of 15 rubrics, five rubrics per task. Task 1 is about "planning for instruction and assessment"; Task 2 is about "instructing and engaging students in learning"; Task 3 is about "assessing student learning" (Pearson, 2019, p. 1). Therefore, it is ever important for preservice teachers to develop solid skills in assessment and feedback, as the major components of edTPA are planning, instruction, and assessment (Pearson, 2019). Task 1 considers a teacher candidate's ability to plan, including a plan for assessment, which assessments should "provide multiple forms of evidence to monitor students' understanding" (Pearson, 2019, p. 18). Additionally, assessments should be designed for both the whole class and students with varied needs, including individual education plans (IEP), 504s, and English language learners (ELLs; Pearson, 2019, pp. 28–29). The edTPA, in task three, assesses teacher candidates' ability to give feedback, focusing on both the strengths of students and their needs (Pearson, 2019, p. 34). Teacher candidates must provide evidence of students' use of academic vocabulary in their assessments, including language function, vocabulary, and either syntax or discourse. Lastly, teacher candidates must be able to target extra support as a result of assessments. Assessments are of prime importance in the edTPA process during residency/student teaching, as the preservice educator must indicate how they will use student responses to content to reteach, modify strategies, or move forward with the content.

In the state of Tennessee, under the career cluster of human service, the dietetics and nutrition program has a course entitled Nutrition Across the Lifespan. Standard 7.2 states the following:

Selection and Preparation of Food: Demonstrate food selection and preparation methods that maximize the nutritional value of foods while minimizing dietary health risks. Plan and conduct nutrition laboratory experiments to determine the physical and chemical changes of food structure through chemical reactions then compare and contrast the results. Demonstrate relationships among concepts including a. Heat b. Acidity level c. Fermentation d. Maillard reactions e. Chemically processed foods f. Preparation techniques and product yield. (Tennessee Department of Education, 2022, p. 6)

A modification of the above standard to meet the IEP requirements for a student with a mild intellectual disability (IQ of 70) could include the following: Demonstrate food selection and preparation skills that follow government recommendations and safe and sanitary food preparation methods and maximize nutrition to promote health.

The learner with the IEP would be held accountable for the modified standard instead of the entire state standard. The educator would modify the assignments and only require parts of the assignment that pertain to the modified standards for a grade. During class, accommodations would be used to keep the student engaged. These accommodations would include the following: peer tutoring (pairing the student with a peer in class); task analysis (breaking down the task into smaller parts); providing extra time for the assignment (e.g., one-on-one time with the teacher), or maybe complete the assignment for homework; and opportunities to redo assignments. The main content for the student would focus on the danger zone of food storage, government websites for safe food handling practices, and personal sanitation techniques. Content would also include the use and care of food preparation equipment and utensils, accurate measurement of ingredients, and food preparation terms and techniques. Meal planning content would include recommended requirements on daily intake of nutrients to maintain health. The learner would also plan menus to meet the requirements, as well as accurate preparation of nutrient-dense recipes. The student would still be accountable for making 100% on the safety test. However, accommodations for this test could include oral testing, opportunities to retake the test, extra time on the test, and/or an alternative setting for the test (Swafford & Giordano, 2017).

By incorporating a modification of the standards and use of accommodations with teaching strategies and assessments, the student with the mild intellectual disability would integrate easily into the general FCS classroom. The modified standard would provide content to improve the life skills of the student in their current family situation and in the future.

SPOTLIGHT: REFLECTIONS OF A PRESERVICE TEACHER DURING RESIDENCY/STUDENT TEACHING

By Kristen Giordano, M.Ed. (Swafford & Giordano, 2017)

This vignette was written by an FCS student-teacher (referred to as a resident by the university) about her Residency II experience during placement in a local school system. Her reflections on

(Continued)

her experience using assessments to identify the individual strengths and needs of her students allowed her to accommodate and modify to meet the diverse needs of her students.

Residency II was approaching, and I began to get excited. A requirement for edTPA in Residency II was to complete a context for learning, which contains detailed information about the school, the community, the students, and the course I was teaching. My placement was in a high school that was located in a rural lower socioeconomic area with 58% of the student body eligible for free or reduced lunch. As I looked through my class roster, I began to realize something quite startling. Out of 18 students, I had eight students with an IEP, and one student who was an English Language Learning (ELL). I thought, "How am I going to do this?" Intimidated was an understatement for how I was feeling. For a brief moment, I began doubting my abilities to take on this challenge. I later recalled my training in teacher education.

After conferring with my mentoring teacher and my university instructor, the first thing I did was to contact the person within my school that had access to the student's IEP and ELL files. This was the chair of the special education department and the ELL teacher. After scheduling a meeting, I brought my notepad and was ready to take as many notes as needed. As we began looking at the IEP and ELL specifications in each student file, many of the students needed the following types of accommodations: information in small/distinct steps, extra prompting, more time on assignments and projects, opportunities to redo assignments, and one-on-one instruction when necessary.

After obtaining the information from the IEP and ELL files, I wanted to know more about students within the class. Therefore, on the first day in the class, I had the students complete an "About Me" assignment, which included questions about their interests, favorite types of activities, and strategies other teachers used to help them succeed in class. The activity also required them to state what they hope to learn within the class. After reviewing student responses, I found that one student did not have a working oven in their home and that many students were interested in learning how to prepare food. Students also completed a learning styles inventory. While I knew what I would be teaching from the course standards, I wanted to know how the students would best learn the information. Results from the inventory indicated that a majority of the learners, within the classroom, were a mixture of kinesthetic and visual learners. This information allowed me to have a starting point to plan lessons that would meet the needs of my students.

Being flexible with planning and delivery of content with all types of students is important; however, with students with disabilities or special needs, nothing can be set in stone. I did not ever want to single a student out; therefore, some accommodations for students with an IEP or ELL were implemented for the entire class. For example, if I needed to make the text larger and more spaced, every student received the assignment or information in that way. Questioning was also an excellent way to conduct formative assessments; however, I learned to provide extra prompting and queues within the question to help trigger memory recall for those who need this accommodation.

When planning the lessons, I made sure to incorporate the types of learning styles assessed from the learning style inventory, as well as provide for the accommodations that were recommended in the IEP. For example, while teaching a unit on quick bread, the first day, I focused heavily on presenting content with class discussion/questioning style teaching while implementing visual components. All students were provided with a notetaker to help with note-taking. When I realized simply explaining the processes to them was not working, on the second and third days of class, I provided more visuals and hands-on activities and included a food lab. I also conducted demonstrations that involved the students to show the students what was expected of them within the foods lab.

For the learning environment, I made sure students had access to all needed materials, equipment, and space to move. For students to learn, they must feel safe within the classroom. Knowing we only had three food labs and 18 students in the classroom, I divided the class into six groups of three. Heterogeneous groups were selected by pairing students who were low achieving or those who may need peer tutoring with students who were natural leaders or high achieving. In regard to the student with the physical disability, safety was of the utmost importance. I also wanted to make sure the classroom was a safe space for sharing various thoughts and ideas.

As a teacher, being able to assess student learning throughout the lesson was important because if something was not working, the student would not be engaged. After teaching a few lessons, I asked my students to evaluate my teaching. Most students revealed they needed to hear the directions repeated (indicating I needed to meet the needs of auditory learners more) and implement even more hands-on tasks. Also, evaluating data allowed me to see trends of how the entire class was doing. For example, after my first assessment, I realized I could not do fill-in-the-blank-style assessments without providing some type of word bank. Instead of blaming the students for not learning. for the next quiz, I made the changes using a word bank, and the students did much better.

Looking back at this experience, I grew so much as a person and as a teacher. At first, it was intimidating. I did not think I was capable of teaching such a diverse group of students in one class. At times it was really hard, as I hit many trials and bumps in the road. I applied concepts from my education classes, and being with students with various needs allowed me to grow with them. Teachers should have the passion to provide students with the best education possible. As educators, we should all strive to know our students so we can best meet their needs in the classroom.

SUMMARY

Assessment is a complex process involving data collection. Assessment is the vehicle educators implement to evaluate students' abilities and understand students' interests and needs. Through the process of assessment, decisions are made regarding curriculum, student placement/grade advancement, funding for programs, and professional development for educators. When planning assessments, one should see a link between the standard, goal/central idea, objectives/learner outcomes, and the assessment. It is important to use a variety of assessment strategies, including performance-based (lab evaluation) and open-ended assessment (think-pair-share, exit tickets, and reflection) as well as portfolios and rubrics. To assess teacher effectiveness, FCS educators should reflect on changes that would be made in the content or materials so that all students are challenged and their needs are met.

KEY TERMS

Formative assessments

Age/grade equivalent scores

Construct validity

Summative assessments

Validity

Norm reference

Stanine

Reliability

Criterion reference

Standard deviation

Content validity

Percentile scores

Assessment

Evaluation

Standardized tests

Rubrics

Double-barrel

Stem

Alternatives

QUESTIONS AND ACTIVITIES

Using the guidelines specified in this chapter concerning the creation of assessment items, complete the following items:

1. Write five true/false items that could be used on an exam for the section titled "Assessment and Evaluation" in this chapter.
2. Write five multiple-choice items that could be used on an exam for the section titled "Program Evaluation" in this chapter.
3. Create a matching set with 10 of the vocabulary words from Chapter 11.
4. Write three short-answer items for the section titled "Formative and Summative Assessments."
5. Write three essay questions about this chapter.
6. Create a Venn diagram on your own. If you struggle to create one, do an internet search for examples of Venn diagrams to see examples. After creating a Venn diagram, compare and contrast formative and summative assessments. Provide an example of each.

REFERENCES

Brame, C. (2013). *Writing good multiple choice test questions*. Vanderbilt University: Center for Teaching. https://cft.vanderbilt.edu/guides-sub-pages/writing-good-multiple-choice-test-questions/

Broemmel, A. D., Jordan, J., & Whitsett, B. M. (2016). *Learning to be teacher leaders: A framework for assessment, planning, and instruction*. Routledge.

Edutopia. (2008). *Why are assessments important?* George Lucas Educational Foundation. https://www.edutopia.org/about/word-george-lucas-edutopias-role-education

Hitch, E. J., & Youatt, J. P. (2002). *Communicating family and consumer sciences*. Goodheart-Wilcox Company, Inc.

Kelly, M. (2019). *Creating and scoring essay tests.* ThoughtCo. https://www.thoughtco.com/creating-scoring-essay-tests-8439

Logsdon, A. (2020). *Different types of scores on standardized tests.* Very Well Family. https://www.verywellfamily.com/what-are-standard-scores-2162891

Mulvahill, E. (2021, June 17). *20 Creative Ways to Check for Understanding.* We Are Teachers. Retrieved from https://www.weareteachers.com/ways-to-check-for-understanding/

Pearson. (2019). *edTPA. Family and consumer sciences: Assessment handbook* (version 06.1).

Swafford, M., & Giordano, K. (2017). Universal design: Ensuring success for all FCS students. *Journal of Family and Consumer Sciences, 109*(4) 47–52. https://doi.org/10.14307/JFCS109.4.47

Tennessee Department of Education. (2022). *Nutrition across the lifespan.* https://www.tn.gov/content/dam/tn/stateboardofeducation/documents/2021-sbe-meetings/july-23%2c-2021-sbe-meeting/7-23-21%20II%20E%20CTE%20Course%20Standards%2

Terra Nova. (n.d.). *Home page.* Retrieved October 12, 2021, from https://terranova3.com/

University of Wisconsin. (n.d.). *Multiple-choice & matching test.* Retrieved September 25, 2021, from https://www.uww.edu/learn/restiptool/multiple-choice-and-matching

Weber State University. (n.d.). True/false questions. https://weber.instructure.com/courses/351442/pages/true-slash-false-questions

Wiggins, G., & McTighe, J. (2005). *Understanding by design* (2nd ed.). Association for Supervision and Curriculum Development. https://doi.org/10.14483/CALJ.V19N1.11490

Figure Credits

Advocacy

Elizabeth Ramsey, PhD, CFLE, and Melinda Swafford, PhD

FIGURE 12.1 Advocacy

Chapter 12 Objectives

Upon completion of this chapter, learners should be able to

- define and provide examples of the different types of advocacy,
- describe how advocacy can be performed,

- analyze and describe how advocacy can be effective,
- describe ways to include advocacy with students,
- compare and contrast advocacy to lobbying,
- define Family Career Community Leaders of America (FCCLA),
- identify individual and group Students Taking Action with Recognition (STAR) events, and
- analyze how FCCLA prepares students to be advocates for individuals and families.

Introduction

This chapter contains content on how advocacy can influence political, social, and economic support for the profession of family and consumer sciences (FCS) education. This chapter is usually not included in a textbook that is devoted to pedagogy. However, after reviewing the history of the profession and how legislation has impacted the growth, funding, and changes in the profession, it is evident that it has become necessary to advocate for FCS education to ensure and maintain awareness of our profession and all that is encompassed in our work with individuals and families.

Advocacy

What is **advocacy**? It is an activity that tries to influence a position within political, economic, and social systems and institutions (AAFCS, n.d.). This influence may be of support or rejection of a cause. There are two types of advocacy: individual and collective. An **individual advocate** is a paid or unpaid individual who is not affiliated with any service or agency that supports a cause. A **self-advocate** is a person who speaks on their own behalf (Stewart & MacIntyre, 2013). This person may be trained or untrained in advocacy. **Collective/peer advocates** are groups of individuals with common views who join together and become involved in a cause that addresses the well-being of those who need support in the community or make their voices heard about a cause (Stewart & MacIntyre, 2013).

Advocacy has many purposes. Individual advocacy promotes individual rights to have control over their lives, as it provides opportunities for individuals to speak for themselves and others. In the FCS profession, collective advocacy can be used to obtain funding and increase awareness and visibility of the profession. Both individual and collective advocacy can influence legislation by providing awareness of obstacles faced that impact quality of life for individuals, families, and communities (AAFCS, n.d.).

Advocacy involves many actions (see Figure 12.2). Letters of support, letters to the editor, or white papers include content on analysis of issues or provide information or make recommendations for reform. Media campaigns may include the development of educational materials and/or provide forums for discussion and awareness. Other advocacy actions may include direct action such as doing public service announcements, joining professional associations/coalitions, serving on boards of organizations/coalitions, and being involved in direct actions to influence change or benefit a cause (AAFCS, n.d.).

FIGURE 12.2 Advocacy Promotes Individual Rights

The American Association of Family and Consumer Sciences (AAFCS) supports advocacy in teacher preparation programs. As stated by Couch and Alexander (2009), FCS professionals cannot opt for neutrality. In our professional work, we must embrace "the responsibility to help individuals develop the capacity to address the … issues they encounter in their own lives" (Couch & Alexander, 2009, p. 70). Viewing the AAFCS tool kit located on the website under the link of "Advocacy", members will find information on how to write a position paper, advocacy letters, the legislative process, and how to obtain copies of legislation, as well as how to set up meetings with Congress. Also in the AAFCS tool kit, one will find information on how to conduct a public policy workshop that includes sample handouts and fact sheets that advocate for FCS in secondary schools (AAFCS Advocacy, n.d.).

Lobbying is a form of advocacy that involves a direct approach to influence legislators to take a specific position on the legislation. There are two types of lobbying: direct, as previously described, and grassroots, which includes public opinion. The difference between advocacy and lobbying is that advocacy is making others aware of a problem and how the problem is impacting families, whereas lobbying is asking them to vote for or against specific legislation (National Council on Aging, n.d.). A lobbyist can be a paid position.

ADVOCATING FOR SOCIAL HEALTH EDUCATION
By Elizabeth Ramsey

Oftentimes, the need for advocacy becomes obvious through everyday experiences and situations, and it is through these experiences that professionals have the opportunity to advocate. One such case for advocacy occurred in a rural middle school in Tennessee in 2017. I was hired to teach

(Continued)

fifth-grade English language arts (ELA). I am licensed general education, kindergarten through sixth grade, and licensed FCS education, sixth through twelfth grade. It is important to note that the county had lost funding for FCS education at the middle school level and had pulled Social Health, once known as Teen Living, from the school system more than a decade earlier. Within the first few weeks of school, I noticed many extreme behavior issues, including theft, outbursts of anger, aggression, and violence. What was most telling was the same children displayed the same behavior issues repeatedly. The middle school had an organized system of tracking behavior that was grade-wide. It was helpful because as data was entered into the system, I found that the same behavior was occurring for other teachers in their classrooms as well, not to mention the behavior was occurring outside of the class-rooms, in the halls, cafeteria, bus/car line, and playground. The school administrators were quick to address behavior issues and enforce consequences, such as recess and lunch detention, after-school detention, and in-and out-of-school suspension. However, after students experienced consequences, their behavior did not change, the behavior remained consistent. With my FCS background, I began to recognize very quickly that the students who struggled with these behavior issues needed help. They needed to learn how to regulate their behavior, resolve conflicts in a productive manner, manage their anger, and simply learn how to be a friend. I recognized the need to teach these students other alternatives to their actions, and I knew that the behavior would not change until the students got the help they needed, which was social health education. Thus, the need for advocacy began.

I requested a meeting with my administrators, who welcomed my ideas. I shared with them the state standards for social health education, along with primary information about the social learn-ing theory, how children imitate modeled behavior, and information from Bronfenbrenner's eco-logical theory that supported the idea for social health education. It did not take any convincing, as the administrators saw the need and were honestly thrilled that a teacher was willing to help. In that meeting, the decision was made to implement social health during remediation time, targeting the Tier 2 and Tier 3 behavior students who needed it the most. Keep in mind, many times children who have extreme behavior issues are also suffering academically. These students were currently enrolled in remediation targeting math or reading but not seeing gains. Perhaps if the students' social health needs were met, gains could potentially be made in academic areas as well because social health addresses not only the areas mentioned above but also time management, memory strategies, and goal setting.

Thus the academic year ensued. I diligently worked with the children in social health during the remediation period, along with my ELA students during regular class periods. I borrowed textbooks from my local university that had an FCS licensure program, as there was no money to support the program at the school. I not only had the FCS background needed to implement social health but but also was trained in adverse childhood experiences (ACEs) and trauma-informed care. I created a trauma-informed classroom and saw gains with my social health students. I implemented morning meetings and peace corners, which can be read about in Chapter 2, along with "Fun Fridays" where the students had an opportunity to put their newly learned skills into practice. Fridays became a day when the students in social health played games, worked on school community projects, and had special visitors, such as mentor examples and therapy dogs.

But this is not the rest of the story. I saw such a need for social health and was so burdened by the rest of the schools in the county that I did not stop. I began to advocate for the entire county, which resulted in the entire state. I began to share the story of what I was doing at the school and how important the content was for the students. I shared with anyone who would listen. I networked with people, shared with school board members, a local representative, and eventually made my way to a state senator. It was the state senator who took the idea and ran with it. Together, we wrote a bill that he sponsored. The bill required that social health education be taught in every middle school in Tennessee. Through the COVID-19 pandemic, the bill was tabled, and as the draft of this textbook was written, the outcome of the bill is still unknown due to the pandemic. While waiting on the bill, I continued advocating and rallying community support by working with state agencies, Tennessee Association of Family and Consumer Sciences (TAFCS), email campaigns, and other key stakeholders such as teachers, administrators, and parents. The bill was tabled again this year by the senator sponsoring the bill. His colleague in the house (who was the cosponsor) did not introduce the bill for a vote by the house members. Our plans are to not give up but to continue to advocate. Plans are to work with the senator but contact a different House of Representatives member for the next legislative session.

FCS Professionals and Advocacy

Because FCS education does not fall under the category of general education, FCS is vulnerable. The current push in public education is to focus on science, technology, engineering, and math (STEM). When budgets need to be cut, programs such as FCS courses and other career technical education courses, along with art, music, and physical education, are all vulnerable to being cut or having their funding reduced. This results in the need for FCS professionals to advocate for increased funding for FCS programs and, oftentimes, even keeping courses from being cut altogether.

Benefits of Advocacy

Advocacy has benefits on the personal level, as well as on the professional level. It is worth the time and effort as a professional to make advocacy part of your professional career. Referring back to Chapter 1, advocacy fits into the FCS body of knowledge. Advocacy leads to capacity building on a professional level. Knowledge and skills are gained when professionals become aware of current research and current societal needs. Through this awareness, they gain self-efficacy as professionals and become confident when sharing current and relevant information. Professionals incorporate capacity building when collaborating with individuals/families to use their own strengths and encourage the individual to explore available options in order to make the best decisions for well-being. The action of advocacy has the ability to trickle down to influence individuals/families. When professionals incorporate capacity-building skills in their practice, results include individuals/families with increased confidence and problem-solving skills. They use capacity building when they encourage individuals/families to use their own strengths and current abilities to meet their needs. Families with increased self-confidence and effective problem-solving skills may be better equiped to avoid trauma (Turnbull & Turnbull, 2005).

Networking

Networking is an exchange of ideas and collaboration of services among individuals, groups, or agencies. (Merriam-Webster, n.d.). Networking aids in advocating and can be on the local, state, and national levels. Advocacy can never be successful without joining with other people and groups to help champion the cause.

Joining professional organizations such as the AAFCS, Association of Career Technical Education (ACTE), National Association Teachers of Family and Consumer Sciences (NATFCS), and LeadFCS Education (formerly National Association of State Administrators of Family and Consumer Sciences Education [NASAFACS]) provide opportunities for networking on the national level, as well as opportunities for professional development and leadership. These professional organizations often provide tool kits, sample letters, and press releases to aid in advocacy (ACTE, n.d.). Often, these organizations have state-level associations that provide similar resources. On the local level, consider networking with organizations that have similar goals or missions. Networking with professional organizations can provide the following benefits: diversity in contacts, new avenues for advocacy, and a light workload by sharing the task.

However, Menon (2017) cautions against **social narrowing**, the idea that humans tend to flock to people like them, with similar backgrounds, education, skin color, nationality, and even style (Menon, 2017). Although there is nothing wrong with this tendency, because there is strength in numbers and we need our like-minded national and state organizations, it can be challenging when we need new ideas or need to be challenged. It's often not the strong ties, the people in our daily lives, but rather the people who are the weak ties who make connections for us (Menon, 2017). It is those weak ties that can bring a connection to an entirely new group. The danger of cliques is that they can keep professionals from reaching their potential, especially when advocating, because we need a connection to people outside of our immediate groups. Thus, understanding the importance of networking and applying both inside and outside of the field is important.

With this said, yes, we need to connect with the same, like-minded FCS professionals to build our ideas and to carry them forth through our professional organizations at the state and national levels, but to truly see change, we must be willing to connect with individuals outside of our field. "This entails respecting and honoring their lay knowledge while instilling the merit of letting it go to make room for discipline and profession-specific knowledge" (McGregor, 2019, p. 30). Forming relationships with key stakeholders through networking is vital in getting FCS education recognized as both preventive and restorative for the betterment of society. Because FCS professionals carry content, tools, and strategies that prevent so many societal woes, we, as FCS professionals, must be willing to share our knowledge and ideas in nonthreatening ways that help build a stronger society.

Elevator Speech

While relationships are foundational to networking and meaningful connections should be strived for and nurtured, FCS professionals should be ready to share their profession through the use of an elevator speech when meeting new people or connecting with interested stakeholders. Frankel (2014) explains how well-educated professionals fail to reach their potential because of their inability to define their brand. FCS professionals need to be prepared to answer the question, "What is

FCS?" Therefore, FCS professionals need an elevator speech that is effective and explains the value of FCS in under 3 minutes. The idea is to prepare an explanation about the FCS profession during the comparable time of an elevator ride (Frankel, 2014). The elevator speech needs to convince others that FCS makes a difference, but to do that, we first must believe that FCS indeed makes that difference.

Koontz (2016) explained an elevator speech from a cattle raiser's perspective, which is a tough business, and like FCS, many cattlemen don't have time for advocacy. Koontz (2016) recommended four suggestions for an effective elevator speech that can be applied to FCS professionals. First, be compelling. Illustrate the purpose of FCS. Second, be clear. Connect the purpose of FCS to the listener so that it becomes meaningful. Third, be convincing. Use statistics and meaningful stories so that the listener will grasp the importance of FCS. Last, be concise by getting to the point and end with some sort of call to action.

In another example, Pagana (2013), who wrote from the perspective of the nursing profession, expressed the need for nurses to have an elevator speech, which likewise can be applied to FCS professionals. Pagana's (2013) advice was to "describe what you do, what you're interested in doing, and how you can be a resource to someone" (p. 14). According to Pagana, a good elevator speech grabs the listener's attention and makes the listener want to know more about what you do. She suggested limiting your speech to only 60 seconds, to have an attention grabber, express your passion, and include what you need.

Applying this information to FCS should be easy because there are many societal issues that FCS professionals can either mitigate or offer solutions—piquing someone's interest by mentioning some social need like obesity or ACEs can start a valuable conversation that may lead to people seeing the value in FCS education. Showing your passion helps to sell the listener on the need and your ability to make a difference. When considering what you need, this may be support for your program, a meeting, a referral, support for education reform—in essence, anything that is crucial to the next step. One last point: Do not forget to practice your elevator speech so that you are

SOCIAL HEALTH ELEVATOR SPEECH

By Elizabeth Ramsey

I teach social health education, and I cover content areas that are such a need in today's society. Did you know that more than 61% of all Tennessee children have experienced at least one adverse childhood experience (ACEs) and that 46% of children have experienced at least one trauma (Tennessee Department of Education, 2018; SAMHSA, 2018) and oftentimes struggle with self-regulation because of their experiences? I teach students about conflict resolution, anger management strategies, and productive ways to manage their emotions so that kids who have experienced trauma and ACEs can learn these important skills. I love what I do, and I see a difference every day in the lives of students who are getting the help they need from the content I teach. Would you be willing to support the upcoming bill that would require social health education in all middle schools? Our students desperately need this content!

comfortable sharing it at a moment's notice. Also, it is acceptable to home in on one aspect of FCS as your passion, as seen in the example of the social health elevator speech in the Spotlight above. FCS is a field that has so many wonderful content areas, and if you find yourself more passionate about an area, do not be afraid to home in on that area and make it your specialty.

A Challenge to All FCS Professionals

The cold hard historical truth of FCS education dates back to Ellen Swallows Richards. Although she was a trailblazer in championing sanitization and safe food handling through her brilliant knowledge of chemistry, she was held at arm's length by the Massachusetts Institute of Technology. Her contributions were only allowed into certain areas, and her labs were held back and only applied within the home setting. One could argue that we still suffer the same fate today—held at arm's length when applying our knowledge, yet we are experts in child development, family relationships, ACEs, and trauma-informed care. We are experts in social health education and FCS pedagogy. We are experts in nutrition and dietetics, food safety, and handling. We are experts in merchandising, retail, and design. Yet, still, we see our programs cut and belittled. We have the answers that prevent major child and family societal issues. We have answers that build resilience in families, children, and communities. Therefore, it is time that we demand a seat at the table. No longer should FCS professionals be secluded to certain areas deemed acceptable by society like in the days of Ellen Swallows Richards. Yet doing this requires that we move from social narrowing and connect with individuals who see our profession's potential. For example, society needs to accept the FCS mission as an agent of change. "It goes against people's intuitive senses to ask them to accept that FCS is anything more than technical skills for cooking and sewing" (McGregor, 2019, p. 28). FCS professionals are charged with bringing about a conceptual change or socialization of society to fully understand the mission of FCS education as a source of knowledge to help individuals and families become empowered through wise decision making and resource management (McGregor, 2019; Swafford & Giordano, 2017).

Referring back to the Spotlight on social health, not a single person who heard the message had a negative response. In fact, people were pleasantly surprised to know that there were state standards and curricula with licensed teachers who are more than capable of implementing such a needed class for middle schoolers. What FCS professionals have to offer, society needs. It is our responsibility to network not only with other FCS professionals but especially with individuals outside of our social circle and to get the message to people outside of our FCS world.

Family Career Community Leaders of America

Family Career Community Leaders of America (FCCLA) is included in this chapter on advocacy. Students Taking Action with Recognition (STAR) events can be a vehicle to teach advocacy, promote the profession, and prepare students for careers in FCS content areas. See Figure 12.3 of FCCLA members meeting with a senator. Furthermore, FCCLA is an opportunity to promote capacity building in your students. FCCLA is a nonprofit national career technical student organization (CTSO) for young men and women in FCS education in public and private schools from

FIGURE 12.3 U.S. Senator Meeting With FCCLA Members

grades 6–12. FCCLA is an integral part of a quality FCS educational program and was founded in 1945 under the name of Future Homemakers of America. The name was changed in 1994 to reflect societal needs and to make the CTSO gender-friendly. (See Chapter 1 for a review of legislation.) Currently, there are 48 state associations with 5,283 chapters (each school has a chapter) and more than 182,000 members (FCCLA, n.d.-a).

STAR Events

The purpose of FCCLA is to provide opportunities for students to expand in cognitive, social, and emotional growth by providing leadership opportunities for student members' service-learning projects. These projects, known as **STAR events**, address pertinent personal, family, work, and societal issues through FCS education while also promoting FCS careers and related occupations. STAR events focus on four of the 16 career pathways: human services, education and training, hospitality and tourism, and visual arts and design. With more than 30 STAR events, students in chapters compete individually or in groups with other chapters at the regional/district, state, and national levels. The competitive events for FCCLA may be viewed using the following link: STAR Events | FCCLA (fcclainc.org).

Topics on the management of diverse roles within the family, character development, topics of concerns for youth and families such as teen pregnancy, substance abuse, peer pressure, the environment, family relationships, nutrition/fitness, and careers can fit in well with the competitive STAR events. During the competition, participants are recognized for their knowledge, skills, and ability to actively identify an issue concerning families, careers, or communities, through researching a topic, along with developing and implementing a project to advocate for positive change. Students must use the **FCCLA planning process**, which is a template that indicates requirements that are used to help students be successful when planning, implementing, and presenting the project. (See the Spotlight titled "FCCLA Planning Process.") The projects support critical thinking, interpersonal communication, leadership development, advocacy, and research strategies (FCCLA, n.d.-c).

SPOTLIGHT: FCCLA PLANNING PROCESS (FCCLA ADVISOR B, N.D.)

- Identify concerns.
- Set goals—what are you doing to address the concerns.
- Form a plan—who, what, when, where, and why.
- Act—carry out the plan.
- Follow up— evaluate the plan, thank those involved, recognize participants.

See the following website for more information.

https://fcclainc.org/sites/default/files/Planning%20Process%20Summary%20Page%20Template%20Fillable.pdf

FCCLA Advisor

The role of the FCS educator is to be the advisor of the chapter. The advisor is responsible for organizing chapters, heading fundraisers, helping with the election of officers, planning trips/events, and completing paperwork. It is important to note that projects in STAR events should be student driven with teacher guidance. FCS educators/advisors should not do the work for the students. Students working with just guidance from the educator leads to their own development of capacity building. As they work to address the issue in competing events, they will gain self-confidence and knowledge through the planning process and presenting the content. The educator's role in FCCLA STAR events will be modeled by the students during their careers as they work in human services, hospitality and tourism, education and training, and visual arts and design.

During the competition, FCS educators judge STAR events at district, state, and national levels or may serve as lead consultant of a STAR event. When judging an event, refer to the planning process and FCCLA guidelines, check to ensure the project meets the guidelines of the planning process, evaluate the project and presentation with a rubric, and provide the competitors with constructive criticism and ways to improve the presentation. See the Spotlight titled "Planning Process."

SPOTLIGHT: STAR EVENT: AFFIRMATION BOOK PROJECT

By Melinda Swafford

I caution you to not think of FCCLA as another task required of FCS educators. I remember how busy it is to be a public school teacher in middle or high school. Keep an open mind, and you will soon realize the benefits of FCCLA for both your students and for you as an educator. When I was an FCS educator in the public school system, I had two children, a son active in high school sports and extracurricular activities and a daughter with a cognitive and physical disability who was attending public school. Her disability required multiple doctor appointments along with occupational, physical, and speech therapy. I was concerned about the amount of time it would take to have an active affiliated FCCLA program. My school was located in a small rural town (population 2,800), with 20% of the population being ELLs. In addition, the school demographic included over 50% of students qualifying for free and reduced meals, and 25% of the students received special education services. I wondered if my students would be able to compete with other schools in the district.

After considering these factors, I began incorporating projects that met the course standards and could also be appropriate to be used for STAR events. The entire class would participate in the projects; however, the students who joined FCCLA could use the project as a STAR event. One project was the Affirmation Book (Figure 12.4). The Family Dynamic/Child Development course I was teaching had 18 students and included a learning segment on preschool development. The learning segment began by teaching the term **affirmation**, which is the positive proclamation of the worth and value of an individual (Swafford et al., 2006). Lessons in this learning segment included the critical role affirmation has in the development of children, factors that placed children at risk, the relationship between affirmation and self-esteem/self-acceptance, the mission of Head Start, and the impact of parent/child reading.

As a class project, the Affirmation Book promoted affirmation of each child, promoted language development, and enhanced parent/school collaboration. The students would design an affirmation book for each child who attended the local Head Start center. Criteria were established, and the students began volunteering 2 days a week at the local Head Start center located two blocks from the school. During the visits, each student kept a journal that included specific attributes, interests, and abilities of each child assigned to them. The FCS students wrote and illustrated a book for each child. The content of the book affirmed the many positive qualities and attributes of the child, and each page included the child's

FIGURE 12.4 Affirmation Book

(Continued)

name. If the child was Hispanic, the books were made bilingual and translated by the students in my class who were ELL.

Upon evaluation, the students determined that affirmation should be a part of each child's life. On the last day of our visit to Head Start, the FCS students delivered thank you notes to the Head Start teachers, gave the books to their specific child, and read the book to the child. The project was publicized in the school newspaper and the project was used by several of the students in the class for the STAR event, Focus on Children.

The Affirmation Book Project served as advocacy in the following ways: awareness and direct action. In awareness, the school and community were made aware of the FCS program and projects used to teach students through the use of the school newspaper. Students in the course were made aware of factors that put children at risk for learning, learned about the benefits of family/school collaboration, and discovered the benefits of reading to children on social, emotional, and cognitive development. Direct action was implemented by the student making the book that focused on positive qualities of the child, making the book bilingual, and sending the book home.

SUMMARY

In conclusion, FCS professionals work to empower and strengthen individuals, families, and communities and make a difference every day. Unfortunately, many outside of the FCS profession never know the important contributions FCS professionals make. That is why FCS professionals must learn to advocate, network, and share their passion for FCS. Oftentimes, it is as simple as sharing your story with others outside of our circle. FCCLA is an opportunity to showcase your program and your students. Through project-based learning, many classroom activities can be used in STAR event categories. Through integrating FCCLA in the classroom, all students, not just FCCLA members, benefit from the project, and students learn valuable skills in networking and advocacy.

KEY TERMS

Advocacy

Networking

Affirmation

Individual advocate

Family Career Community Leaders
    of America (FCCLA)

Social narrowing

Lobbying

STAR events

Self-advocate

Collective/peer advocates

FCCLA planning process

QUESTIONS AND ACTIVITIES

1. Select a topic of interest that you have as an FCS preservice educator; identify networking agencies on the national, your specific state, and local levels.
2. Conduct a web search on the professional organizations AAFCS, ATCE, NATFCS, and FCS lead education that support FCS education. Which organization has information on advocacy? What resources do they provide? Which ones would you consider joining as a new FCS educator? Why?
3. Conduct a web search on FCCLA. Identify resources available for an advisor. Make a graphic organizer using the STAR events. What are the benefits of formulating an FCCLA chapter in your school? Identify three benefits each for FCS students and for the FCS educator.
4. After reading the Spotlight on the Affirmation Book Project, complete the FCCLA planning template using content from the Spotlight. As a class, identify another project that could be used in a different course.
5. Create an elevator speech about the importance of FCS and deliver it to the class.

REFERENCES

American Association of Family and Consumer Sciences. (n.d.). *Advocacy.* https://www.aafcs.org/resources/advocacy

Association for Career Technical Education. (n.d.). *Advocacy.* https://www.acteonline.org/advocacy/

Couch, S., & Alexander, K. L. (2009). Professionalism: Ethical professional practice for teachers of family and consumer sciences. *Journal of Family and Consumer Sciences Education, 27*(National Teacher Standards 4), 60–76. http://www.natefacs.org/JFCSE/v27Standards4/v27Standards4Couch.pdf

Family, Career, and Community Leaders of America. (n.d.-a). *About.* https://fcclainc.org/about

Family, Career, and Community Leaders of America. (n.d.-b). *Advisors.* https://fcclainc.org/sites/default/files/Planning%20Process%20Summary%20Page%20Template%20Fillable.pdf

Family, Career, and Community Leaders of America. (n.d.-c). *STAR events.* https://fcclainc.org/compete/star-events

Frankel, L. P. (2014). *Nice girls still don't get the corner office: Unconscious mistakes women make that sabotage their careers.* Grand Central Publishing.

Koontz, C. (2016). Elevator speech. *The Cattleman, 103*(6), 10. https://issuu.com/thecattleman

McGregor, S. L. T. (2019, Summer). Conceptual change during the professional socialization process. *Journal of Family and Consumer Sciences Education, 36*(1), 21–33.

Menon, T. (March 2017). The secret to great opportunities? The person you haven't met yet [Video]. TED Conferences. https://www.ted.com/talks/tanya_menon_the_secret_to_great_opportunities_the_person_you_haven_t_met_yet/reading-list#t-11615

Merriam-Webster. (n.d.). Networking. In *Merriam-Webster.com dictionary.* Retrieved January 24, 2021, from https://www.merriam-webster.com/dictionary/networking

National Council on Aging. (n.d.). *Nonprofit rules and regulations. Advocacy vs lobbying.* https://elder-law. laws.com/organizations-for-older-adults/national-council-on-aging

Pagana, K. D. (2013). Ride to the top with a good elevator speech. *American Nurse Today, 8*(3), 14–16. https://www.myamericannurse.com/

Stewart, A., & MacIntyre, G. (2013). *Advocacy models and effectiveness Insight 20.* Iris.

Substance Abuse and Mental Health Services Administration. (2018, May 10). *Helping children and youth who have experienced trauma: National Children's Mental Health Awareness Day.* https://www.samhsa. gov/sites/default/files/brief_report_natl_childrens_mh_awareness_day.pdf

Swafford, M., Thomas, R., & Bailey, S. (2006). Affirmation book project: Impacting diversity, literacy, and collaboration. In R. R. Harmon (Ed.), *International family studies developing curricula and teaching tools* (pp. 165–173). Haworth Press.

Swafford, M., & Giordano, K. (2017). Universal design: Ensuring success for all FCS students. *Journal of Family and Consumer Sciences, 109*(4), 47–52.

Tennessee Department of Education. (2018). *Six-hour building strong brains for secondary schools: Facilitator guide.*

Turnbull A., Turnbull, R., Erwin, E., J., & Soodak, L., C. (2006). *Families, professionals and exceptionality: Positive Outcomes Through Partnership and Trust* (5th ed.). Prentice Hall. 100–111.

Figure Credits

Appendix A. Conversation Stems

Clarifying

- Is it your position that ...?
- To be clear, you're saying that ...?
- I'm confused when you say ___. Can you clarify?

Paraphrasing

- Put another way, you're saying ...
- Is it accurate to say that you believe ...
- I hear you saying that ...

Agreeing

- I agree with ___ because ...
- ___'s point about ___ was important because ...
- You and I are coming from the same position because ...

Disagreeing

- I see it differently because ...
- There is no evidence to suggest that is true because ...
- We see ___ differently because ...

Elaborating

- Yes, and furthermore ...
- Adding to what you said, ...
- I agree, and I want to add that ...

Summarizing

- Overall, what I'm saying is ...
- My whole point in one sentence is ...
- To summarize ...

Adapted from Learn Zillion (2017). 6–8 Conversation Stems | LearnZillion https://learnzillion.com/p/

Appendix B. Sample Teacher Evaluation Rubric

General Educator Rubric: Instruction

	Significantly Above Expectations (5)	At Expectations (3)	Significantly Below Expectations (1)
Standards and Objectives	• All learning objectives are clearly and explicitly communicated, connected to state standards and referenced throughout lesson. • Sub-objectives are aligned and logically sequenced to the lesson's major objective. • Learning objectives are: (a) consistently connected to what students have previously learned, (b) know from life experiences, and (c) integrated with other disciplines. • Expectations for student performance are clear, demanding, and high. • There is evidence that most students demonstrate mastery of the daily objective that supports significant progress towards mastery of a standard.	• Most learning objectives are communicated, connected to state standards and referenced throughout lesson. • Sub-objectives are mostly aligned to the lesson's major objective. • Learning objectives are connected to what students have previously learned. • Expectations for student performance are clear. • There is evidence that most students demonstrate mastery of the daily objective that supports significant progress towards mastery of a standard.	• Few learning objectives are communicated, connected to state standards and referenced throughout lesson. • Sub-objectives are inconsistently aligned to the lesson's major objective. • Learning objectives are rarely connected to what students have previously learned. • Expectations for student performance are vague. • There is evidence that few students demonstrate mastery of the daily objective that supports significant progress towards mastery of a standard.
Motivating Students	• The teacher consistently organizes the content so that it is personally meaningful and relevant to students. • The teacher consistently develops learning experiences where inquiry, curiosity, and exploration are valued. • The teacher regularly reinforces and rewards effort.	• The teacher sometimes organizes the content so that it is personally meaningful and relevant to students. • The teacher sometimes develops learning experiences where inquiry, curiosity, and exploration are valued. • The teacher sometimes reinforces and rewards effort.	• The teacher rarely organizes the content so that it is personally meaningful and relevant to students. • The teacher rarely develops learning experiences where inquiry, curiosity, and exploration are valued. • The teacher rarely reinforces and rewards effort.

(Continued)

General Educator Rubric: Instruction (Continued)

	Significantly Above Expectations (5)	At Expectations (3)	Significantly Below Expectations (1)
Presenting Instructional Content	Presentation of content always includes: • visuals that establish the purpose of the lesson, preview the organization of the lesson, and include internal summaries of the lesson; • examples, illustrations, analogies, and labels for new concepts and ideas; • effective modeling of thinking process by the teacher and/or students guided by the teacher to demonstrate performance expectations; • concise communication; • logical sequencing and segmenting; • all essential information; • no irrelevant, confusing, or non-essential information.	Presentation of content most of the time includes: • visuals that establish the purpose of the lesson, preview the organization of the lesson, and include internal summaries of the lesson; • examples, illustrations, analogies, and labels for new concepts and ideas; • modeling by the teacher to demonstrate performance expectations; • concise communication; • logical sequencing and segmenting; • all essential information; • no irrelevant, confusing, or non-essential information.	Presentation of content rarely includes: • visuals that establish the purpose of the lesson, preview the organization of the lesson, and include internal summaries of the lesson; • examples, illustrations, analogies, and labels for new concepts and ideas; • modeling by the teacher to demonstrate performance expectations; • concise communication; • logical sequencing and segmenting; • all essential information; • no irrelevant, confusing, or non-essential information.
Lesson Structure and Pacing	• The lesson starts promptly. • The lesson's structure is coherent, with a beginning, middle, and end. • The lesson includes time for reflection. • Pacing is brisk and provides many opportunities for individual students who progress at different learning rates. • Routines for distributing materials are seamless. • No instructional time is lost during transitions.	• The lesson starts promptly. • The lesson's structure is coherent, with a beginning, middle, and end. • Pacing is appropriate and sometimes provides opportunities for students who progress at different learning rates. • Routines for distributing materials are efficient. • Little instructional time is lost during transitions.	• The lesson does not start promptly. • The lesson has a structure, but may be missing closure or introductory elements. • Pacing is appropriate for less than half of the students and rarely provides opportunities for students who progress at different learning rates. • Routines for distributing materials are inefficient. • Considerable time is lost during transitions.

	Significantly Above Expectations (5)	At Expectations (3)	Significantly Below Expectations (1)
Activities and Materials	Activities and materials include all of the following: • support the lesson objectives; • are challenging; • sustain students' attention; • elicit a variety of thinking; • provide time for reflection; • are relevant to students' lives; • provide opportunities for student-to-student interaction; • induce student curiosity and suspense; • provide students with choices; • incorporate multimedia and technology; and • incorporate resources beyond the school curriculum texts (e.g., teacher-made materials, manipulatives, resources from museums, cultural centers, etc.). • In addition, sometimes activities are game-like, involve simulations, require creating products, and demand self-direction and self-monitoring. • The preponderance of activities demand complex thinking and analysis. • Texts and tasks are appropriately complex.	Activities and materials include most of the following: • support the lesson objectives; • are challenging; • sustain students' attention; • elicit a variety of thinking; • provide time for reflection; • are relevant to students' lives; • provide opportunities for student-to-student interaction; • induce student curiosity and suspense; • provide students with choices; • incorporate multimedia and technology; and • incorporate resources beyond the school curriculum texts (e.g., teacher-made materials, manipulatives, resources from museums, cultural centers, etc.). • Texts and tasks are appropriately complex.	Activities and materials include few of the following: • support the lesson objectives; • are challenging; • sustain students' attention; • elicit a variety of thinking; • provide time for reflection; • are relevant to students' lives; • provide opportunities for student to student interaction; • induce student curiosity and suspense; • provide students with choices; • incorporate multimedia and technology; and • incorporate resources beyond the school curriculum texts (e.g., teacher-made materials, manipulatives, resources from museums, etc.).

(Continued)

General Educator Rubric: Instruction (Continued)

	Significantly Above Expectations (5)	At Expectations (3)	Significantly Below Expectations (1)

Questioning	Teacher questions are varied and high-quality, providing a balanced mix of question types:
	  • knowledge and comprehension;
	  • application and analysis; and
	  • creation and evaluation.
	• Questions require students to regularly cite evidence throughout lesson.
	• Questions are consistently purposeful and coherent.
	• A high frequency of questions is asked.
	• Questions are consistently sequenced with attention to the instructional goals.
	• Questions regularly require active responses (e.g., whole class signaling, choral responses, written and shared responses, or group and individual answers).
	• Wait time (3–5 seconds) is consistently provided.
	• The teacher calls on volunteers and non-volunteers, and a balance of students based on ability and sex.
	• Students generate questions that lead to further inquiry and self-directed learning.
	• Questions regularly assess and advance student understanding.
	• When text is involved, majority of questions are text based.
		Teacher questions are varied and high-quality providing for some, but not all, question types:
		  • knowledge and comprehension;
		  • application and analysis; and
		  • creation and evaluation.
		• Questions usually require students to cite evidence.
		• Questions are usually purposeful and coherent.
		• A moderate frequency of questions asked.
		• Questions are sometimes sequenced with attention to the instructional goals.
		• Questions sometimes require active responses (e.g., whole class signaling, choral responses, or group and individual answers).
		• Wait time is sometimes provided.
		• The teacher calls on volunteers and non-volunteers, and a balance of students based on ability and sex.
		• When text is involved, majority of questions are text based.
			Teacher questions are inconsistent in quality and include few question types:
			  • knowledge and comprehension;
			  • application and analysis; and
			  • creation and evaluation.
			• Questions are random and lack coherence.
			• A low frequency of questions is asked.
			• Questions are rarely sequenced with attention to the instructional goals.
			• Questions rarely require active responses (e.g., whole class signaling, choral responses, or group and individual answers).
			• Wait time is inconsistently provided.
			• The teacher mostly calls on volunteers and high-ability students.

	Significantly Above Expectations (5)	At Expectations (3)	Significantly Below Expectations (1)
Academic Feedback	• Oral and written feedback is consistently academically focused, frequent, high-quality and references expectations. • Feedback is frequently given during guided practice and homework review. • The teacher circulates to prompt student thinking, assess each student's progress, and provide individual feedback. • Feedback from students is regularly used to monitor and adjust instruction. • Teacher engages students in giving specific and high-quality feedback to one another.	• Oral and written feedback is mostly academically focused, frequent, and mostly high-quality. • Feedback is sometimes given during guided practice and homework review. • The teacher circulates during instructional activities to support engagement, and monitor student work. • Feedback from students is sometimes used to monitor and adjust instruction.	• The quality and timeliness of feedback is inconsistent. • Feedback is rarely given during guided practice and homework review. • The teacher circulates during instructional activities, but monitors mostly behavior. • Feedback from students is rarely used to monitor or adjust instruction.
Grouping Students	• The instructional grouping arrangements (either whole-class, small groups, pairs, individual; heterogeneous or homogenous ability) consistently maximize student understanding and learning efficiency. • All students in groups know their roles, responsibilities, and group work expectations. • All students participating in groups are held accountable for group work and individual work. • Instructional group composition is varied (e.g., race, gender, ability, and age) to best accomplish the goals of the lesson. • Instructional groups facilitate opportunities for students to set goals, reflect on, and evaluate their learning.	• The instructional grouping arrangements (either whole-class, small groups, pairs, individual; heterogeneous or homogenous ability) adequately enhance student understanding and learning efficiency. • Most students in groups know their roles, responsibilities, and group work expectations. • Most students participating in groups are held accountable for group work and individual work. • Instructional group composition is varied (e.g., race, gender, ability, and age) to most of the time, accomplish the goals of the lesson.	• The instructional grouping arrangements (either whole-class, small groups, pairs, individual; heterogeneous or homogenous ability) inhibit student understanding and learning efficiency. • Few students in groups know their roles, responsibilities, and group work expectations. • Few students participating in groups are held accountable for group work and individual work. • Instructional group composition remains unchanged irrespective of the learning and instructional goals of a lesson.

(Continued)

General Educator Rubric: Instruction (*Continued*)

	Significantly Above Expectations (5)	At Expectations (3)	Significantly Below Expectations (1)
Teacher Content Knowledge	• Teacher displays extensive content knowledge of all the subjects she or he teaches. • Teacher regularly implements a variety of subject-specific instructional strategies to enhance student content knowledge. • The teacher regularly highlights key concepts and ideas and uses them as bases to connect other powerful ideas. • Limited content is taught in sufficient depth to allow for the development of understanding.	• Teacher displays accurate content knowledge of all the subjects he or she teaches. • Teacher sometimes implements subject-specific instructional strategies to enhance student content knowledge. • The teacher sometimes highlights key concepts and ideas and uses them as bases to connect other powerful ideas.	• Teacher displays under-developed content knowledge in several subject areas. • Teacher rarely implements subject-specific instructional strategies to enhance student content knowledge. • Teacher does not understand key concepts and ideas in the discipline and therefore presents content in an unconnected way.
	▢		
Teacher Knowledge of Students	• Teacher practices display understanding of each student's anticipated learning difficulties. • Teacher practices regularly incorporate student interests and cultural heritage. • Teacher regularly provides differentiated instructional methods and content to ensure children have the opportunity to master what is being taught.	• Teacher practices display understanding of some student anticipated learning difficulties. • Teacher practices sometimes incorporate student interests and cultural heritage. • Teacher sometimes provides differentiated instructional methods and content to ensure children have the opportunity to master what is being taught.	• Teacher practices demonstrate minimal knowledge of students anticipated learning difficulties. • Teacher practices rarely incorporate student interests or cultural heritage. • Teacher practices demonstrate little differentiation of instructional methods or content.
	▢		

Thinking	Significantly Above Expectations (5)	At Expectations (3)	Significantly Below Expectations (1)
	The teacher thoroughly teaches two or more types of thinking:	The teacher thoroughly teaches one type of thinking:	The teacher implements no learning experiences that thoroughly teach any type of thinking.
	• analytical thinking, where students analyze, compare and contrast, and evaluate and explain information;	• analytical thinking, where students analyze, compare and contrast, and evaluate and explain information;	The teacher provides no opportunities where students:
	• practical thinking, where students use, apply, and implement what they learn in real-life scenarios;	• practical thinking, where students use, apply, and implement what they learn in real-life scenarios;	• generate a variety of ideas and alternatives; or
	• creative thinking, where students create, design, imagine, and suppose; and	• creative thinking, where students create, design, imagine, and suppose; and	• analyze problems from multiple perspectives and viewpoints.
	• research-based thinking, where students explore and review a variety of ideas, models, and solutions to problems.	• research-based thinking, where students explore and review a variety of ideas, models, and solutions to problems.	
	The teacher provides opportunities where students:	The teacher provides opportunities where students:	
	• generate a variety of ideas and alternatives;	• generate a variety of ideas and alternatives; and	
	• analyze problems from multiple perspectives and viewpoints; and	• analyze problems from multiple perspectives and viewpoints.	
	• monitor their thinking to insure that they understand what they are learning, are attending to critical information, and are aware of the learning strategies that they are using and why.		

(Continued)

General Educator Rubric: Instruction (*Continued*)

	Significantly Above Expectations (5)	At Expectations (3)	Significantly Below Expectations (1)
Problem-Solving	The teacher implements activities that teach and reinforce three or more of the following problem-solving types: • Abstraction • Categorization • Drawing Conclusions/Justifying Solutions • Predicting Outcomes • Observing and Experimenting • Improving Solutions • Identifying Relevant/Irrelevant Information • Generating Ideas • Creating and Designing	The teacher implements activities that teach two of the following problem-solving types: • Abstraction • Categorization • Drawing Conclusions/Justifying Solution • Predicting Outcomes • Observing and Experimenting • Improving Solutions • Identifying Relevant/Irrelevant Information • Generating Ideas • Creating and Designing	The teacher implements no activities that teach the following problem-solving types: • Abstraction • Categorization • Drawing Conclusions/Justifying Solution • Predicting Outcomes • Observing and Experimenting • Improving Solutions • Identifying Relevant/Irrelevant Information • Generating Ideas • Creating and Designing

General Educator Rubric: Planning

	Significantly Above Expectations (5)	At Expectations (3)	Significantly Below Expectations (1)

Instructional Plans	Instructional plans include:
	
	• measurable and explicit goals aligned to state content standards;
	
	• activities, materials, and assessments that:
	
	  • are aligned to state standards.
	  • are sequenced from basic to complex.
	  • build on prior student knowledge, are relevant to students' lives, and integrate other disciplines.
	  • provide appropriate time for student work, student reflection, and lesson unit and closure;
	
	• evidence that plan is appropriate for the age, knowledge, and interests of all learners; and
	
	• evidence that the plan provides regular opportunities to accommodate individual student needs.
		Instructional plans include:
		
		• goals aligned to state content standards;
		
		• activities, materials, and assessments that:
		
		  • are aligned to state standards.
		  • are sequenced from basic to complex.
		  • build on prior student knowledge.
		  • provide appropriate time for student work, and lesson and unit closure;
		
		• evidence that plan is appropriate for the age, knowledge, and interests of most learners; and
		
		• evidence that the plan provides some opportunities to accommodate individual student needs.
			Instructional plans include:
			
			• few goals aligned to state content standards;
			
			• activities, materials, and assessments that:
			
			  • are rarely aligned to state standards.
			  • are rarely logically sequenced.
			  • rarely build on prior student knowledge.
			  • inconsistently provide time for student work, and lesson and unit closure; and
			
			• little evidence that the plan provides some opportunities to accommodate individual student needs.

Student Work	Assignments require students to: • organize, interpret, analyze, synthesize, and evaluate information rather than reproduce it; • draw conclusions, make generalizations, and produce arguments that are supported through extended writing; and • connect what they are learning to experiences, observations, feelings, or situations significant in their daily lives both inside and outside of school.	Assignments require students to: • interpret information rather than reproduce it; • draw conclusions and support them through writing; and • connect what they are learning to prior learning and some life experiences.	Assignments require students to: • mostly reproduce information; • rarely draw conclusions and support them through writing; and • rarely connect what they are learning to prior learning or life experiences.

(Continued)

General Educator Rubric: Instruction (*Continued*)

	Significantly Above Expectations (5)	At Expectations (3)	Significantly Below Expectations (1)
Assessment	Assessment Plans: • are aligned with state content standards; • have clear measurement criteria; • measure student performance in more than three ways (e.g., in the form of a project, experiment, presentation, essay, short answer, or multiple choice test); • require extended written tasks; • are portfolio-based with clear illustrations of student progress toward state content standards; and • include descriptions of how assessment results will be used to inform future instruction.	Assessment Plans: • are aligned with state content standards; • have measurement criteria; • measure student performance in more than two ways (e.g., in the form of a project, experiment, presentation, essay, short answer, or multiple choice test); • require written tasks; and • include performance checks throughout the school year.	Assessment Plans: • are rarely aligned with state content standards; • have ambiguous measurement criteria; • measure student performance in less than two ways (e.g., in the form of a project, experiment, presentation, essay, short answer, or multiple choice test); and • include performance checks, although the purpose of these checks is not clear.
Expectations	• Teacher sets high and demanding academic expectations for every student. • Teacher encourages students to learn from mistakes. • Teacher creates learning opportunities where all students can experience success. • Students take initiative and follow through with their own work. • Teacher optimizes instructional time, teaches more material, and demands better performance from every student.	• Teacher sets high and demanding academic expectations for every student. • Teacher encourages students to learn from mistakes. • Teacher creates learning opportunities where most students can experience success. • Students complete their work according to teacher expectations.	• Teacher expectations are not sufficiently high for every student. • Teacher creates an environment where mistakes and failure are not viewed as learning experiences. • Students demonstrate little or no pride in the quality of their work.

	Significantly Above Expectations (5)	At Expectations (3)	Significantly Below Expectations (1)
Managing Student Behavior	• Students are consistently well-behaved and on task. • Teacher and students establish clear rules for learning and behavior. • The teacher overlooks inconsequential behavior. • The teacher deals with students who have caused disruptions rather than the entire class. • The teacher attends to disruptions quickly and firmly.	• Students are mostly well-behaved and on task, some minor learning disruptions may occur. • Teacher establishes rules for learning and behavior. • The teacher uses some techniques, such as social approval, contingent activities, and consequences, to maintain appropriate student behavior. • The teacher overlooks some inconsequential behavior, but other times addresses it, stopping the lesson. • The teacher deals with students who have caused disruptions, yet sometimes he or she addresses the entire class.	• Students are not well-behaved and are often off task. • Teacher establishes few rules for learning and behavior. • The teacher uses few techniques to maintain appropriate student behavior. • The teacher cannot distinguish between inconsequential behavior and inappropriate behavior. • Disruptions frequently interrupt instruction.
Environment	The classroom: • welcomes all members and guests. • is organized and understandable to all students. • supplies, equipment, and resources are all easily and readily accessible. • displays student work that frequently changes. • is arranged to promote individual and group learning.	The classroom: • welcomes most members and guests. • is organized and understandable to most students. • supplies, equipment, and resources are accessible. • displays student work. • is arranged to promote individual and group learning.	The classroom: • is somewhat cold and uninviting. • is not well organized and understandable to students. • supplies, equipment, and resources are difficult to access. • does not display student work. • is not arrange to promote group learning.
Respectful Culture	• Teacher-student interactions demonstrate caring and respect for one another. • Students exhibit caring and respect for one another. • Positive relationships and interdependence characterize the classroom.	• Teacher-student interactions are generally friendly, but may reflect occasional inconsistencies, favoritism, or disregard for students' cultures. • Students exhibit respect for the teacher, and are generally polite to each other. • Teacher is sometimes receptive to the interests and opinions of students.	• Teacher-student interactions are sometimes authoritarian, negative, or inappropriate. • Students exhibit disrespect for the teacher. • Student interaction is characterized by conflict, sarcasm, or put-downs. • Teacher is not receptive to interests and opinions of students.

Appendix C. Sample edTPA Lesson Plan Template with Completed Lesson Plan

Template Created by Tennessee Tech University (TN Tech, 2021)

Sample Lesson Plan Created by Kayleigh Beasley, MS (2021)

Lesson Title: Effective Instruction for Students with Disabilities	Grade/Level: Teaching as a Profession 1
Curriculum Standards	**Central Focus Question/Big Idea/Goal**
State Curriculum Standards (Include the number and text of the standard. If only a portion is being addressed, then only list the relevant parts.) TAP I Standard 12: *"Create an annotated visual representation of the key indicators, diagnostic tests, and most important features of effective instruction for students diagnosed with:* *Intellectual disabilities* *Developmental disabilities* *Learning disabilities* *Emotional/behavioral disorders* *Autism spectrum disorders* *Communication disorders* *Hearing loss or deafness* *Low vision or blindness* *Attention Deficit Hyperactivity Disorder (ADHD)"*	*What question(s), big idea(s), and/or goals drive your instruction?* After the lesson, the learner will (TLW) present an annotated graphic detailing the key indicators, diagnostics tests, and appropriate instruction for each of the given diagnoses, meeting 85% of the requirements included in the grading rubric.

Lesson Objective(s)

Objective 1:
To begin the lesson, TLW define each of the listed diagnoses found in the course standard.

Objective 2:
After reviewing the characteristics of the listed diagnoses, TLW correlate key indicators, diagnostic tests, and effective instruction for each of the given diagnoses.

Objective 3:
After researching the key indicators, diagnostic tests, and effective instruction for the listed diagnoses, TLW create a visual representation of the information for each of the given diagnoses. *Objectives are measurable.*

Vocabulary/Academic Language (Language Function) The language function for this lesson requires learners to define, research, analyze, and synthesize information.

What opportunities will you provide for students to practice content language/vocabulary and develop fluency?

Language Function: Synthesize. TLW synthesize content regarding various types of disabilities.

Vocabulary list: Intellectual disabilities, developmental disabilities, learning disabilities, emotional/behavior disabilities, and autism

Discourse: Throughout this lesson, the educator will engage the learner to orally use academic language discourse when posing questions during formative assessments, while monitoring learners in independent work, and when providing feedback on learner responses. Learners will use discourse when composing the visual representation and during the presentation of the content to the class members.

Syntax: For instance, at the beginning of the lesson, the students have to define the various types of disabilities to distinguish one from the other. By conducting research, students are analyzing the content to learn more about each of the diagnoses. And finally, students synthesize the content as they bring everything together in their annotated visuals.

After conducting research and during synthesis of the content for presentation, the learners will use syntax as they complete an annotated infographic that requires them to identify key factors of the diagnoses in a presentation with content and visuals.

Assessment/Evaluation

Formative (Informal): *How will students demonstrate understanding of lesson objective(s)? How will you monitor and/or give feedback?*

The following formative assessments are used. By prompting a think-pair-share activity at the beginning of the lesson, students share existing knowledge about each of the diagnoses, which allows the teacher to gauge the students' prior knowledge and therefore know how to proceed. Asking questions of higher order thinking throughout the lesson also ensures that students are finding and comprehending the information needed for the content of their graphics. And finally, basic observation of the sources students are reviewing, notes being taken, and small-group discussions taking place guide the teacher in providing any additional assistance that the students might need.

Summative (Formal): *What evidence will you collect, and how will it document student learning/mastery of lesson objective(s)?*

Students are to create an annotated visual that illustrates what they have learned in regard to the listed diagnoses. Scoring criteria in the rubric will reflect the learning outcomes in the learning objectives. The rubric will include grading criteria related to the students' definitions or descriptions of each diagnosis and criteria for the organized breakdown and synthesis of information on the key indicators, diagnostic testing, and effective instructional methods for each diagnosis.

Set/Motivator: *How will you engage student interest in the content of the lesson? Use knowledge of students' academic, social, and cultural characteristics.*

Motivator: The Teacher Will (TTW) provide a sample piece of text that represents the difficulty of reading for students with dyslexia (various samples can be found online). TTW call on students to take turns reading the text. After reading the passage, TTW ask the class to explain how they felt attempting to read the jumbled text aloud. TTW ask how this impacted their ability to comprehend what they were reading. After discussion, TTW explain that knowing how to identify and then obtain the appropriate diagnosis for various disabilities is key to planning appropriate instruction for students with specific learning needs.

Overview: TTW call on students to read Standard 12 and the learning objectives for the lesson. TTW provide a basic preview of what will be done to meet the objectives and the anticipated timeline for completing each part of the lesson.

Review: TTW ask students to recall the steps of the admission, review, and dismissal process, the purpose of IEPs, and basic aspects of an LRE, all studied in Standard 11. TTW ask students how this prior knowledge might be used as they learn more about meeting the needs of various special populations listed in Standard 12.

Instructional Procedures/Learning Tasks: *Provide specific details of lesson content and delivery.*

To transition to the supervised practice portion of the lesson, the teacher will prompt students to engage in the think-pair-share activity previously mentioned with formative assessment. From there, the teacher will use the smartboard to demonstrate how to find more information on each diagnosis by researching credible resources online; this could be considered the "I do" portion of the lesson. After that, students will be divided into groups to conduct their own research on their assigned diagnoses. Following the research, each group will be expected to share their findings and sources with the class. The group work will be counted as the "we do" portion of the lesson. And finally, following all group presentations, the independent practice portion of the lesson will consist of students working individually as they complete their annotated visuals mentioned for the summative assessment; this would be the "you do" portion of the lesson.

Questions and/or activities for higher order thinking: *These cannot be answered by yes or no.*

The teacher could ask the class basic questions such as, "What was the most challenging part of this assignment?" or "How will you use what you learned throughout this lesson in your lesson planning moving forward?" or "Why is it critical for teachers to recognize the key indicators of these disabilities at a young age?" Posing such questions would help reinforce the purpose of the lesson, making it relevant to the students as they recognize the significance of learning this content as future teachers.

Closure: Verbalize or demonstrate learning or skill one more time. *May state future learning.*

The teacher will follow up with students after they complete their annotated visuals. Since they have already demonstrated their level of mastery through their work, this does not have to be overly elaborate. For instance, the teacher should explain that in TAP 2, the students will be in alternate placements in other classrooms where there will likely be varying student needs. By using the content learned in this lesson, the TAP students should have better insight into the types of instruction and adaptations that could be used to meet these needs in their alternate placements.

Material/Resources: *What do you need for this lesson?*

Chromebooks, printer, computer software, posterboards, trifold displays, markers, scissors, glue, visuals examples of disabilities, slide deck, handouts over different diagnoses, and suggested online resources.

Adaptations to Meet Individual Needs: Grammarly on Chromebooks will help with spelling and punctuation for students with learning disabilities in written expression. Students who need help with reading comprehension will receive one-on-one help from the teacher during independent work. Peer tutoring will be used when specified by the student's IEP.

Management/Safety Issues: *Are there any management and/or safety issues that need to be considered when teaching this lesson?*

Due to the nature of the lesson, the teacher will monitor the room to ensure that conversations regarding various disabilities are respectful. Students will have previously covered person-first language to ensure appropriate, respectful verbiage will be used in student work. The teacher will ensure adequate supplies will be available for students to limit wait time.

REFERENCES

Beasley, K. (2021). *Effective instruction for students with disabilities. Teaching as a Profession 1.* Macon County High School.

Tennessee Tech University. (2021). *edTPA lesson plan template.* Office of Teacher Education. Tennessee Technological University. http://edTPALessonPlanTemplate.docx (live.com)

INDEX

ABOUT THE AUTHORS

Dr. Melinda Swafford is Professor Emerita of Tennessee Technological University (TTU), School of Human Ecology, in Cookeville, TN. She received her PhD in education with an emphasis on exceptional learning from Tennessee Technological University. Dr. Swafford has over 30 years of teaching experience in family and consumer sciences (FCS) content that includes nutrition, family service, early childhood, and early intervention. As a public school teacher for 12 years, Dr. Swafford was a middle and high school FCS teacher with an inclusive program as well as a special education teacher. She has 20 years of experience teaching in higher education and was the interim director of the TTU Women's Center for 2 years. While at TTU, her role was to prepare preservice students for careers in FCS education and child and family service. She also served as a consultant with the Tennessee Department of Education Career Technical Education grant from 2005–2013. Dr. Swafford has received national recognition for her work in FCS, has been published in several academic journals, and is an author of book chapters. She retired in 2019. She is still a member of the American Association of Family and Consumer Sciences.

Elizabeth Ramsey, PhD, CFLE, is a professor at Tennessee Technological University in the School of Human Ecology. She leads the concentration of family and consumer science education along with contributing to the concentration of child development and family relations. Additionally, Dr. Ramsey is a Certified Family Life Educator (CFLE) and a Rule 31 Family Mediator, carrying the domestic violence endorsement. She is a dual-licensed educator in Tennessee, endorsed in both Kindergarten–6th grades and Family and Consumer Sciences Education, 6th–12th grades. Dr. Ramsey is a trained scorer for Pearson's edTPA in family and consumer sciences content. She is a trainer in adverse childhood experiences (ACEs) and trauma-informed care. She has experience in early intervention, family mediation, teaching middle school, parent education, and higher education. While teaching middle school, she implemented a trauma-informed classroom. Dr. Ramsey's research and project interests include the training and education of foster parents, social health education in public school systems, implementation of trauma-informed care in helping professions, the mitigation and prevention of ACEs, and building resilience in children and families who have experienced ACEs and/or trauma. Dr. Ramsey is a published author in several academic journals and textbooks. She currently serves as president of the Tennessee Association of Family and Consumer Sciences.